The Cottage Ownership Guide

The Cottage Ownership Guide

How to Buy, Sell, Rent, Share,

Hand Down & Retire to Your Waterfront Getaway

By Douglas Hunter

Cottage Life BOOKS

Library and Archives Canada Cataloguing in Publication

Hunter, Douglas, 1959-

   The cottage ownership guide : how to buy, sell, rent, share, hand down & retire to your waterfront getaway / by Douglas Hunter.

Includes bibliographical references and index.

ISBN-13: 978-0-9696922-5-6

ISBN-10: 0-9696922-5-0

   1. Vacation homes. 2. House buying. 3. House selling. 4. Home ownership. 5. Real estate business. I. Title.

HD1379.H845 2006   643'.12   C2005-907474-4

Publisher Cataloging-in-Publication Data (U.S.)

Hunter, Douglas, 1959-

   The cottage ownership guide : how to buy, sell, rent, share, hand down & retire to your waterfront getaway / by Douglas Hunter.

[256] p. : ill. ; cm.

Includes bibliographical references and index.

Summary: Guide to finding, financing and managing a waterfront cottage.

ISBN-13: 978-0-9696922-5-6

ISBN-10: 0-9696922-5-0

   1. Home ownership. 2. House buying. 3. House selling. 4. Vacation homes. I. Title.

643.12 dc22   HD1379.H845   2006

Published by Cottage Life Books
54 St. Patrick St.
Toronto, Ontario, Canada
M5T 1V1
www.cottagelife.com

Trade distribution by
Firefly Books Ltd.
66 Leek Crescent
Richmond Hill, Ontario
L4B 1H1

Printed in Canada

Published in the United States by Cottage Life Books
Box 1338
Ellicott Station
Buffalo, N.Y., U.S.A. 14205
www.cottagelife.com

Trade distribution by
Firefly Books (U.S.)
Box 1338
Ellicott Station
Buffalo, N.Y., U.S.A. 14205

Illustrations by Doug Panton

Drawings by Richie Tripp

Edited by Ann Vanderhoof and David Zimmer

Design by Steve Manley, Overleaf Design Ltd.

Printed and bound in Canada by Friesens Corporation Altona, Manitoba

Cover photograph courtesy Ontario Tourism (2005)

Topographic map, p. 46, reprinted with permission of Natural Resources Canada

Hydrographic chart, p. 46, reprinted with permission of the Canadian Hydrographic Service

Bottom-contour map, p. 47, reprinted with permission of Adventure Fishing Maps, Bridgenorth, ON

Planning and zoning map, p. 47, courtesy of Kandiyohi County, Willmar, MN

Real estate forms, pp. 72–73 and 201, reprinted with permission of the Ontario Real Estate Association

Survey, p. 102, reprinted with permission of Coote, Hiley, Jemmett Limited, Ontario Land Surveyors, Bracebridge, ON

"Summarizing the Options," p. 240–241: A version of this chart, by Brenda Spiering, first appeared in *Cottage Life* magazine; reprinted with permission of the author

Table of Contents

1 Introduction *15*

2 Getting started *19*
Determining your "needs" and "wants"

The "needs": How much and how far? 20
　　How much are you willing to spend? **20**
　　Chart: Surprise, surprise: How additional costs add up **23**
　　How far are you willing to travel? **23**
The "wants": Making your wish list 25
　　Do you want a cottage you can use year-round? **26**
　　Drive-to or water-access? **26**
　　What is your vision of "cottage country"? **28**
　　Are you willing to rough it? If so, how much? **28**
　　How many people do you want to fit into your cottage? **29**
　　The L.Q. test: What is your luxury quotient? **30**
　　What do you want to do for fun? **32**
　　Are kids part of your cottage picture? **32**
　　The Cottage Wants Checklist **34**
Cross-border shopping: Issues affecting Americans buying property in Canada 37
　　Taxation **37**
　　Restrictions on non-resident land ownership **38**
　　Borrowing from Canadian institutions **39**
　　Health care and retirement **39**
Caution for Canadians buying from a non-resident 39

3 Choosing your lake or river *41*
How to make sure a specific place fits your wish list

How to be a lake detective 42

Mining cottage association reports for nuggets of buyer-helpful information **42**

Who's in the know? Where to turn for info **43**

What's your lake like? **44**

Area maps: Essential tools for lake detectives **46**

How much does the water level change? **49**

Matching your lake with your planned activities **51**

Sample lake analysis **54**

Do you even need a lake? **56**

Hot-button local issues **57**

Where to turn for info on local issues **59**

4 The property search process   *61*

Finding what's on the market and finding an agent

Looking for love in all the right places **61**

The Multiple Listing Service on-line **62**

When is there too much liquidity? **62**

Realty web pages **63**

Independent commercial websites **64**

How to snag a property where cottages rarely come up for sale **64**

Print media **65**

The "With Contents" Purchase **66**

How to choose an agent **68**

Two bottom-line must-haves **68**

Understanding the agent's role **68**

The birth of the buyer agent **70**

What a seller's agent is obligated to show you **71**

Choosing the agent relationship that's right for you **75**

5 Taking a test drive   *79*

Your first trip to see a property

Testing the location **79**

Is this where you want to be? **80**

Where does the sun set? **80**

Which way does the wind blow? **81**

Case study: Off-season buying requires more detective work **82**

How close are the neighbors? **83**

How do you get to the property? **84**

Questions to ask about a property's road access **85**

Questions to ask about a property's water access **86**

Testing the neighborhood **87**

Who are the neighbors? **87**

What is the boat traffic like? **89**

Is the water used by transient boaters? Or anglers? **90**

Testing the cottage 91
    How does the cottage get its power? 91
    Where does the cottage get its drinking water? 92
    Questions to ask about the water system 93
    How does the cottage treat sewage? 93
    Questions to ask about the waste system 94
    What sort of communications systems are available? 95
    Is the cottage suitable for year-round use? 96
    How is the cottage insulated? 96
    How is the cottage heated? 97

6   The property survey   *99*
What it tells you and why every cottage needs one

Survey basics 100
    Different types, different levels of information 100
    How recent is recent? 100
    Who pays for the survey? 103
Survey issues 103
    Encroachments and boundary disputes 103
    The shoreline road allowance 106
    Other road allowances 108
    Cottages on leased land 108
    Restrictive covenants and easements 109
    Ownership beneath and on the lake 111
    Where does the waterfront end and the lake begin? 111
    Aboriginal land claims 112

7   Inspecting the cottage   *113*
What a professional inspection tells you

Why inspect? 114
    When to inspect 115
    Goals of an inspection 115
Who inspects cottages? 116
    Finding a cottage inspector 117
    What an inspector does not (or might not) do 118
    No-nos for home inspectors 118
The inspection process 119
    Arrange to go along 119
    What an inspector is looking for 120
    Got 'em covered? 120
Evaluating the inspection report 121
    Structural 122
    Q & A: Problem discovered. Is it time to walk away? 123
    Mechanical 123
    Pumps and plumbing 123

Septic smarts: The snowball effect **124**
Seller disclosure: Telling it like it is **125**
Heating systems **126**
Getting the green light on woodstoves **127**
Inspections and options for closing **128**
Getting the repairs done **128**

8 Buying a lot or tear-down   *131*

How to approach other cottage purchase options

"Non-resale" options **131**
Vacant land **132**
Q & A: Can you rebuild a tear-down that breaks
  current rules? **132**
Tear-down/renovation **133**
Planned subdivisions **133**
Heading off headaches **134**
Will you be allowed to build? **134**
What to do before buying **135**
How much will it cost? **136**
Tax tips for Americans buying land and building a cottage **138**
Deducting interest charges **138**
Undeveloped land as an investment property **139**
Deductions for a home under construction **139**
Tax tips for Canadians **140**
Case study: Reducing the buy-now, build-later tax hit **141**

9 Financing the cottage purchase   *143*

How to do it to your best advantage

Risk assessment in cottage real estate **143**
How big a mortgage will you need? **144**
Who gets the best financing deals? **145**
Types of loan products available for cottages **146**
Conventional mortgages **146**
Insured mortgages **147**
Collateralized mortgages **147**
*Cross-border financing: American buyers and Canadian
  banks* **147**
Conditions that concern banks **148**
Chart: Risky business **149**
Other forms of financing **152**
Use your home as collateral **152**
Using other assets as collateral **153**
Working with a line of credit **154**
Sample spreadsheet: Using a line of credit to buy cottage
  furnishings **155**

Financing land   156
Mortgage interest deductibility for American buyers   157
    Q & A: Can we claim the deduction?   **157**

10 Sharing a cottage   *159*
Co-ownership with friends, family – or strangers

Prerequisites for success   159
    A compatible vision for how the property will be used   **160**
    A compatible vision for change   **160**
Co-ownership structures   161
Issues in co-ownership   162
    Financing the purchase   **162**
    Who gets to use it when?   **163**
    Chart: Choosing time slots   **164**
    How will expenses be divided?   **165**
    Changes in ownership   **166**
Where trouble lies   166
    Don't sweat the small stuff   **167**
    Play to the partners' strengths   **167**
    There's a difference between breakage and breakdown   **167**
    Other common causes of discord   **168**
    Co-ownership agreements: Dealing with the what-ifs   **168**
    Case study: A solid friendship is no guarantee of a
        trouble-free co-ownership   **171**
Time-sharing and fractional ownership   170

11 Renting out your cottage   *173*
Steps towards a trouble-free rental

Finding renters   174
    Who will your renters be?   **174**
    Getting the word out   **175**
    When are you going to rent?   **176**
    Case study: Getting a good fit   **176**
Increasing the odds of a trouble-free rental   177
    Is your cottage renter-friendly?   **177**
    Establishing the conditions of rental   **178**
    What to include – and not include – in the rental   **179**
    Basic cottage gear for renters   **179**
    Giving renters the information they need   **180**
    Managing risk when renting   **181**
Using a professional rental service   182
    Types of rental services   **182**
    Items to consider when hiring a rental services company   **183**
    Screening the renters   **183**
    How much does it cost?   **184**

Renting and the tax man 184
Reporting rental income **184**
Rental expenses and Canadian taxpayers **185**
Renting and capital gains on Canadian property **185**
Eligible U.S. rental expenses **186**
Rental income and U.S mortgage interest deductibility **186**

12 Selling your cottage *187*
Strategies to decrease the headaches and increase the reward

Who's going to handle it? 187
Choosing an agent **188**
Selling privately **188**
Red-flag reasons for deciding to do it yourself **189**
Got a buyer in mind? Then selling it yourself makes sense **189**
Downsides to selling privately **191**
Six for the sale **192**
Advantages an agent offers **192**
Q & A: Getting a "for sale by owner" property on MLS **193**
Playing to your own strengths **194**
The Return on Equity Rule: Holding out for the right price costs you money **194**

Getting the price right 196
Appraisal + market forces = asking price **197**

Putting together an information package 198
The basic facts **198**
Pictures are worth a thousand words **198**
The value-addeds **199**
Provide documentation **199**

Vendor disclosure documents and vendor due diligence 200
Sample: Seller Property Information Statement **201**
A vendor due diligence checklist **202**

Boosting market appeal 203
Adding value to the property **203**
Tips from the frontline: Where to focus your renovation efforts **204**
Getting the cottage ready for showing **205**

Selling and taxation 206
Taxes in Canada **206**
Taxes in the U.S. **207**
How to build a cottage operating manual **208**

13 Relocating to vacation country *211*
Making the cottage your full-time home

Bottom-line basics 211
If you're buying a property now for retirement later **212**
A starter kit of questions for year-round cottage living **213**

Assessing local services **213**

Lifestyle "transference" **214**

Case study: Retooling the retirement dream **214**

Making a cottage retirement work **215**

Year-round versus seasonal occupancy **216**

For Americans: Make sure you're covered **216**

Fretting over fitting in **217**

Assessing the cottage: Is it ready for year-round living? **218**

Retirement retrofits **218**

Special considerations for the working set **221**

14 Handing down the cottage *223*

How to structure a cottage inheritance to reduce taxes – and family disputes

Planning ahead for the tax bite **224**

Using the cost of cottage improvements to offset capital gains **225**

Using residence/home status to reduce capital gains **226**

Practicalities of bequest **227**

Did you use these loopholes? **228**

Treating heirs equally doesn't mean treating them the same **228**

Leaving a cottage to one of several offspring **229**

Number-crunching for Canadians: How to estimate the capital gains tax **230**

Case study: Using the principal-residence designation to reduce the tax bill **232**

Avoiding family friction once the offspring take over **233**

"Pre-bequest" changes in ownership **234**

Number-crunching for Americans: Being wise to capital gains reduction **235**

Using life insurance to pay capital gains tax **238**

Specialized strategies **238**

Non-profit organization **239**

Testamentary trusts **239**

Living trusts **239**

Chart: Summarizing the options: The pros and cons of various bequest strategies **240**

Protecting against loss of the property through mental incompetence **242**

Charitable bequests and public donations **244**

15 For more information *245*

Acknowledgments **249**

Index *250*

1. Introduction

Vacation homes have been with us for as long as humankind has needed a vacation. The Romans had their villas. The Elizabethans couldn't wait to escape the crowds and pestilence of London and head for their country retreats. Somewhere in our deep past, whenever breaks in the mammoth-hunt schedule permitted, a cave dweller probably grabbed spouse and kids and shambled off to a quiet spot with a drop-dead view by the tar pits.

The cottage is supposed to be about "getting away from it all," but clearly you don't have to be cooped up in one of Milton's Dark Satanic Mills before you start yearning for a respite at the lake. Most people who own a vacation property have a perfectly nice home elsewhere. The change they're looking for is not just about fresh air and a place to paddle a canoe, but about a different set of priorities. A cottage is about sleeping in – or getting up even earlier than usual to do some fishing. It's about having a haven for family and friends – or a haven from the rest of the world entirely. Cottages are where batteries are recharged, where harried souls can decompress – regardless of where they're located or their degree of sophistication.

The cottage is synonymous with escape. And with a perfect cottage, the escaping is *to*, not *from*. You stop thinking about getting away from town – it's not just that any port in a storm will do – and, instead, about getting *to* the lake.

Some of you reading this book have probably had years of experience with cottages. Some of you own one already. For those of you interested in buying your first cottage, perhaps your family had one that evokes fond childhood memories. Others will have little experience with cottages at all – perhaps a visit to a friend's getaway or a summer rental has piqued your interest in becoming an owner. You may be single or half of a couple, or surrounded by kids...or grandkids. Your idea of the perfect retreat is going to differ from the next person's. And depending on where in North America you live, so too will the types of retreats on offer. But regardless of who you are, where you live, and where you plan to buy a property, you all share some common cottage concerns.

Balancing emotional attraction with solid advice

Owning a cottage is – and should be – an affair of the heart. But when we've fallen in love, sometimes we give clear thinking and logical planning a back seat. That's where *The Cottage Ownership Guide* comes in, helping you balance the emotional appeal of a cottage with solid information. It will guide you through the common-sense aspects of purchasing and ownership, as well as the hard financial decision-making that goes along with them.

Some of you are looking for an undeveloped piece of lakefront land, others for a remote cabin or a simple cottage on the water. Still others are in the market for what amounts to an all-the-bells-and-whistles lakeside home. Some of you only imagine using it for a few weeks every summer. Maybe you're thinking of renting it out occasionally, perhaps selling it eventually. Others plan to retire to it now or in the near future – or even 30 years from now. Perhaps you face issues related to sharing a cottage, or you're wrestling with how best to hand it down to your kids. Whatever your situation, this book aims to provide sensible and practical advice.

People buy vacation properties for many reasons, and this book is directed specifically at one broad group: those who seek a waterfront property *for their own personal use*. All real estate is an investment of sorts, but this is not a manual for buying a cottage exclusively as an investment property. This book also does not attempt to address vacation-property specialty markets such as condominiums and ski chalets (unless the chalet is a lakeside cottage doing double-duty as a winter getaway). Think of the classic waterfront getaway (which may or may not be winterized, and may not even be right on a lake), and you're in the right book.

The goal of the guide: Helping you ask the right questions

Nevertheless, the scope of this book is hardly narrow. It takes a deep breath and plunges into the North American cottage market. Theoretically, that means dealing with properties in 10 different Canadian provinces and 48 continental American states, with owners who might live in one country and own a cottage in another. It means a myriad of taxation, financing, zoning, building-code, boating, and environmental-protection regulations at several different government levels – from the municipal right up to the federal. This guide doesn't attempt to describe every rule and situation, but instead is intended to alert you to possible concerns and steer you in the right direction for specific information.

Consider this book a primer on the issues involved in purchasing, owning, selling, sharing, renting, retiring to, and bequeathing a cottage. Much of its information will be handy, no matter what sort of property you're looking for, or own. By the same token, this book doesn't deal with aspects of buying and selling real estate in general (such as the structure of an offer to purchase), precisely because the information is general. Cottage properties are a specialized branch of real estate, and this book aims to help you understand the many nuances of that branch.

In many areas, the information in this book will be the beginning of your search for detailed answers that depend on your specific circumstances and the laws that apply where you live. Not only are laws and regulations specific to particular jurisdictions, they are also fluid. Generally speaking, "big-picture" issues, such as the application of capital gains tax to property or (for American taxpayers) mortgage interest deductibility on vacation properties, are bound to be with us for some time. What will change to varying degrees is the way these issues operate at the fine-print level.

The book strives to explain the essential issues, knowing that circumstances on a property on any given lake can change at any given time. And while in some cases an explanation of a particular financial issue is made with a sample worksheet, keep in mind that the precise calculation could change in the near future. In these complex areas, the book will give you a useful appreciation of the essential issues, and from there you can turn to your accountant, lawyer, banker or other professional to fill in your particular picture.

Watch for the flags

Particularly when it comes to tax issues, what you need to know changes dramatically depending on which side of the border you're on. Information that's specific to one country or the other is flagged with the appropriate national symbol.

How this book works

Most of us learn best through example, and from experience. This book draws on the specific experiences of cottage owners and the seasoned advice of industry professionals to bring facts to life and illustrate many unwritten rules of the cottage market. Along with the straight text, you'll find Tips, Cautions, Case Studies, Q&As, Charts, and Sample Calculations – as well as checklists, to assist you in working out your own plans.

The book is organized in a somewhat linear way, taking first-time buyers from the beginning of their search for the perfect property right to the point of estate planning. This structure attempts to impose some order on the process, but we all know that life isn't so neat. You may not follow the precise process the book outlines – and certainly this book's way isn't the only way – but by absorbing that process, you'll pick up useful information, and gain directions to other chapters for more on related issues. Even if you've already begun the search process by the time you pick up this book, I encourage you to start reading at the beginning.

TIP:

**Selling your cottage?
Be sure to read about
the buying process**

If you've picked up this book
because you want to sell your
cottage, don't read just the
"Selling Your Cottage" chapter.
You should also read the
chapters about *buying* a cottage,
as they will give you a valuable
heads-up on purchasers'
expectations and the process
of searching for a cottage.
(And watch for the "Seller's Tips"
scattered throughout the
chapters.)

Ultimately, however, this book isn't meant to be read straight from front to back. You will find directions within chapters sending you elsewhere in the book for more information, particularly where a subject isn't necessarily exclusive to the theme of one chapter. Different chapters will be more important to you at different stages of your cottage ownership, and if you're just starting the search process for a property, I hope this book can be useful to you for years to come. And many issues require foresight, sometimes years of it. For example, if you are in the market for a cottage and are thinking about retiring to it in 20 years or so, read the retirement chapter now, not when your pension is fully vested.

I have stuck to the masculine gender when referring in the singular to cottage owners, buyers, real estate agents, and various professionals. This does not imply anything about who actually occupies those roles – only a desire for simplicity and space-saving readability.

Finally, do your utmost to enjoy the process of becoming a vacation property owner. Much of the advice in this book runs toward avoiding unhappy circumstances. When I was nearing its completion, I was in a meeting with executives of the largest consulting firm in the world, and the topic of this project came up. The people around the table perked up in interest, asking what it was going to be about. I explained that part of it was helping people avoid pitfalls in the cottage property market. Almost as one, they learned forward and demanded, *"Like what?"*

"Where can something go wrong?" is a primary interest of anyone contemplating a major investment, and I do hope this book addresses that concern. But owning a vacation property is about something going *right*. This book can help you make it as right as possible.

2. Getting started

Avacation property is one of the largest investments you can make. In fact, for most people, only the purchase of their home is likely to be larger. On the face of it, all you're buying is real estate, no different from a house in town. But just as cottages are blessed with a shining lake, sweet breezes, and peace and quiet, they also come with a host of considerations you don't encounter in the city.

Never fear: Rather than being problems, those considerations are part of what makes the cottage so special. Still, they do require some serious forethought to make sure the property you decide on is the right one for you. By approaching the purchase in a pragmatic way – as much as an affair of the heart can be called pragmatic – you can greatly simplify the decision-making process.

Searching for the perfect cottage is a bit like pushing a locomotive; sometimes just getting started is the hardest part. This book is here to help nudge the process along and get you thinking about the criteria that are truly important to your enjoyment of a cottage property. There's no point becoming an expert on drinking-water systems or financing options if you haven't first assessed what you need and want in a getaway. Get the "needs and wants" right, and other concerns will fall neatly into line, allowing you to avoid working through a lot of knotty issues that ultimately have no bearing on your purchasing decision.

Needs and wants: Two words, two different sets of issues. Needs, of course, relate to necessity. Wants are in the realm of desire – your wish list.

The line between the two can blur – for many of us, aesthetics and gut feel are just as important as any hard data – but in most cases certain "need" criteria *must* be met before the "want" criteria can be met.

Defining your needs and wants is an exercise to be worked out on paper, if only because the act of writing it all down will help you clarify your own requirements, help you avoid overlooking something, and – perhaps most importantly – make sure your spouse and your kids (and anyone else involved) are just as happy and confident about the decision as you are. It's all part of the cottage-shopping process, and should be done in pencil because you'll find that your needs and wants will shift along the way.

This is not a rigorous science, and you may disagree with the importance we give to some of the criteria – in which case, feel free to move them around. Beyond giving you, the buyer, some solid parameters for your search, the exercise ensures that everyone involved in the purchase is on the same page when it comes to selecting the property. Couples need to agree on what they're looking for. They have to appreciate which criteria their partners are dead-set on achieving, and which ones they themselves can be flexible about in order to reach a satisfying compromise.

The "needs": How much and how far?

In the "needs" category, we're going to put just two basic criteria: How much can you afford to spend? And how far are you willing to travel?

These are the make-or-break items – and there's less room for flexibility than with other criteria. In short, you only have a certain amount of money to spend, and the property you seek must be within a certain distance from your main residence.

Note that both these "needs" are based on your particular circumstances, and are independent of the property itself. If your circumstances change, these needs can as well, and a property that wasn't suitable on first inspection might become suitable down the road. Repeat this exercise in five years, and your needs may be entirely different.

How much are you willing to spend?

When searching for a cottage, you need to first establish what you can afford. If you're working with a real estate agent, his or her first question is going to be, "What are you willing to spend?" It's an entirely sensible question because there's no sense schlepping you around to properties you can't afford, even if they meet the wish list you've provided. Once price range is settled, you'll be able to align your ambitions with your budget and direct your search accordingly.

TIP:

Do the Driveway Test

Have a look at the driveway of a happy couple and you may notice that Partner A is driving a half-ton pickup, while Partner B is buzzing around in a two-seater convertible. Totally different vehicles, but they manage to fit in the same driveway.

As you go through the needs and wants process, think of the cottage in terms of that driveway, accommodating very different personal criteria in the purpose it serves. But you have to be sensitive and realize that if the property becomes too aligned with one person's criteria, the other person's priorities may not be accommodated at all.

In other words, while a pickup might be okay, a dump truck would squeeze the convertible into the ditch.

Keep in mind that a budget of $200,000 can get you a turnkey resale cottage, fully furnished, complete with boats, appliances, and furniture – or it can get you an empty waterfront lot. So can $75,000. By "budget," we mean what it will cost you to have a habitable cottage, regardless of the nature of the initial purchase.

Visit your banker

In deciding how much you want to spend, the key factor (for most of us, at least) is calculating how much you can (and want to) borrow, and what the money will cost. So before you crunch the numbers too far, set up an appointment with a banker. *(See Tip, at right.)*

If you have a good credit rating (and good equity), he or she will be only too happy to discuss financing strategies, and you'll get a pretty quick idea of what you're capable of buying. It might give you sober second thoughts, for instance, when you realize the rustic island retreat you envision owing isn't eligible for the bank's best loan interest rates. On the other hand, you might learn a few surprising things about financing strategies that give you the confidence to look at more-expensive properties you otherwise wouldn't have considered. *(See Chapter 9 for more on financing.)*

Look beyond the purchase price

While your eyes might be tightly focused on the purchase price, you also need to consider the accompanying one-time and ongoing costs. Although some (such as legal and closing costs) will be familiar to homeowners, others are more likely to come into play with a cottage purchase and may not be expected by a first-time cottage buyer.

TIP:

Do your cottage loan shopping in your cottage area

Consider dealing with a bank in the area where you're contemplating a purchase – perhaps a branch of the bank you use at home. Bank officers in urban settings can access standard internal bank documents that provide guidelines on loan approvals for vacation properties, but they don't necessarily have the feel for the local real estate market that an area banker will.

TIP: Buy the cottage that suits you right now

If there's a single inviolate rule in acquiring a vacation property, it's this: Buy what you can use now, not what you think you'll need in 20 or 30 years. Your needs and wants (and those of your family) evolve with time. Such changes influence the kind of cars we drive, the homes (and communities) we live in, the recreational activities we pursue, the vacation destinations we prefer. We have little problem accepting that we might choose to drive a minivan for a few years while the kids are growing up, then switch to a small sedan when the nest empties, or that a particular neighborhood is desirable right now because of the school district, but that another will be more appealing later in life because of its proximity to shopping areas or recreational facilities. Investing in a vacation property should be approached with the same sense of lifelong flexibility.

It *is* possible to find a property that suits you at every stage of your life, but a one-size-fits-all purchase should not be an absolute goal. Many vacation property purchasers have an idyllic retirement in the back of their minds as they shop around, but as we'll explore in Chapter 13, retirement properties have specific criteria that can't or shouldn't necessarily be met when searching for something that suits, for example, an active young family.

Pre-purchase:

• **Survey:** Depending on the age of the property and the number of times it has been bought and sold, it may not have an official survey on record. A new survey is crucial to determine the exact boundaries of the property, to make sure none of the structures encroaches outside property lines, and to locate any points of deeded access or rights of way. If the seller doesn't provide a recent survey – smart sellers will, but they're not legally required to – it's wise to have one done yourself. Budget $1,500–$2,500, more for a large property with multiple structures. *(See Chapter 6.)*

• **Building inspection:** A professional assessment of the mechanical and structural systems of the cottage can help identify problem areas that need to be addressed, whether right away or in the future. (Major deficiencies can often be subtracted from the purchase price.) Additional specialized assessments of the septic system, drinking-water quality, and wood-heating system may also be in order before you purchase. Budget at least $400 for a home inspection, plus additional funds for specialized inspections of individual cottage systems. *(See Chapter 7.)*

Post-purchase:

• **Property taxes:** While you expect property taxes to be part of cottage ownership, and a standard sales listing will include the amount of current property taxes, it's important that you check their status. As market values soar and municipalities are burdened with services formerly provided by other levels of government, taxes can rise quickly. Also, areas that are making the transition from seasonal to permanent occupancy are particularly prone to leaps in tax rates.

• **Road maintenance:** Not all roads in cottage country have been assumed by local government. Many of the ones that provide access from a municipal road to a neighborhood of cottages (as well as the individual cottage laneways) are private concerns. They occasionally have to be graded, sometimes graveled and, where there is winter occupancy, plowed. Cottages that share a private access road also share the costs of maintaining it. *(For more on private roads, see Chapter 5, p. 84.)*

• **Property maintenance:** Because many cottages are responsible for their own water and sewage systems (and sometimes their own power production, too), ongoing maintenance can be more costly than with an urban dwelling. And urban dwellings usually don't come with docks and other waterfront structures. They, too, will require ongoing maintenance. Also, take a good look at the condition of the trees on the property you're considering. Dead or dying ones will need to be cleared away for basic safety – and the trimming and removal can be expensive.

If you're handy, you'll probably want a complete second set of tools to keep at the cottage, as well as some you would never use at home.

More on being moneywise

• For information on deductibility of interest on vacation-property mortgages and other loans by U.S. taxpayers, see Chapter 9, p. 157.

• For information on the tax implications of buying vacant land or "tear-down" property, see Chapter 8, p. 138 (U.S.), p. 140 (Can.).

• For information on the importance of keeping detailed records of cottage expenses from day one of ownership, see Chapter 14, p. 200.

• **Caretaker services:** Your insurance coverage may require you to contract caretaker services to keep an eye on the place during the off-season. (And even if your insurance doesn't demand it, you may decide it's a good idea.) Usually this isn't a huge cost, though it depends on the services and the frequency with which they're rendered.

• **Utilities:** How you intend to use (or not use) the property in the off-season has costs attached. If you "mothball" the place for winter, costs will be far lower than if you opt to keep the heat turned on and the plumbing fully functional to accommodate winter visits.

Surprise, surprise: How additional costs add up	
Annual road maintenance fee	$400
Yearly cost of boat storage at local marina	800
Fuel and maintenance for ski boat	850
Fuel and maintenance for kids' fish boat	250
Septic system pumpout (every 2 years)	100
Jimmy, the guy who shovels snow off the roof	200
Annual outlay you didn't bargain for	**$2,800**

• **Insurance:** Vacation property insurance can rarely be folded into the coverage of the owner's principal residence. Depending on a property's location, how it is built, and the way it is heated, you may find yourself facing very high premiums (or forced to make upgrades to even secure coverage). Check with your insurance company on the availability and cost of coverage before making a final offer.

• **Powerboats:** If the cottage is water-access, you'll need to budget for a seasonal dockage charge to keep a boat at the marina, and likely an additional charge if you store it there in the winter. Even if you don't have a water-access property, you may require the services of the local marina for maintenance, winter storage, and spring commissioning. And we haven't even talked about fuel or boat insurance. The powerboat component of a cottage can easily run into four figures annually.

A good real estate agent who is knowledgeable about the area should be able to ballpark some of these expenses for you.

How far are you willing to travel?

Everybody knows this one: The mantra of real estate is "location, location, location." Where a property is located is the foundation of its value, and that's never more true than in vacation country. But when we're discussing needs, "location" has a slightly different context in a cottage purchase versus an urban residential one. At this point, we're not concerned with the "neighborhood" – the specific lake – or the nature of the shoreline, or the particular view. (We'll cover those all-important aspects in Chapters 3 and 5.) What we're talking about right now is *distance* from your main residence. And by *distance* we really mean not raw mileage, but the amount of *time* it takes you to get there. So the second "need" question is really: "How much time am I willing to spend on the road?"

Answering that question also requires you to reply to: "How frequently

CAUTION:
The 30-Minute Trap

As you strive to determine the appropriate driving distance, beware of the 30-Minute Trap. You might set a maximum driving time of three hours, then discover that by just going 30 minutes more, an appealing property can be reached. It's comparable to what we'd call the 50-Dollar Rule of household budgeting. You know the tune: You set an upper limit on some aspect of the monthly budget, and then decide that you can squeeze out an extra 50 bucks for movies-on-demand on the TV, or a slightly more expensive car. But it's amazing the budgeting train wreck that 50 extra dollars can cause. When you set an outer limit of travel time, be clear why you did so, and only go beyond it with due caution.

do I plan to make the trip?" If you plan to withdraw for weeks or months at a time, a long trip is far more tolerable. Not only are you doing it less frequently, but you can also plan the drive for off-peak hours. With a weekend-use property, you're pretty much locked into driving up on Friday and back on Sunday. If you plan to make frequent weekend visits, travel time is a front-burner purchase consideration. And time, unfortunately, is money: All else being equal, the farther you drive from a major urban center, the less expensive vacation properties become.

How far is too far?

A road map and a compass from your kid's geometry set will help you limit your search for your getaway. Start with a rough as-the-crow-flies guesstimate. Using the compass, draw a circle for every hour of highway road travel, making them a realistic 60 miles (or 100 kilometers) in diameter, with the center point being your house. You can quickly see how far you can get in one, two, three, four, or more hours. That is, if you're a crow flying at 60 miles or 100 klicks an hour... which you're not. But at least you've gained a heads-up that suggests the cute cabin out on the far edge of circle number seven probably isn't a wise choice.

To figure out how

Crow-flies estimate: 2 hrs. 45 mins. Actual time: 3 hrs. 50 mins.

fast, but Friday and Sunday night jams

long & winding cottage road

no passing lane (farm vehicles)

slow city traffic

Lake of Isles

Neartown

Chain Lake

Lake Worthy

Bass Lake

Littlefield

Lakeville

Outerburg

Scape City

Round Lake

MUSHMETRO

Biggish Lake

60 MILES

THE CIRCLE GAME: Concentric 60-mile circles with your home as their center will help you find possible lakes within your range. Driving the route will confirm your actual travel time

TIP: **Take a test drive. On a Friday night.**

While a compass and map can help get you started in determining travel time, the only way you're really going to get a handle on reality is to make the drive when you expect to be making it. And if that means a Friday night, so be it. It's better to know now rather than later that the getaway you thought might be two hours door-to-door turns out to be four hours at peak periods. Test drive the return trip on Sunday afternoon or evening, too.

long you're *really* going to need to get from A to B, try to work out the distance along the actual roads. In vacation country, there's seldom a straight line from A to B, and the meanderings are going to add up. Then you need to face the reality that you probably won't be driving at top speed the whole way, that there will be pit stops, and that rush hour will considerably increase the travel time.

Next, contact a real estate agent in the area you're considering and flat-out ask how long it takes to drive there. Unless you live at an obscure address, the agent should be able to give you a reasonable (if optimistic) estimate. Once you're seriously considering a purchase in the area, you'll be making the drive yourself to look at listings. Just remember the Friday-night factor: If you're going to be routinely making the trip at the busiest times, you really need to make your test drives under those conditions.

The "wants": Making your wish list

Tallying up your "wants" forces you to figure out exactly why you want a cottage – something more specific than simply "to get away from it all." Sure, in a perfect world most of us want some privacy and peace and quiet, with a sunny exposure and a sweet little swimming spot. And a splendid view. And some birds and other wildlife. Those are the basics – and they are features you can find at radically different properties. To make sure you find a place that works for you and your family, it's important to get a more nitty-gritty feel for your requirements.

Does your interpretation of "getting away from it all" just mean finding a place outside the city, or do you crave the utter solitude of a more remote location? Is the social scene important to you? Do you enjoy meeting the neighbors and sharing a meal or two, or do you prefer keeping your own company? Is the cottage you seek a tiny hideaway for two or a rambling place chock full of extended family and visiting guests? Do you want total comfort or is roughing it in the bush more your style? Does your wildlife

TIP:
MapQuest can help
Go to www.mapquest.com and plug in your home address and the closest town to the lake you're considering. Click on "Get directions," and MapQuest will obligingly provide not only a total distance but also an approximate travel time. Great for ballpark estimates.

threshold end with chipmunks and loons or does it encompass bears and water snakes? How about your spouse's?

To get a better handle on what you're looking for, use the **Cottage Wants Checklist** on p. 34. Unless you have an unlimited budget, there will undoubtedly have to be compromises. Here are some of the major items you'll need to think about:

Do you want a cottage you can use year-round? Or are you happy to stick with the traditional May–October cottage season?

A four-season cottage is, for all intents and purposes, a fully serviced home. Buying a cottage suitable for four-season use will raise the expense of the purchase and eliminate many otherwise appealing three-season properties. If you're thinking of a winterized cottage, be sure you have solid reasons, beyond imagining it would be nice to spend Christmas in the woods. One or two visits totaling only a few days per winter are probably not going to justify its cost. That said, there are good reasons for going the winterized route:

• Even if you're not planning to use it in the dead of winter, a winterized cottage, with proper heating and insulation, can stretch its comfortable use well into the early-spring and late-fall shoulder seasons.

• If the cottage will be used as a retirement home, either immediately or in a few years' time, it only makes sense to look for a four-season property – even if it turns out you don't want to occupy it for more than six or eight months of the year. As noted above, the winterizing will be more than appreciated in the spring and fall. (*See Chapter 13 for more on assessing the cottage for retirement living.*)

• You're unlikely to go wrong with an investment in a four-season property. As vacation properties overall become more sophisticated, should you ever decide to sell, being able to offer a year-round retreat will be rewarded with strong buyer interest.

• In snow-belt areas, the local tourism economy does a complete changeover in the winter, bidding adieu to the cottagers and welcoming the skiers and snowmobilers (although in many cases they are the same people). Many cottages are located near excellent groomed cross-country ski trails, snowmobile trails, and downhill ski areas. A summer cottage can do double-duty as a ski chalet without having to be at the base of the mountain. Being within a reasonable drive of a ski area may be a compelling reason to buy a particular property and use it as a weekend winter retreat.

Drive-to or water-access?

This is one of the great cultural divides in cottage properties. Water-access properties appeal to people who see cottaging as a real getaway, a retreat

TIP:
"Time to get there" doesn't just involve driving time

When you're considering how long you're willing to travel to get to your getaway, you need to build in the time required for a bathroom break (or two), a dinner stop, or a detour for last-minute groceries. Will the family pet have to be watered and walked along the way? Can you perform diaper diagnostics on the fly or will they require roadside pit stops? And don't forget to take your own personality into account: Are you a straight-line driver or a more unhurried type who likes to stop at antique shops and garden centers along the way? Budget your time accordingly – and enjoy the drive.

from civilization that requires a separate mode of transportation. Drive-to properties, no matter how remote the cottage or bumpy the trip, generally offer a greater measure of convenience and ease of access. (For starters, you don't have to pack and unpack everything twice as you do with a water-access place.)

But it's far from that cut and dried. Certainly many water-access properties involve a significant boat trip into the wilds. But many others are on islands close to the mainland or on lakes where road access has proved impossible to provide in some areas, and the boat ride is just a jaunt of a couple minutes in sheltered water. At the same time, "drive-to" doesn't have to mean suburban comfort. Some cottages are on fully assumed municipal roads, complete with weekly trash pickup and recycling, while others are accessed from privately maintained bush roads that challenge the suspension of the typical family sedan. (*See Chapter 5 for more considerations regarding access when you're looking at a particular property.*)

Whether water-access or drive-to, the following pricing rule applies: The easier it is to get to (and from) a cottage, the more expensive it will be. Island properties have a particular cachet, and have seen stronger demand in recent years, but it doesn't change the fact that a comparable property on the mainland in the same area that can be reached by car is going to command substantially more money. And while some water-access cottages can be used year round – with the notable exception of those times in early winter and spring when the ice is not solid enough to allow safe crossing – most remain three-season retreats. A buyer who can tolerate (or embrace) the strictly seasonal use of a water-access property can save significantly on the purchase price.

Other factors to consider about water access:

• **Will the reality of your work and family schedules mean you will regularly arrive after dark?** Particularly on a large lake, you may not want to face a trip across open water at night.

• **Do you plan to entertain frequently?** Guests will have to be picked up and dropped off at the marina, which entails a level of coordination and timing that doesn't fit with everyone's vision of a laidback retreat. And some of your potential guests will view a mandatory boat ride with less enthusiasm than others.

• **Do you have flexibility in your schedule?** With some places, you simply may not be able to get in and out exactly when you want. Cottagers at some water-access spots on eastern Georgian Bay, for example, can literally wait for days for the weather to improve enough to allow a small boat to navigate safely back to the marina. Needless to say, such logistics aren't compatible with inflexible weekend schedules – including those of guests. (It may not always be possible to pick them up at the marina on Friday night and whisk them back there on Sunday afternoon.)

CAUTION:
Water-access limits rental potential

The inconvenience and limitations on use that come with a water-access cottage might be just fine with the owners, but can severely diminish the appeal of a property to potential renters and, consequently, affect how much rent you can ask for the place. If renters are helping to finance your dream retreat, water-access might not be for you. (*See Chapter 11 for more on renting out your property.*)

TIP:

"Roughing it" goes beyond the property

When you think about how rustic a cottage you want, you also need to decide how far you're willing to be from the nearest town – from services such as medical facilities and shopping. At the same time, consider how big that nearest town needs to be. Does it require a supermarket or will a general store suffice?

TIP:

How handy are you?

A cottage doesn't have to be described as a "fixer-upper" or a "handyman's delight" to benefit from a do-it-yourselfer's mentality. "Remote" also equates with a greater degree of do-it-yourself skills. If a cottage is located a distance from town and the pump stops working, it will be up to you to figure out what's wrong.

Generally, the less turnkey and the more rustic the place, the more it requires an owner who is familiar with tools. So think about your (and your spouse's) "handiness factor" before you start shopping.

What is your vision of "cottage country"?

We all love cottages for the way they bring us closer to nature. And most of us have fairly specific ideas about the sort of nature we want to be brought closer to. Finding a property that's the right price and the right distance from home isn't going to make you happy if it places you in an environment that doesn't fulfill your perception of cottage country.

The cottage has to speak to *your* sense of cottaging. For some people, this is the classic rock-and-pine landscape of the Precambrian Shield (also known as the Canadian or the Laurentian Shield), where glaciers scoured lakes from some of the oldest rock on the planet. For others, the ideal cottage is on a vast swath of beach, where small fry can safely swim and grown-ups can sunbathe to their heart's content. Making one group settle for the ideal of the other isn't going to produce happy cottage owners.

If you have fairly specific ideas about what kind of cottage terrain you want, you need to factor this into your search from the beginning. For some buyers, accessing this perfect terrain is going to present a logistical stretch. (The Precambrian Shield, for example, only extends so far south, into the Adirondacks of upstate New York, Michigan's Upper Peninsula, and the "Superior Uplands" in northern Minnesota and Wisconsin.) But other buyers will find striking differences in the landscape within their search area. The leading edge of the Shield, for example, slants across south-central Ontario, atop the Kawartha Lakes system, and the transition in some locales is so abrupt that one side of a lake can be rock-and-pine, while the other side is more gently rolling countryside built on a sedimentary foundation.

Are you willing to rough it? If so, how much?

Henry David Thoreau loved his fabled cabin at Walden Pond – or at least he loved writing about how he loved it. But the first name in "back to nature" could always walk back to town when nature got a little too red in tooth and claw or he needed his laundry done.

By and large, the cottage experience is still considered a celebration of simplicity – but people differ greatly on what, exactly, that means. As you narrow down your choices, you need to be honest with yourself, and especially with any significant other, about how far from the amenities of your normal urban/suburban existence you're willing to go. (Take the **"luxury quotient" test** on p. 30 to determine your "roughing it" persona.)

Aesthetics can also be a flashpoint of disagreement. Some people have decided ideas about what a cottage should look like, and their ability to enjoy it is tied to the architecture and decor. Others don't give a hoot about the place's appearance, so long as the basic bits are in working order and the location is right.

If two people are involved in the purchase, they need to be in agreement on the physical *and* aesthetic aspects of "roughing it." If a property falls short of one person's expectations, the other needs to be prepared to make changes to bring it up to those expectations. And if that's the case, there has to be a realistic, affordable plan for doing so. Otherwise, one of them isn't going to want to be there, and the purchase will become a source of aggravation.

There's no strict divide between "roughing it" and living in luxury. It's not an all-or-nothing decision. Many options exist, for example, between hand-pumping your water from a well and enjoying pressurized municipal service. You might also have a combination of amenities: full electric service from a utility, but a private septic system and water pumped from the lake (albeit delivered thanks to an electric pump). You can exist totally off-grid, with wind and solar power, and do so in fairly sumptuous surroundings. You can also be totally on-grid, with full utility service for electricity, water, and sewage, and be in a two-bedroom seasonal retreat furnished with hand-me-downs, with a single canoe in the way of water toys.

In short, it's not easy to be cut-and-dried in defining how much you want in the way of creature comforts, and coming to an agreement with your spouse can be a challenge. In some cases, your desires for a particular style of property will be self-limiting. With an island property, you may well be able to find one with service from an electrical utility, but you're likely on your own when it comes to drinking water and waste treatment.

Also keep in mind that certain upgrades are possible within a very basic property. If the electrical service is there, and waste-water treatment is appropriately scaled, you may be able to add a dishwasher. And the most humble cottage interiors can be remade in fine style without requiring any changes to the property itself.

How many people do you really want to fit into your cottage?

Many people buy cottages because they are looking for a retreat not only for themselves, but also to entertain friends and extended family. Be realistic about how many people you plan to play host to, and how often. If it's just the occasional visit from your brother's family, a foldout couch and some floor space (or tents for the kids) can take care of things.

But if regular visitors are going to be a fact of life, think about a cottage with extra bedrooms, a second building on the property, or enough room on the property to allow the construction of one. Kids may enjoy the hobbit-sized loft open to the sights and sounds of cottage activity, but your elderly in-laws might not appreciate it, and if you want them to visit you'll need an alternative.

Depending on the zoning, limiting the second building to a simple "bunkie" that doesn't require its own septic system or the expansion of the existing one can make a building permit far easier to obtain. (*See Chapter 6 for more on zoning issues.*)

Continued on page 32

The L.Q. test: What is your luxury quotient?

Every person's idea of "roughing it" is different, and a cottage property that's out of step with your personal comfort level won't be enjoyable for long. Take our informal test to see what might work for you. Choose the answer that comes closest to your mindset, then score yourself at the end.

1. *Is it crucial that your cottage has a clothes washer and dryer?*
a) No, not at all.
b) Yes, I'd like one.
c) I send all my laundry to the dry cleaners.

2. *Would you be comfortable using an outhouse for a few years until proper plumbing can be arranged?*
a) No problem – that *is* proper plumbing!
b) Well, okay...for now. But proper plumbing is in the cards.
c) Are you crazy? You don't expect me to wait until I get back to the city, do you?

3. *On a water-access property, wind and weather can sometimes leave cottagers "shorebound" for extended periods. Can you handle this?*
a) Sure! Kind of exciting actually.
b) I could handle that for a while.
c) But how will I get into town for the fresh croissants and Sunday *New York Times* I've ordered?

4. *Are you prepared to get by with a limited selection of kitchen appliances?*
a) Absolutely. Barbecues are us. Besides, we still have our camping stove.
b) It's not a problem as long as there's a regular fridge and stove.
c) I suppose I can live without double ovens for a short time, but I'll need a microwave. And a dishwasher. And a refrigerator with an ice-maker on the front.

5. *What are some good activities during a power outage?*
a) I'd go for a paddle on the moonlit lake.
b) Stargazing is great. And if the kids are in bed...well, you know.
c) Isn't there a back-up generator? I'll miss "Wall Street Week."

6. *The only place within an hour's drive where you can shop for groceries is a little corner store. Does this pose a problem?*
a) No. Once I'm away from it all, I like to stay that way.
b) Not a big deal. We'll just make sure we pack carefully.
c) Do they carry triple-crème cheeses and pâté?

7. *How much wildlife contact are you comfortable with?*
a) The closer to nature, the better.

b) I love all creatures great and small – as long as they stay outside the cottage.

c) Chipmunks and squirrels, okay. Surely if we keep the land around the cottage cleared, we won't have to worry about anything else?

8. *In many parts of cottage country, cell phone service is unreliable or non-existent. How do you feel about this?*

a) Couldn't be happier. I hate the things!

b) Fine by me...I'm on vacation.

c) You're kidding, right? If I can't use my cell and BlackBerry, I'll lose my edge!

9. *At many cottages, distance from town means contractors and repair people can't arrive immediately. How handy are you?*

a) Puttering is my hobby. I can rebuild anything with my Leatherman and a roll of duct tape.

b) I can do some basic plumbing and electrical repairs if I have to.

c) My father gave me a hammer when I got married. It's the little silver one that rings the dinner bell.

10. *You've found a cottage with great frontage and a stupendous view over the water. Only thing is, it's a 1960s bungalow that hasn't seen a reno – and, given the price of all that lovely waterfront, your budget won't allow it. Problem?*

a) Not at all. We'll be spending most of our time outside anyway.

b) If it's a sunset view, I can live with avocado appliances. After all, retro is in.

c) How can I invite my boss and her husband for the weekend?

To calculate your Luxury Quotient, tally 1 point for each "A" answer, 2 points for each "B" answer, and 3 points for each "C" answer. If you scored:

10-16   With a luxury quotient as low as yours, it's a wonder you've chosen cottage ownership instead of wilderness camping. The good news is that because you don't require a lot of amenities, your cottage-buying options are wide open; properties that are unsuitable to more finicky buyers tend to be offered at lower prices. A long-term renovation would be right up your alley.

17-23   You're a regular Joe or Joanne: Not surprisingly, you represent the majority of cottage purchasers, able to put up with a certain degree of "roughing it" if comes with other rewards. A place that needs upgrades or renovations is an acceptable option, but they must be governed by a strict timetable. The bad news is that because your profile is shared by many other cottagers, competition for similar properties can be intense.

23-30   You should limit your cottage search to fully turnkey places, close to town, with all the amenities. You'll pay a high price for all that convenience, but a narrower market means fewer buyers vying for the same property. A word of warning: If you scored at the top end of this category, you might reconsider whether any cottage is right for you. Monaco might be more your style.

What do you want to do for fun?

Most cottagers are recreational generalists – they like to swim, paddle a canoe or kayak, do a bit of fishing, knock about in a sailing dinghy or on a sailboard, and try some water-skiing. And it's more than fine to want a cottage just so you have a retreat where you can watch the sun go down – or stare at the Perseid meteor shower in August. But if family members have specific recreational interests that are real priorities, the cottage location needs to satisfy them.

We'll deal with how those different recreational activities affect your search for a property in Chapter 3. For now, you need to identify them – the **checklist** on p. 34 will help – so that one family member's desire for great bass fishing doesn't negate another's dinghy-sailing ambitions. Clearly understanding what it is you want to do at the cottage will help to focus your search and avoid conflict.

Are kids part of your cottage picture?

If you have a young family, the suitability of the property to kids is going to make or break your enjoyment of it. A cottage is supposed to provide a relaxing getaway, not an injection of high anxiety. In vacation areas on the Canadian Shield, for instance, you might be tempted by properties with spectacular views set on shorelines with rocky drop-offs, both above and below the water. Granted, young children can never be left unsupervised – anywhere – but think carefully about how much fun you're going to have if you're constantly making sure your toddlers don't toddle off a 30-foot cliff. And a property with a beach isn't necessarily the answer if it also comes with a lot of boat traffic that threatens children swimming and venturing out in kayaks and pedal boats.

TIP: Kid-friendliness is more than a "danger rating"

Rather than accepting or rejecting a potential property based on how dangerous you think it might be, also look at it from another, more positive direction. Ask yourself whether it has what it takes to build happy memories – what it has to offer that could be engaging and fun for your children for summers to come:

• Are there lots of kid-friendly sunfish and rock bass to be caught right off the dock?

• Is there a marsh nearby that kids can explore with dip nets?

• Is there a natural attraction you can use as a hiking or boating destination? A berry patch? A picnic spot? A lookout? A beaver pond?

• Is the water calm enough to allow kids to learn to paddle a canoe and sail? And is there a sailing club nearby that will teach them? (*See "Look Beyond the Property," next page, for more things to think about when you evaluate the possibilities for family fun.*)

TIP: Look beyond the property to gauge the fun potential

- A cottage area's road system can be a real hoot for mountain-biking, and provide an additional incentive for buying, especially if you have teens with energy to burn.
- Nearby parks can offer trails for hiking and skiing; they may also have interpretive centers with nature programs of interest to young and old, from stargazing to wolf-call outings. A local naturalists' club can also provide options.
- Some cottage locations put you in close proximity to cultural draws. Is there summer theater? A concert series? An art gallery or annual tour of artists' studios? A good local library? First-class entertainment often tours through (or is based in) cottage country. Some cottage locations put you in close proximity, and some don't. State and provincial tourism promotion programs do a good job of outlining date-specific attractions, and can give you an overview of what's going on where and when.
- Find out if the lake has an association or clubs that offer swimming or sailing lessons or environmental activities for kids.

Geography is rarely homogeneous: You can often find a variety of waterfront types within any area – even on the same small lake. (Even classic Canadian Shield terrain has its share of beaches.) Don't give up on a particular area because you think it might be too rocky for your toddlers. You can also adapt yourself to your children's needs in their early years by taking them to a beach near the cottage. They'll thank you later for having had the foresight to buy a property with a rock outcrop from which they can execute cannonballs.

That said, the issue of "child appropriate" vacation properties doesn't have to be so complicated. Sure, toddlers will fare better with even a small stretch of beach where they can putter about in the shallows and fling pails of sand in your hair. But children are adaptable and parents are resourceful, and generations of cottage youngsters have been safely introduced to a wide variety of environments and activities with proper precautions, training, and supervision. Because there is no way to avoid risk completely, no vacation property is 100% "child safe" – just as no city or suburban street is.

Finally, while many buyers are seeking isolation, solitude isn't necessarily the best option for a young family. Some seasonal communities stand out because they allow children to socialize, both formally and informally – which can be a big plus if your young ones are at an age where siblings need more than each other for company. New friendships can develop at a community beach, and some local owners' associations even offer a calendar of activities that will keep the kids engaged and entertained. When considering a particular property, ask the real estate agent if there are families with children of ages similar to your own in the immediate area. Who knows? That kid quotient could seal the deal.

The Cottage Wants Checklist

Use this checklist to get a picture of what's important to you – and what's not. If you're wise, you'll have your spouse fill out the checklist, too. Then compare notes. Unless you're extremely like-minded, some discussion will undoubtedly need to follow. Then, as you begin to look at listings, refer to the checklist to see how well a property matches your priorities.

Rate the importance of each item:
1. I agree strongly; **2.** I agree somewhat; **3.** I disagree somewhat; **4.** I disagree strongly

Cottage usage	1	2	3	4	I want a four-season cottage
	1	2	3	4	I'm happy with a May–October cottage
	1	2	3	4	The cottage will be used primarily on weekends, plus a couple of one- or two-week vacations
	1	2	3	4	I plan to stay there for long stretches or an entire season
	1	2	3	4	I want to retire there right away or in the near future
Getting there	1	2	3	4	I want road access
					If by road...
	1	2	3	4	It's important that the cottage is on a municipally assumed road
	1	2	3	4	It's important that the cottage is on a private road
	1	2	3	4	I want water access
					If by water...
	1	2	3	4	I want to travel to the cottage on sheltered water
	1	2	3	4	Some "big" water is okay
	1	2	3	4	I'm happy if the boat ride to the cottage is part of the adventure
Services					**Electricity**
	1	2	3	4	The property must have electrical service of some kind
	1	2	3	4	The electrical service must be from a utility
	1	2	3	4	The electrical service must be capable of supporting typical home appliances
	1	2	3	4	The electrical service can be "off-grid" (solar, wind, or generator power, for example)
					Water
	1	2	3	4	There must be a potable water supply from a utility
	1	2	3	4	The water can be drawn from a well or the lake
	1	2	3	4	Water from a well or lake must be treated by an in-line purification system
	1	2	3	4	I'm happy to bring in my own potable (bottled) water
					Sewage
	1	2	3	4	The property must be serviced by a municipal waste system
	1	2	3	4	The property can have a septic bed
	1	2	3	4	The property can have an above-ground septic tank
	1	2	3	4	The property can have a composting toilet or other alternative toilet
	1	2	3	4	The property can have just an outhouse

Condition					
	1	2	3	4	The cottage must be in turnkey condition
	1	2	3	4	The cottage can require minor renovations (less than $10,000)
	1	2	3	4	The cottage can require substantial renovation (more than $10,000)
	1	2	3	4	The cottage can be a "tear-down" and require complete replacement
	1	2	3	4	The property can be occupied by a trailer or mobile home
	1	2	3	4	The property can be vacant, without a cottage on it

Remoteness					
	_____	minutes			Maximum acceptable travel time to the nearest full-service town (e.g. food and beverage shopping, hardware store, medical facilities)
	_____	minutes			Maximum acceptable travel time to the nearest store with basic supplies
	1	2	3	4	I want neighboring cottages within easy walking distance
	1	2	3	4	I prefer not to have neighbors close by

Waterfront

My preferences for a cottage are...

	1	2	3	4	Rock-and-pine landscape
	1	2	3	4	At least some beachfront
	1	2	3	4	On a high, rocky slope
	1	2	3	4	On level ground at water's edge
	1	2	3	4	On a small water body
	1	2	3	4	On a large water body
	1	2	3	4	On a chain of lakes
	1	2	3	4	On a water body with some restrictions on motorized vessels
	1	2	3	4	On a water body with lots of boating opportunities
	1	2	3	4	Shallow "walk-in" entry to the water
	1	2	3	4	Steep drop-off at water's edge requiring entry from a dock

View

	1	2	3	4	The property must have a sunset view
	1	2	3	4	The property must face the sunrise
	1	2	3	4	I don't want to see other cottages when I look out my front window

Location

	1	2	3	4	The cottage must occupy waterfront property
	1	2	3	4	I want an island property
					If on an island...
	1	2	3	4	I want a private island
	1	2	3	4	A multi-cottage island is fine
	1	2	3	4	The cottage could be on a river rather than a lake
					If on a river, it must...
	1	2	3	4	be navigable by powerboat
	1	2	3	4	be navigable by sailboat
	1	2	3	4	be navigable only for purposes of paddle sports
	1	2	3	4	grant access to a larger water body
	1	2	3	4	The cottage could be a backlot property

Continued on next page

				If a backlot property, it must...
1	2	3	4	have publicly accessible waterfront within walking distance
1	2	3	4	have a public boat launch area within short driving distance
1	2	3	4	have a marina nearby where a boat can be kept

Waterfront structures				
1	2	3	4	A large dock is important
1	2	3	4	A small dock is okay for now, as long as it's feasible to put a larger one in later
1	2	3	4	A small dock is all I need
1	2	3	4	A boathouse is important

Recreation				
				The following activities are critical to the enjoyment of the property...
1	2	3	4	Swimming
1	2	3	4	Sailing
1	2	3	4	Paddle sports
1	2	3	4	Waterskiing
1	2	3	4	Wakeboarding
1	2	3	4	General powerboating (taking lake cruises, tubing, etc.)
1	2	3	4	Fishing
1	2	3	4	—There must be good fishing opportunities in close proximity to the cottage
1	2	3	4	—Fishing areas may be on an adjoining lake or river system, accessible by boat
1	2	3	4	—I just want "fun" fishing for me and my family
1	2	3	4	Hunting
1	2	3	4	Hiking
1	2	3	4	Birdwatching
1	2	3	4	Relaxing on the dock
1	2	3	4	Snowmobiling
1	2	3	4	Cross-country skiing
1	2	3	4	The cottage must serve as a chalet in the winter for skiing
				If it is to serve as a chalet...
1	2	3	4	I want to be within a 30-minute drive of the ski area
1	2	3	4	it can be greater than 30 minutes away from the ski area

Accommodation				
				The cottage must provide private accommodations for...
			_____ *number*	couples and single adults
			_____ *number*	children and youth (under 21)
1	2	3	4	Children and youth may share a room
1	2	3	4	Children and youth may occupy an outbuilding
1	2	3	4	Overnight guests are expected frequently
1	2	3	4	Guests may occupy an outbuilding

Rental				
1	2	3	4	The property will be rented out occasionally
				If so, property will be rented out...
1	2	3	4	only to family and friends
1	2	3	4	on at least some occasions to strangers

Cross–border shopping: Issues affecting Americans buying property in Canada

Canadians and Americans have been crossing the world's longest unde-fended border in search of vacation properties for decades. (Franklin Delano Roosevelt had a lovely summer getaway on New Brunswick's Campobello Island. It's now a park jointly administered by Canada and the U.S.) In some Canadian vacation areas, American ownership represents a large proportion (sometimes even a majority) of properties, and some Canadian real estate ads give prices in both Canadian and U.S. dollars. The investment flow in the opposite direction is far more limited, especially for summer vacation properties, as a result of concerns over health-care coverage, the purchasing disadvantage of the Canadian dollar, and a robust supply of properties north of the border. (Canadians have been investing in ski chalets in the U.S., and the American South is home to an abundance of Canadian-owned winter getaways, but neither category falls within the parameters we've set for this book.)

Beyond the scenery and the fishing, a favorable exchange rate has en-couraged spending of greenbacks in Canada. Cross-border buying has also been boosted by the 1997 repeals of a 20 percent land-transfer tax in Ontario and a 33 percent land-transfer "duty" in Quebec on properties purchased by non-residents. The repeal of these charges has, in recent years, produced heavy promotion of vacation property opportunities for Americans by On-tario and Quebec realtors.

Some of the main issues that affect Americans buying in Canada are:

Taxation

This a complex and confusing area, so consult your tax accountant before you start cross-border shopping. Here are the essential concepts to keep in mind:

• A property owner must pay property taxes to the local municipality, re-gardless of his or her citizenship or residency status.

• A cottage in Canada – or anywhere else outside the U.S. – can qualify as an American taxpayer's main or second home, and generate all the appropriate expense deductions on personal income tax available to such residences in the U.S. These deductions include the property taxes paid to a Canadian municipality, as well as borrowing costs associated with the property. *See Chapter 9 for more.*

• Canadian properties owned by American citizens are not subject to the estate laws of Canada. They are, however, subject to capital gains taxes, which are paid to the Canadian government. *See Chapter 14 for more.*

• Under the 1997 tax treaty between Canada and the U.S., Canada can collect taxes on revenue earned by Americans in Canada and on gains realized on the sale of Canadian property. Taxable items include rental income from a property and, as mentioned above, capital gains realized on its sale. But non-resident taxpayers cannot be double-taxed. U.S. taxpayers receive credits for the taxes they have paid in Canada to offset any taxes to which they are subject at home. *See Chapter 11 for more on taxation of rental revenue, and Chapter 14 for more on capital gains taxation.*

Restrictions on non-resident land ownership

• Some provinces have restrictions on property acquisition in Canada that apply to Americans. This is a confusing area of Canadian property law, and regulations could change in individual provinces at any time. Make sure you know the limitations before you get your heart set on a property. *From east to west across the country:*

Newfoundland and Labrador: No restrictions.

Nova Scotia: No restrictions. At the moment, foreign owners (meaning not a Canadian citizen, landed immigrant, or permanent resident under Canadian law) of property outside municipal boundaries must sign in with the Foreign Land Registry Office.

New Brunswick: No restrictions.

Prince Edward Island: Non-resident purchases are limited to five acres and a shore frontage of 165 feet; larger purchase proposals must be submitted to the Island Regulatory and Appeals Commission for approval.

Quebec: Non-residents are restricted to 10 acres of agricultural land, which can affect some vacation properties.

Ontario: No restrictions, except for grants of provincial Crown land.

Saskatchewan and **Manitoba:** Non-Canadian non-residents are restricted to 10 acres of agricultural land.

Alberta: The province's Foreign Ownership of Land Regulations restrict the acquisition of "controlled" lands, which are private, agricultural, and recreational lands outside municipal boundaries. Ownership by non-Canadian non-residents of these controlled lands is capped at two lots totalling 20 acres, although exemptions are available. From the perspective of vacation properties, Crown land is available only to Canadian citizens.

British Columbia: No restrictions, except for grants of provincial Crown land.

CAUTION:

Canadians, take note

If you're thinking of buying property outside your home province, be aware that restrictions on ownership in some provinces have nothing to do with citizenship but apply to *all* non-permanent residents of that particular province. (*See list at right.*)

Borrowing from Canadian institutions

• Non-residents of Canada can secure mortgages from a Canadian financial institution, but their borrowing is limited by the Canada Mortgage and Housing Corporation to 75 percent of appraised value, unless they have an ownership partner who has residency status.

• A portion of mortgage interest payments made by an American to a Canadian bank must be withheld from the lender and remitted to the IRS. *See Chapter 9, p. 147.*

Health care and retirement

Purchasing a vacation property in Canada – even if you use it as a retirement home – won't qualify you for provincial health insurance coverage unless you secure permanent residence status or otherwise meet strict residency requirements. *(See Chapter 13 for more on public health coverage and permanent residency.)* Canadian hospitals won't turn you away at the emergency room if you drop a load of firewood on your foot or suffer a heart attack while chopping it. But you *will* have to figure out how to pay the bill.

American property owners must take care to ensure that their private health-care coverage extends beyond the U.S. border. Even at that, many Canadian hospitals will insist that the bill is settled by the patient, and will not direct-bill a U.S. insurance company.

Caution for Canadians buying from a non-resident

Canadians who buy a vacation property in their own country from any non-resident can be in for a major tax shock if they don't take care at the closing. The non-resident owner is obligated to pay tax to the Canadian government on the capital gains realized on the sale. The person buying the property is responsible for remitting a tax of either 25 or 50 percent (depending on the property ownership category) of the entire purchase price – not simply of the capital gain – unless the seller provides a tax clearance from the Canada Revenue Agency (CRA). Standard practice for Canadians buying Canadian property from a non-resident owner who doesn't come up with a tax clearance at closing is to withhold the higher 50 percent portion of the purchase price and remit it to the CRA, then let the seller get back whatever portion of that remittance he's entitled to by filing a Canadian tax return.

Any astute real estate lawyer should be aware of this – but don't let it slip between the cracks. If you don't hold back and remit the 50 percent of the purchase price and the vendor hasn't paid the capital gains tax, the CRA will come to you looking for it. This remittance requirement also applies to a non-resident who buys a Canadian property from another non-resident.

3. Choosing your lake or river

In the previous chapter, we discussed some basic preparatory work for buying a vacation property. We touched on setting a budget, determining a search area, and narrowing down the qualities your ideal property would have. Now we want to take that information and begin to translate it into a specific place.

No matter where you start, do your due diligence

The search process set out in this book starts with identifying target price and driving distance and establishing a wish list (Chapter 2), and then moves to identifying potential locations that meet those criteria. However, for many cottage buyers, the process starts with a specific real estate listing: They are attracted to a particular lake because of a particular property for sale on it.

If this is your situation, even though the property has tugged at your heartstrings, it's crucial that you still go through the exercises of (a) analyzing your needs and wants, and (b) finding out all you can about the lake or river the property is on. Back the emotional appeal of the cottage with some solid homework to make sure it satisfies your criteria and is the right place for you and your family.

When choosing a vacation property, you shouldn't start with the building. Instead, the emphasis should lean heavily towards the location. You can renovate, rebuild, or even tear down and replace an existing cottage, *but you can't change the characteristics of the lake.*

If you fall in love with a cottage, make sure you can also fall in love with the body of water sitting in front of it.

How to be a lake detective

The most important factors when considering a chunk of waterfront property are the overall nature and well-being of the lake or river that makes it waterfront in the first place. Before you can determine whether the body of water will mesh with your hoped-for activities, you need to do a little research to determine its general character.

Trouble is, depending on your locale, it may be impossible to find a

Mining cottage association reports for nuggets of buyer-helpful information

It's remarkable how much you can learn about a lake from one publicly available document, whether it's a cottage association's newsletter or the minutes of its annual general meeting. Here's what a potential buyer could glean from one single AGM report, available on the association's website. (Names have been changed to protect the vexed.)

• "Brad gave an excellent PowerPoint presentation on black bears, focusing on mothers and their cubs...."

(Note to self: Ask cottage association or local office of department of natural resources: Does this mean the cottage is in a healthy wilderness area? Or is it signaling a problem with bears breaking into cottages? Or both?)

• "It was noted that crayfish have disappeared from the lake.... Members were asked to report their views on this and frog disappearance. These species are sentinels and might indicate water quality or fish predators are a problem."

(Red flags! Worth investigating to make sure there isn't a water-quality problem. But don't overreact – the declines could be a natural cycle.)

single source that will succinctly "rate" a lake, since many governments are loath to make such pronouncements. That said, there are other ways to perform a health check on the lake of your dreams, most of them requiring only some common sense and a detective's nose.

Who's in the know? Where to turn for info

• **A knowledgeable realtor who lives in the area** can be a great source of information on everything from how weedy the lake gets in summer to how high or low its levels can fluctuate. Is your agent an angler? If so, start asking fishy questions.

• Even if fishing isn't really an interest, you can get some good info simply by dropping into a **local bait shop** or **tackle store**. Ask the owners – or other customers – about the water quality and you'll probably learn more than you ever imagined about average depth, fish populations, weeds, and turbidity (how clear or murky a lake is). Nine times out of ten, you'll also learn something about the lake's history.

TIP:
"Name" lakes cost more
Whether you're shopping for shoes or a cottage, certain names carry a cachet − and that cachet comes at a cost. Well-known, high-profile lakes in popular vacation areas command more than their lesser-known cousins. (Simply put, you pay a premium when you want Manolos or Muskoka.)

If you don't want to pay for a name, check out the lesser-known or "sleeper lakes" in the same area, which can offer similar landscape and a similar overall feel. They may be smaller and a little farther afield than the "name" lakes, but they may also be less crowded − and a lot less expensive.

• "Mary talked about the possible reallocation of police officers to the Northeastern Regional Office. She is concerned that service in our area might be adversely affected."

(Maybe Mary is a worrywart. But maybe she's not. Why is a police presence so necessary in this little town? Has there been a history of cottage break-ins or vandalism?)

• "Blackheart Paving Co. has applied for approval of a portable asphalt plant at the quarry on the highway. Council is split on this issue, but Randy is very much against it. There was a concern that people on Buzzard Bay might notice an asphalt odor and there could be some environmental pollution at the site."

(Better check which way the prevailing winds blow – and prevailing political winds, too. Will runoff into the lake be a problem?)

• "Wayne noted that the township's Official Plan has not yet been accepted. However, it is true that the proposed plan will state there is a 100-foot setback for all new buildings. Carol said she was concerned that the association had spoken against the plan and that a change to it could make development on the lake much easier. Emile noted that the association position was that the designation of the lake as 'nearing capacity' should remain, but that allowance should be made for the current setback of 66 ft. to remain. The Board would also vigorously oppose any attempt to sell Crown land on the lake."

(Whoa! If that 100-foot setback passes, will you be able to build onto the front of the cottage as you planned? On the other hand, maybe modifying your own plans is a worthwhile trade-off for strict development controls.)

TIP:

It's nice to have a big umbrella

In some states and provinces, lake associations and ratepayers' groups get together to form even larger "umbrella organizations" that allow them to lobby governments with more clout and combine their efforts on things such as environmental initiatives. In Ontario, for example, the Federation of Ontario Cottagers' Associations (FOCA) represents more than 500 individual lake associations. By contacting the umbrella organization, you can find out if there is an association on the lake you're interested in and get put in touch with its members.

• Many lakes have a **ratepayers' group** or **lake association** made up of full- and part-time residents who care enough about the lake they live on to form an official group and pay dues. By contacting a lake association member, you can learn a great deal about the human side of things from someone who perhaps has raised children and grandchildren on the very lake you're thinking about buying on. Some lake associations participate in environmental programs such as those that monitor water quality and conduct ecological inventories of flora and fauna. You'll also find out about local issues. (*See "Hot-Button Local Issues," p. 57.*) An invaluable resource for cottage detectives.

To find the association on a lake you're interested in, ask locally (e.g., a real estate agent or the municipal office), or let your fingers do the walking: Type the name of the lake or lake area and "ratepayers" or "association" into a search engine such as Google. (*Also see the Tip, at left.*)

• Another research technique is to contact **the relevant state department** or **provincial ministry**. (In the U.S., the national Fish and Wildlife Service can also be a helpful gateway.) You'll often find a distinction between the departments and ministries that are concerned with environmental issues, and ones that address natural resources, which include sportfish and game. In Ontario, for example, the overlap is between the Ministry of the Environment and the Ministry of Natural Resources. In Michigan, it's between the Department of Environmental Quality and the Department of Natural Resources. The "natural resources" department or ministry is usually your main information node. Check its website; the Minnesota Department of Natural Resources, for one, has an online "lake finder" tool that provides a wealth of data, including topographic and bottom-contour maps and info on fish populations, water levels, and water quality.

• **Maps** and **charts** can provide a wealth of information to potential cottage owners. See p. 46 for the main types and the clues they can offer about the area you're considering.

What's your lake like?

As you snoop around to get a basic idea of your lake's general characteristics, here are a few areas to think about, as they will affect how the lake will match your version of cottaging.

Size matters: What's the depth?

The shape of a lake, what scientists call morphology, can have a profound effect on how suitable a body of water might be for a prospective cottager. Deep lakes, for example, tend to be cooler and have lower nutrient levels and more dissolved oxygen than shallow lakes, making them good places to find cold-water species of fish such as lake trout. Warmer, shallower lakes with their high nutrient levels will support a much wider variety of species (making them great for anglers), but they'll also tend to be weedier (which isn't so good for squeamish swimmers).

Nutrient levels: Well fed or overfed?

The levels of phosphorus and nitrogen in a lake are directly related to its ability to support biological growth. Higher levels mean more growth, which can mean more weeds. On the positive side, this can mean more fish, but too much growth can also backfire; as aquatic plants sink and decompose, they create an unpleasant stew and gobble up dissolved oxygen that fish need to survive. Too few nutrients however, are just as bad. Without sufficient nutrients to support biological growth, a lake can lose its ability to maintain a healthy fish population.

To classify lakes according to their levels of nutrients, water scientists (called limnologists) divide them into three categories. **Oligotrophic** lakes have very low nutrient levels, **mesotrophic** lakes have moderate levels, and **eutrophic** lakes have high levels. You might like an oligotrophic lake for its crystal-clear, weed-free waters, but you won't have much luck fishing for largemouth bass. And while the fish-rich waters of a eutrophic lake might appeal if you're an angler, a weed-choked swimming area and funky-smelling water are a big turn-off. What most cottagers are looking for is a mesotrophic lake – one that, as Goldilocks would put it, is "just right."

These lake types are involved in a long-term process called eutrophication, in which bodies of water gradually turn from oligotrophic to mesotrophic to eutrophic. Left to its own devices, nature generally requires thousands of years to turn a lake from oligotrophic to eutrophic. But human activities can ratchet up the process to such a degree that serious eutrophication can unfold well within a cottager's lifetime. The main culprit is nutrient loading from agricultural runoff, septic systems, and lawn fertilizers.

CAUTION: Algae alert

In a few lakes, eutrophication has reached a crisis point, becoming so severe that it leads to blooms of blue-green algae (otherwise known as "pond scum"). Some varieties produce a dangerous toxin as they die and decay, and when such a bloom occurs, health authorities can take aggressive steps on a lake until it goes away – ordering people not to drink the water (boiling it first won't eliminate the toxins; special filtration generally is required) or even swim in it (and to keep pets out as well). Not what you're looking for in a cottage lake.

The type of lake most susceptible to these toxic blooms is shallow and warm, with minimal circulation. If you're considering purchasing on such a lake, find out if it has any history of algae blooms, and how persistent the problem is. (A 1999 study of 130 lakes in upstate New York found that 20% of them showed evidence of potentially toxic blooms – and that once a lake had experienced a bloom, the odds were 50-50 that it would have another.) If a lake has had problems in the past, determine what measures are being taken to control their reoccurrence.

Area maps: Essential tools for lake detectives

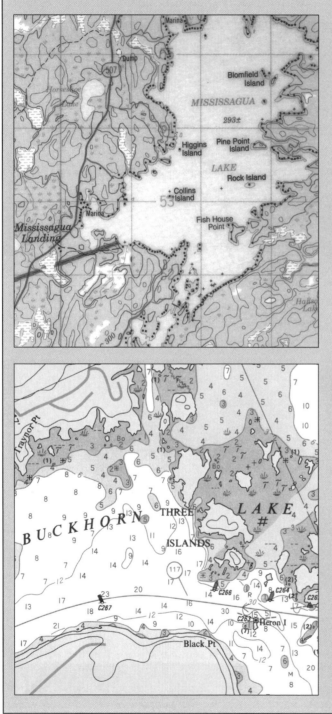

Topographic

No cottage search is complete without an up-to-date "topo" map. Available in scales from 1:10,000 to 1:50,000 (the smaller the second number, the greater the detail), they can convey a tremendous amount of information about surface features.

In addition to land elevations, you'll find lakes, ponds, rivers, creeks, marshes, and swamps. All manner of roads are marked, along with railroads, power corridors, dams, marinas, waterfalls, rapids, fish ladders, and much, much more. Outside of urban areas, you'll find individual buildings marked. Those black squares indicating every known home, cottage, barn, and shed can tell you a lot about the density of a lake community. (Just pay attention to the map date. A lot of construction can happen in 10 to 20 years.)

Federal and provincial/state parks and First Nations reserves are also marked, further filling in the picture of land use in the area. While actual zoning information isn't included, structures such as airports, sewage treatment plants, municipal dumps, and aggregate quarries are – interesting information to the potential purchaser of property.

A topo map doesn't have lake-depth contours or individual soundings, though some companies are producing maps that blend topographic and hydrographic information. Your best bet to finding these specialized maps is to look in the Yellow Pages or on the Internet for a dedicated map store.

Hydrographic

If the lake or other water body that interests you is part of a federal navigable waterway, it will have a hydrographic chart. These are the nautical charts produced for navigation purposes. The information they convey about the surrounding land is fairly limited – they're for navigation, after all – but they can tell you other interesting stuff: They mark marshy areas, for instance (great for paddling; not so great for a cottage on-shore), and underwater hydro cables, which will tip you off to the location of cot-tages. They can also give you a sense of boat traffic (if, say, a buoyed small-craft route is marked in an area you're considering). They usually provide depths and bottom contours, as well as showing general bottom type – mud, sand, rock, etc. – all useful information for prospective cottagers.

Bottom contour

Maps showing bottom contours exist for some lakes, usually those that are fishing hot spots. (They often include fishing information on them as well.) They'll tell you lake depths and bottom topography, including shoals, humps, and deep holes that will pique the interest of keen anglers. (They're not meant for naviga-tion.) From the prospective cottager's point of view, bottom-contour maps hint at the depth and steepness of the drop-off in front of that cottage property you're considering.

Check with the provincial or state de-partment of natural resources or a local bait shop to find out if one is available for your lake.

Planning

This category of maps provides information on zoning, current and future land use, utility easements and other rights of way such as road allowances, individual lot configurations, as-sumed roads, parkland and other public land, and more. Pay attention to zoning definitions, not only for the land occupied by the property you're thinking of buying, but also of the ad-joining lands. (Where applicable, also get a copy of the map that shows flood risk areas.)

Prepared by municipalities and, some-times, by other levels of government, these maps are now downloadable in many cases. Otherwise, you may be able to inspect or make copies of them at the municipal office.

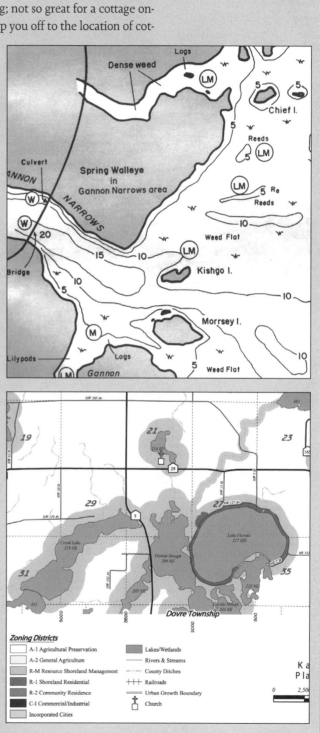

TIP:

Happy fish mean a happy lake

If a lake's fish populations are healthy, it's a good bet the water quality is also in good shape. Lake detectives should check out government publications that cover sport-fishing regulations. Information on open seasons, slot limits, and species restrictions will give you insight into a particular lake's fish populations and whether it has been pressured by overfishing, habitat loss, or more serious water-quality problems. As well, look for publications that provide edibility guidelines for sportfish: species by species breakdowns of toxin levels and safe eating amounts. If you can eat most sizes and species of the fish that live in your prospective lake, it's a safe bet that you can swim in it, too.

Wet your whistle: Can you drink the water?

Many cottagers and lake boosters underscore the pristine qualities of their favorite water body with statements like, "Crystal Lake is so pure you can drink the water right off the dock!"

But, the fact is, you should never drink *any* untreated surface water, even if it's from an undiscovered lake never before seen by human beings. Illness-causing pathogens of all sorts live in even the "purest" waters, courtesy of the wildlife that do their business in and around streams, rivers, and lakes. A short slurp might not do you any harm – this time. But a second slurp from the same spot a few minutes later might leave your stomach in an uproar.

Most surface water, however, *can* be treated to make it safe for drinking, by running it through a cottage-based purification system. (For info on the types of systems available for water treatment – and a host of other water-related subjects – pick up a copy of *Cottage Water Systems: An Out-of-the-City Guide to Pumps, Plumbing, Water Purification, and Privies* by Max Burns.)

Even when treated to the point of meeting provincial or state drinking-water standards, water from a lake (or a well, for that matter) may not measure up to *your* idea of "drinkable" water because of its taste and character. Sulphur and other minerals can impart odors; turbidity – the amount of suspended solids – can cause cloudiness. And the water may have a slight (albeit harmless) tint caused by tannins in plant matter, which you might not even notice until you fill a bathtub. Additional treatment systems can take care of such things, or you may choose to tolerate the differences for showering and doing dishes, and rely on bottled water for cooking and drinking.

Once you get serious about a particular property, you'll want to know more about its water supply. (*See Chapter 5, p. 93, for questions to ask, and Chapter 7, p. 121. for info on having the water tested.*) For now, although general water-quality information for specific lakes can be hard to find, some lake associa-

TIP: **Research through renting**

One of the best ways to really get a handle on a particular cottage area is to rent there. A weekend or week-long visit at a property can tell you a lot more than a one-hour visit with a real estate agent. You might discover that the sound of a babbling brook has cured your insomnia...or the sound of the lake's late-night partiers has worsened it. Good things to know. You also get to try out the fishing and the swimming. If you're highly motivated to buy, trial renting may not be the best strategy, as it can take several summers to line up all the rentals that will allow you to sample various areas. But there's no substitute for first-hand experience. If you can manage the time to use the research-through-rental approach, do so.

tions do conduct their own water audits and may be able to provide helpful data. The local health department can tell you if there have been problems in the past requiring a boil-water advisory or restrictions on use. (*See Caution, p. 45.*)

Wet your whole self: Is it safe for swimming??

The vast majority of North American lakes are perfectly safe to swim in. A history of algae blooms (*see Caution, p. 45*) or persistent outbreaks of giardiasis or "beaver fever" (a parasite-related illness) are possible red flags. If you have reason to suspect a problem, contact the local health department and find out if the lake has been subject to any closures to recreational use.

How much does the water level change?

Changes in water level can have a profound effect on your ability to enjoy a particular property. Shoreline contours change; beaches emerge or disappear; fish and other wildlife habitats can be dramatically affected; docks can be left high and dry. With a water-access property, you might even have trouble getting to the cottage if the water level drops substantially.

Seasonal changes

Most rivers and lakes in vacation country are influenced to some degree by seasonal changes: They begin rising in spring, due to snowmelt and runoff, and decrease as the summer progresses. Depending on the drainage and the importance of the spring snowmelt, the levels can change in any given lake a little or a lot – and it will vary from year to year, depending on precipitation (both snow and rain) and temperature (which affects the amount of evaporation). Some lakes scarcely register the seasonal cycle in their levels; others, like the Great Lakes, typically see a seasonal level change of several feet.

The Great Lakes also see multi-year cyclical changes, with both high-water years (and the attendant beachfront erosion) and low-water years creating problems for property owners.

The ups and downs of feeder lakes

Feeder lakes – lakes that are part of watersheds that feed a controlled system such as Ontario's Trent-Severn Waterway – can see their levels rise and fall dramatically throughout the year. The lakes in the Kawarthas and Haliburton areas that feed the Trent-Severn, for instance, are controlled by a series of dams, some with hydro-generating capacity. When the levels of the waterway drop too low for safe navigation, water will be released through the system – from either a power station or a stoplog dam – to compensate, causing the level on upstream lakes to drop. The lakes may be further drained down in the fall, so that the system can handle the spring highs caused by snowmelt and runoff.

TIP:

Itching to buy on a particular lake?

If you hear about swimmer's itch on a particular lake or see posted notices at its waterfront parks, it's not a reason to avoid purchasing a cottage there. Though swimmer's itch produces a rather unsightly lumpy red rash – which occurs when the larval stage of certain flatworms burrow into the skin – it is *not* an indicator of pollution problems in a lake. On the contrary, it is often touted as a sign of the local ecosystem's overall health. (The flatworm life cycle moves through snails to waterfowl and then into the water.) And because migratory birds are involved, it can't be said to be found in one lake and never in another.

In any case, it can be avoided by vigorously toweling down after a swim.

CAUTION:

You'll pay extra for flood protection

Standard homeowner policies in Canada and the U.S. do not cover flood damage. Additional insurance must be purchased to take care of this risk – or eventuality – and, be forewarned, it doesn't come cheap.

CAUTION:

Sand but true...

Because beaches are so desirable, there's a growing trend in vacation country to put them where they don't belong, by trucking in – or barging in – loads of sand at great expense. Trouble is, if Ma Nature didn't want a beach there in the first place, it won't remain there for long, as winds and waves will soon sweep the sand away. If you're not prepared for the costs of annual beach maintenance, make sure your sand is the real McCoy.

Is the cottage on a system used for power generation?

Across the Laurentian Shield, public and private utilities have harnessed its cascading waters to generate electricity. Ontario is one of the most intensively dammed jurisdictions, with Ontario Power Generation (OPG) operating 29 small hydroelectric plants and 240 dams on 26 different river systems. (Some of these river systems are far removed from vacation areas, but others, such as the Muskoka and the Madawaska, are very much within cottage country.) Wisconsin has an estimated 200 dams of various sizes generating electricity, while Minnesota has 39 hydroelectric operations.

The flow of water is manipulated in the name of power generation, but operators are also supposed to be sensitive to recreational concerns, wildlife, and the fishery. Rapid changes in local levels can be considerable – on the order of several feet. If you are considering a cottage on a watercourse with hydroelectric operations, you should educate yourself on the system and its influence on local water conditions. A good starting place is the website of the utility (OPG in Ontario, for instance) or the state or provincial department of natural resources.

Is the property on a flood plain?

Take heed of properties along river courses (and lakes within river systems) that appear to be either on or overlooking natural flood plains. You can remove the guesswork by contacting the local conservation authority, which oversees flood-control measures, or the provincial or state natural-resources people. Areas prone to flooding are well delineated in disaster-management planning, and flood warnings are regularly issued. Floods are not strictly a spring-runoff phenomenon and can be triggered throughout the summer as well.

In Canada, the federal and provincial governments have entered into agreements to reduce flood damage. The Canada Mortgage and Housing Corporation will no longer finance new developments in designated flood areas, and disaster-assistance programs will no longer cover losses due to flooding of new developments in those areas. Municipalities are also being encouraged or expected (depending on the province) to zone according to flood risk in designated areas and to incorporate flood-hazard information into municipal planning.

Ontario leads the country in flood mapping, with more than 270 designated communities; Quebec is close behind, with about 250. Lists for each province and territory are available on-line (www.ec.gc.ca/water/en/manage/flood/e_fdrp.htm#prov). In the U.S., the Federal Emergency Management Agency (FEMA) maintains and updates the National Flood Insurance Program maps, which identify local risks; you can search for and order them on-line from FEMA's Map Service Center (msc.fema.gov). Also visit FEMA's Multi-Hazard Mapping Initiative at hazardmaps.gov. Its interactive on-line atlas allows you to pinpoint info on flood zones and recent flood data.

Matching your lake with your planned activities

Swimming

When we think of cottages, we think of hitting the water. But not everybody hits the water the same way, and some people don't like to hit it at all. (If you don't swim and don't have to accommodate any family or friends who do, then don't worry about it. Pick a lot with a lovely view.)

For most would-be cottagers, however, the typical waterfront decision is between a rocky shoreline and a sandy beach. Some properties will give you a helpful mix of both, but for the most part, you have to make a choice. Be prepared to be flexible, and take a hard look at the way you really like to swim. If the swim area is mostly for adults, who can dive off a rock or dock for some serious laps, then a shallow entry isn't a necessity. Deep-water swimming also keeps your feet out of the weeds, if that sort of thing bothers you. For small children, or swimmers who like to be able to touch the bottom, it does make sense to have some shallow beach access.

Boating

Cottage boating has as many permutations as there are types of boat. When you're considering a cottage area from a boating perspective, you want to know if a particular kind of boating is both feasible and permissible. If you're keen on waterskiing or wakeboarding, for example, a lake with restrictions on boat speed and wake isn't for you. Eliminating such lakes from your property search area from the get-go will make drawing up a shortlist of prospective properties much simpler.

Choosing a lake that limits boating to certain categories – either by law or because of the nature of the water body – should be done with some caution, especially if your current boating experience is limited. Once you own waterfront property, you may well find yourself getting drawn into all sorts of boating activities that weren't previously in your (or your family's) repertoire, or that weren't in your preconceived notion of how you would entertain yourself.

That said, you want to make sure that the kind of boating you plan to

TIP:

Look before you leap

Make sure you know what your swimming area is like early, mid, and late season. On a shallow, warm, eutrophic lake, a sandy cove that looks so appealing in May might turn into an algae pond come August. On a lake that's subject to large fluctuations in water level, a beach that's lovely in late season may not exist several months earlier.

TIP: **Go for a tour of the lake by boat**

Ask your real estate agent or rent a boat from the local marina. Go for a ride and check out the boats you see at other cottage docks and on the water. Also check out the boats at the local marinas – the ones berthed there and the ones they sell and service. Although such indicators don't tell the whole story, they're a great way to get a feel for the lake's boating culture.

Paddling checklist

☐ How rough does it get? Does your skill level match the average water conditions?

☐ Is the lake big enough – or connected to other waterways – to keep paddling from getting boring?

☐ Will excessive powerboat traffic create unpleasant or unsafe conditions?

☐ Are there bays, marshes, and channels to explore?

☐ Will seasonal fluctuating water levels open or close paddling opportunities?

☐ Is there public land (parkland, for instance, or undeveloped Crown land) that can provide a paddling destination, a place to stop for a picnic or a swim?

☐ Are there opportunities for overnight camping expeditions?

Sailing checklist

☐ Is the lake big enough and open enough?

☐ Is it deep enough and relatively free of rocks?

☐ Will the prevailing wind create a tacking nightmare?

☐ Does the property's shoreline allow easy launching/beaching?

☐ Are there other sailors on the lake, which will allow for some friendly competition?

do matches the kind of boating already taking place on a particular lake. If your idea of vacation bliss is paddling a canoe across still waters, don't invest on a lake where there is an established water-ski or wakeboard culture and then expect to be able to lobby to change the lake to suit your interests. And if you're the one with the wakeboards, go where wakeboards are welcomed, where your towrope acrobatics won't alienate your holiday neighbors and ignite a popular uprising against your type of watercraft.

Paddling

For paddling enthusiasts, there isn't a lake that won't technically accommodate your canoe or kayak, but not all bodies of water are equally paddle-friendly. There may be heavy powerboat traffic, or the lake may be too large and open for your skill level, with waves that discourage venturing out or make it unsafe for children. A large lake can go from flat calm to a chop of two feet or more in just a few hours. You can head out in perfect conditions – and find yourself fighting large waves to get back.

Some lakes also make for more interesting paddling than others. You can only paddle up and down in front of your nearest neighbors' properties so many times before you'll wish you'd bought a place on a lake with an undeveloped, marshy bay to explore. Links to rivers, creeks, and other lakes also increase a lake's paddling potential.

Sailing

The minimum requirements for a sailing dinghy: enough room to tack back and forth, tolerably low powerboat traffic, and enough water depth, especially near the shore around your cottage, to accommodate the draft a rudder and centerboard or daggerboard requires. (Sailboards and beach catamarans require minimal depth.) A beach makes launching and hauling easy.

If you're really keen, you'll want to know the prevailing wind direction and determine how it affects your ability to navigate the lake. A narrow lake with prevailing winds that blow along its length, for instance, will mean a lot of short tacks, probably through boat traffic, to get from one end to the other. A lake that's sprinkled with islands or bounded in part by high cliffs can mean fluky winds and wind shadows that will either test your patience or sharpen your skills, depending on your point of view.

If you're planning to make sailing a priority at your cottage, look for a lake with a sailing club. Even if you're not interested in the organized activities of a club, its presence signals that the local sailing is halfway decent. Beyond that, the regular races, special regattas, and learn-to-sail programs of a club can increase enjoyment of the cottage.

Powerboating

Powerboats are a big part of the cottage experience. Beyond specific sports such as fishing, waterskiing, and wakeboarding, they're used for everything from sunset cruises to towing the kids around on an inflatable toy; from picnic excursions to trips to the local marina store. But not all lakes are created equal, and some pack more wind and waves than an inexperienced boater will be comfortable with. If you're a big-water boater from way back, then just about any lake will do. But for those who either have little boating experience or simply want a more placid cottage pool, some further investigation might spare you a bumpy ride.

Lake size is obviously a big factor in how rough the water can get, but the shape of the lake and its "fetch" – the length of the lake that prevailing winds can bear upon without obstruction – can also contribute to its roughness. If a dock is in an exposed position, directly in line with the lake's fetch, docking, mooring, and possibly even swimming might be next to impossible on a windy day. And just because a lake is relatively shallow doesn't mean it's always tranquil; shallow waters can whip into whitecaps very quickly on a windy day.

If you're not sure what a potential lake has to offer, check out the kinds of boats that other cottagers use. If pontoon boats, aluminum fishing boats, and small open runabouts are common, it's an indication that the lake is usually relatively calm. If there's a trend towards large, deep-vee runabouts with fully enclosed cockpits, expect some heavy weather. Another clue to a lake's turbulence is the presence of mooring devices that keep boats suspended in the air or up on shore via a marine railway, rather than tied up to a dock. There are many reasons for having such a lift, but one of them could be that wave action makes it impossible to leave the boat in the water.

Boating restrictions

If you have certain activities in mind you'll want to find out if the lake has legal restrictions in place that limit the type of powerboat or the manner in which it can be used. And if you're trying to choose a lake that's free from motorized vessels, or where their use is strictly curtailed, the restrictions will be even more important to you.

Restrictions pertain to three things: the nature of the vessel, the nature of the operator, and the way the vessel is operated. Most of those restrictions change according to location.

• **In Canada:** Restrictions on types of craft permitted and maximum speed can be applied to specific bodies of water with the consent of the Canadian Coast Guard. But the Boating Restriction Regulations are based on whether a boat has an engine or its maximum power. They do not provide for singling out a particular class of powerboats, such as personal watercraft, wakeboard boats, or speedboats. Currently, to eliminate a type of boat on a particular lake, a restriction essentially must forbid all motorized vessels, or all motorized vessels of a certain horsepower.

The popularity of bans or power restrictions varies from province to province. Only 27 places in all of Ontario have some kind of ban on motor-

Sailing club links

Lists of clubs are available in Canada from the provincial sailing associations. Go to the national authority, the Canadian Yachting Association (www.sailing.ca) for the individual provincial contacts. In the U.S., contact the United States Sailing Association (www.ussailing.org).

Powerboating checklist

☐ Are there vessel and/or horsepower restrictions on the lake?

☐ Do the shoreline and water conditions allow easy mooring?

☐ Do other cottagers on the lake share the same boating activities?

☐ Is the lake big enough – or connected to a chain of other lakes – to keep your interest alive?

☐ Is there a marina on the lake? Where will you refuel? Where will you launch your boat in spring and haul it in fall?

ized vessels. British Columbia, on the other hand, currently has 264 locations with bans. For the complete list of places with power (and speed) restrictions, go to the Canadian Dept. of Justice website (laws.justice.gc.ca) and search the regulations for "boating restrictions." (*For a discussion of speed restrictions in Canada, see Chapter 5, p. 89.*)

• **In the U.S.:** Although navigation is under federal jurisdiction, authority over the use of specific navigable waters often rests with the state, and municipalities sometimes also pass ordinances that place limits on boating activity. U.S. state and municipal laws are generally far more pointed than Canadian ones and do place restrictions on certain types of vessels. For example, in Vermont, operation of a personal watercraft is forbidden on all waterways between a half-hour after sunset and a half-hour before sunrise. Laws on how close you can operate a boat to shore, an anchored vessel, a swimmer, a surfer (the list goes on and on) vary from state to state. There may also be lake-specific restrictions or outright bans on waterskiing, limitations on noise levels, and no-wake speed limits.

Sample lake analysis: Translating what you hear into what it means

Name: Veronica Lake
Type: oligotrophic
Characteristics:
—about 50 square miles
—mostly steep-sided granite
—generally deeper than 30 feet, and "off the scale" on trolling depth sounders in the middle

What this means for cottagers
Pluses:
• extensive boating opportunities
• classic rock-and-pine character
• cool, deep waters home to trophy lake trout
Minuses:
• a "big-water" lake that can get rough quickly when the wind comes up
• few sand beaches
• deep water is slow to heat for swimming, and surface cools quickly, even at the height of summer, if wind and wave action cause mixing

Name: Hortense Lake
Type: mesotrophic
Characteristics:
—about 25 square miles
—fed by streams and groundwater
—drains from a navigable river that connects to Irving Lake
—mixed bag of landscape: generally steep-sided to the west, but with low sloping shore to the east and an extensive wetland in the southeast
—depths vary widely, from a "hole" of more than 60 feet in the middle to shoal depths

What this means for cottagers
Pluses:
• offers great recreational variety: deep water for boating (just watch out for the shoals), a wetland to explore by canoe and kayak, and connection to another lake when you need a change of scenery or access to another fishing hole

Fishing

Are you looking for a place where the kids can have a summer's worth of fun dunking worms for panfish? Or are you after more sophisticated angling action? As most dedicated anglers already know, word of mouth is the best way to find out what the fishing's like in general, what the top species are in the lake, and even whether a once-productive water body has succumbed to intensive fishing pressure.

Hit the local marina or the tackle shop and ask a few questions. See what the neighbors have to say. And if the nearest town has a big sign that proclaims "Walleye Capital of Canada," it's a safe bet you're onto a good thing. (Unless, of course, you're after lake trout.)

Serious anglers may want to go further: If a tour of the lake with a depth sounder to assess its weed beds, shoals, and underwater structure isn't possible, the keys to its secrets might already be recorded in a hydrographic chart or bottom-contour map. (*See "Area Maps: Essential Tools for Lake Detectives," p. 46.*) General water quality and limnology can also provide clues to a lake's predominant fish species. (*See "What's Your Lake Like?, p. 44.*)

• variety in fish species too, from smallmouth bass lurking in shoreline snags to pike in the weed beds to lake trout in the middle hole
Minuses:
• almost too desirable, making it susceptible to overdevelopment, particularly where the low-slope shoreline is encouraging more suburban-style four-season homes
• might not take much to tip Hortense into the eutrophic state (*see Ethel Lake, below*)

Name: Ethel Lake
Type: eutrophic
Characteristics:
—less than five square miles
—most of the lake is less than 20 feet deep
—a flood-control dam maintains the level
—gently sloping shoreline is fully developed with four-season properties; lots of lawns and deciduous trees

What this means for cottagers:
Pluses:
• suitable for most boating activities

• shallow waters warm up fast in the spring and stay warm all summer for swimming
• small enough that kids in pedal boats aren't going to be caught by surprise by a two-foot chop when the prevailing winds whip up
• lots of sunfish to be caught by the kids right of the dock
• low-slope shorelines allow young ones to wade, but lake is still deep enough for swim rafts close to shore
Minuses:
• too small for larger powerboats
• shoreline subject to wake damage from ski boats
• water tends to be weedy and has a lot of suspended solids, a turnoff for some swimmers and a burden on cottage water-treatment systems
• shallow depth and control dam mean little water circulation, and with the heavy nutrient loading of septic systems and lawn fertilizers, lake is in danger of becoming "hyper-eutrophic" and undesirable for recreational use
• algae blooms are becoming common in the dog days of August

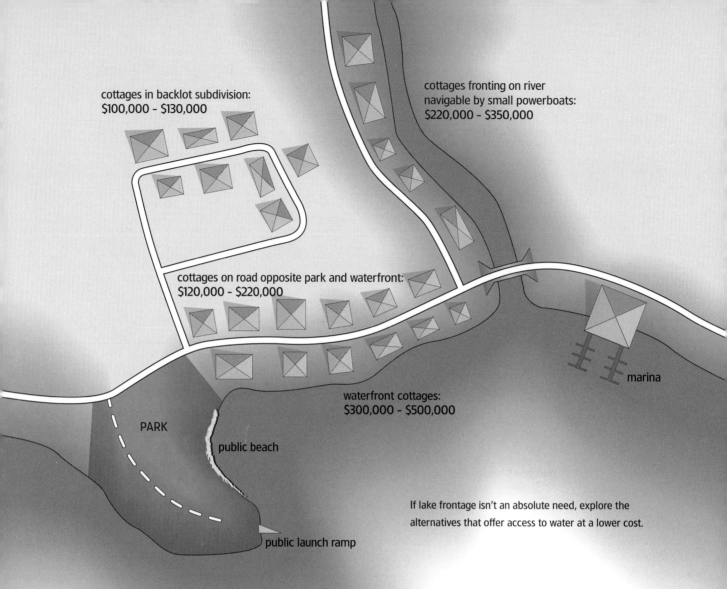

cottages in backlot subdivision:
$100,000 – $130,000

cottages fronting on river
navigable by small powerboats:
$220,000 – $350,000

cottages on road opposite park and waterfront:
$120,000 – $220,000

marina

waterfront cottages:
$300,000 – $500,000

PARK

public beach

If lake frontage isn't an absolute need, explore the
alternatives that offer access to water at a lower cost.

public launch ramp

Riverfront property checklist

☐ Is the river navigable, providing access by boat to a larger lake or lake system?

☐ If the river provides access to a lake or lake system, what is the level of boat traffic? Can you tolerate it?

☐ Is the river itself large enough to accommodate your other recreational needs? (Will its size, depth, traffic, and current permit swimming for your family? Is sailing possible?)

☐ Does its depth fluctuate throughout the season?

Do you even need a lake?

If lake frontage isn't an absolute requirement, you can reduce your spending substantially at the same time as you maximize your enjoyment.

We're not talking about a "dry" rural retreat (which isn't the concern of this book). However, there are alternatives to lake frontage that offer access to water – and can therefore accommodate your recreational "wants" while offering significant savings.

If not a lake…a river?

The image of "the lake" is so ingrained in our concept of cottage country, it's easy to forget that rivers have water in them, too – and cottages on their shores. And riverfront property is often significantly cheaper than lakefront.

"River" has as many connotations as "lake" does. And certainly a property on the St. Lawrence River in the celebrated Thousand Islands area is not going to be cheaper than one on a small lake. But there are other river options: Some might not be able to accommodate anything bigger than a

CAUTION: **Check your right to use the beach**

The catch with a backlot property is ensuring it indeed has a clear right to access the beach – and all of the beach, not just a sidelot shore road access a few dozen feet wide at the water's edge. Where backlots have access to a public waterfront park, right of usage is not an issue. But where beachfront properties have soared in value, owners of those properties have been known to try to defend (or establish) an exclusive right to the waterfront, to the exclusion of the public and backlot owners.

If you're considering a backlot property, be sure to find out whether access is an issue. Conversely, if you're the one investing in a beachfront property, you need to understand your rights, and the rights of others, to access that beach. *(See "Where Does the Waterfront End and the Lake Begin?", p. 111, for more.)*

canoe or small outboard runabout and are an end in themselves as a recreational waterway. Others are navigable by larger boat and offer access (by boat) to other bodies of water.

River properties aren't for everyone. Swimming may be limited, sailing may be impossible, and if the watercourse provides access to a lake, the boat traffic may be intolerable. Currents and seasonal water levels can severely hamper a river's use – or add to its attraction. If you carefully assess your recreational needs, you may find a river setting can fulfill them. Given the amount of boat traffic that a lake can generate, a river that can tolerate only canoes and kayaks may provide the idyllic retreat you crave. Rivers often offer great fishing, as well as opportunities for travel and exploration.

If not waterfront...a backlot?

"Backlot" refers to a property that is close to but not actually on the water. A traditional waterfront property will have the better view and easier access to the lake, but it will also have a much higher price tag. And the price difference between waterfront and backlot property in the same area can be huge: An undeveloped waterfront lot can easily cost more than a backlot with a residence already in place.

Not all vacation areas have backlot properties, but those that do offer a chance to buy what can be a first-class retreat that still delivers water-based recreational opportunities, despite the absence of waterfront. The key is that these backlot properties must provide ready access to the sorts of recreation you're interested in. (*See checklist at right and caution at the top of the page.*)

Hot-button local issues

Doing your homework on a particular area also means keeping an eye peeled for local issues that might make you think twice about choosing one

Backlot checklist

☐ Is there a readily accessible public beach nearby?

☐ Does some kind of deeded access exist to the waterfront?

☐ Is the access guaranteed? Does the municipality have a history of selling off public land?

☐ Is there a public launch ramp or a marina nearby?

☐ Are there trails near the property for cross-country skiing or snowmobiling that could enhance the property's use in winter? Could it do double-duty as a ski chalet?

location over another, or could provide unpleasant surprises after you close the deal. Here's a Yogi Berra-like motto to help you along: "The more you know, the less you don't."

• **Property taxes:** As property values increase, so naturally do assessments. An increase in an assessed value doesn't necessarily translate into a proportionate increase in taxes, but as waterfront values go up, many cottage owners have become concerned about the shift of the overall local tax burden in their direction. Taxes are a fact of life, and it would be unwise to decide not to buy a particular property solely because of a tax issue. But you should know the lay of the land to avoid being surprised by a major increase.

• **Development:** The area may look quiet and pristine, but what does the future hold? Is there a proposal afoot to have an old rural property at the other end of the lake rezoned so that a resort can be built? Is a marina planning a major expansion? Not all development activities are bad, and some are quite beneficial, but you need to know if a fundamental change in the area's character could be on the way.

• **Water and beach access:** In some communities, right of access to local beaches has become a huge issue and, unfortunately, property deeds and old surveys aren't always clear on who's entitled to what. Waterfront property owners may think they own the beach out front. Backlot owners may think they have right of access. The general public may think, based on historic use, that they're entitled to drive to the area, park on the roadside, and use the beach as well. In areas where this has emerged as a flashpoint issue, the consequences of any final legal ruling affect all parties, and in the meantime, tensions can run high.

If there's the slightest hint of a dispute over beach and general shoreline access in an area, do plenty of homework before you buy. (*See "Where Does the Waterfront End and the Lake Begin?," p. 111.*)

• **Municipal services:** Some townships that were once largely cottage areas, with the majority of their residents seasonal, have been finding that their population growth is now being driven substantially by the conversion of seasonal waterfront properties to year-round residences. This demographic and residential shift is being driven by retirement living, and the trend can only grow.

Municipalities are striving to manage the resulting environmental impact and demands on their services. As waterfront areas, particularly ones with significant backlot neighborhoods, become more developed, pressure can mount to move away from private wells and septic systems in favor of municipal water and sewage.

It's crucial for prospective buyers to be aware of such initiatives. At the very least, you want to avoid unpleasant financial surprises in a year or two. One-time compulsory charges to pay the capital costs of big-ticket municipal services can be difficult to recoup in property value over the near or medium term. And once services are introduced, property taxes (and possibly separate utility charges) are going to increase.

Another reason to find out as much as you can about what might be coming is to avoid an unrecoverable major expense. More than one property owner has drilled a new well or refurbished a septic system, only to learn shortly thereafter that compulsory municipal water or sewage service was on the way.

Where to turn for info on local issues

• **Local cottagers' and ratepayers' associations:** These are treasure troves of critical information. Where cottagers' associations used to be mainly concerned with social events and perhaps a cooperative firefighting system, taxes and municipal services have increasingly come to the fore, in some cases spurring the creation of separate ratepayers' groups that concern themselves with political issues. A lot can be going on at an association level that you might want to know about before you buy. Occasionally, the issues may be so serious that you might decide to look elsewhere for a property.

Get in touch with the association that covers the lake you're considering (*see p. 44*) and see if you can arrange to receive some of their recent newsletters. Many associations have websites, and what pertinent news can't be gleaned simply by browsing the site may be available in a downloadable newsletter. (*See "Mining Cottage Association Reports," p. 42.*)

• **The municipality:** Municipal governments large and small have discovered the cost efficiency of distributing information electronically, by creating websites that allow you to read or download helpful documents such as the budget, the official plan, and minutes from meetings of council and the committee of adjustment. Go back at least a year to get a sense of developing issues. The bigger issues usually take time to build up a head of steam.

An official plan (if available) can give you a general sense of the local government's approach to development issues. You might discover, for example, that the municipality intends to introduce water and sewage service to shoreline properties; that it opposes or welcomes new marinas; that it pledges to encourage or restrict commercial development in resort or cottage areas.

• **Local media:** Small-town and community newspapers can be a great source of local information...or they can be utterly useless. It's hit-and-miss. But if you're considering a purchase in a cottage area that supports a local paper, be sure to read it – and not just for the real estate listings: Watch for things – positive and negative – that will affect your cottage lifestyle. Have cottage B & Es skyrocketed in the last year? Is council about to pass a new official plan that will affect development on your lake? A local paper is a great place to learn about the lighter side of the local community, too: community events such as regattas and fundraisers, strawberry socials and turkey dinners. And don't forget to read the ads: It never hurts to know who the local septic tank expert is.

• **The real estate agent:** An important reason to consider securing a local agent in your search for the perfect property is that a good one will know the local issues and where the proverbial bodies are buried, politically speaking. Experienced realtors who have been selling in the same area for years can have a depth of knowledge about the local community that can really speed up your research. They're certainly not going to actively discourage you from buying in the area, but they'll be a big help in sketching out the local peculiarities, knowing that repeat business and referrals result from satisfied customers. Do enough homework yourself first, so you can ask specific questions about local issues.

4. The property search process

As you research a particular lake or area, it's important to get a sense of local liquidity: the availability of resale properties in any given year. You don't want to waste a lot of time and energy getting to know a particular lake that's caught your fancy, only to realize that properties in your price range hardly every come up for sale there. So hand in hand with your lake research, you want to start searching for available properties in the area(s) you've identified as fitting your criteria.

Looking for love in all the right places

Real estate listings and ads are your starting point for the cottage property search. They alert you to many of the spots available, and give you a clue to the supply of places in your price range in a given area. In fact, odds are good that a property you actually want to buy will be found in listings or ads. But there's no single place to discover everything that's on the market.

The Multiple Listing Service on-line

The most effective place to begin is on-line, using the Multiple Listing Service, or MLS. Agents rely on MLS to get the word out to other agents using the service that they have a property available. In this way, everyone's clients are effectively pooled.

In pre-Internet days, a buyer generally had access to MLS only through a real estate agent. Agents usually kept the printed listing sheets on hand only for the area in which they worked.

The on-line version of MLS – **www.mls.com** in the U.S., **www.mls.ca** in Canada – has signaled a major change in the way the market operates. Now MLS can be accessed directly by consumers, and features readily searchable databases of properties based on region, type (including building lots), price range, number of bedrooms, and whether or not you want waterfront and a fireplace, to name just a few search fields.

With MLS on-line, a person in New Jersey can look at vacation properties in Alberta. Someone in British Columbia can mull over listings in upstate New York. It's the easiest way to gather a snapshot of the kinds of properties available (and the prices) in a particular area.

Individual listings provide far more detail than any print ad can. They usually include several interior and exterior photos to give you a sense of the place and a reasonably detailed list of features; sometimes a lot plan is even included.

While MLS is not going to capture every single available property for sale, it's a simple, painless way to start your property search. You can very quickly determine what the general resale supply is like, and what opportu-

TIP:

The prospect of a buyer can lead to a property being listed for sale

Some cottage properties may only become available because you happen to be looking. It will be your interest, working in concert with a real estate agent, that might shake loose a property that hasn't yet been listed. See "The Real Estate Agent as Matchmaker," p. 69.

When is there too much liquidity?

Have you ever driven down a street and been struck by the number of homes with For Sale signs on the lawn? If it happens to be your street, you start to wonder what the neighbors know that you don't.

The same thing can happen in a cottage area. Some places just seem to have a steady supply of resale properties – a little too steady, it can seem. Why are so many owners so eager to sell? It's an excellent question, and if you come across this phenomenon, you need to find the answer.

Here are a few possible reasons:

• **Market testing.** When property values spike, owners can be tempted to dip a toe in the market waters to feel the temperature. A lot of owners can be motivated to try this at the same time. Their selling motivation, however, isn't high, and if they don't attract a top-dollar offer, they'll take the sign down and try again in a year or two.

• **"Starter lake."** Some places have a high number of entry-level cottages. People hold onto them for a few years, get their feet wet in cottaging, and then move on to something bigger and better. Turnover is constant, and entry-level prices are a sure sign of this phenomenon.

nities exist in your price range. Just keep in mind that MLS listings aren't the sum total of available properties. (*See Tip, at right.*)

Realty web pages

Beyond MLS, you will find on-line listings at three other levels:

1. the major real estate firms

2. their individual real estate offices, as well as offices of independent brokers

3. individual salespeople

Although MLS handles an estimated 80 percent of all property sold in North America, agents do occasionally hold back properties as exclusive listings. So it's worth looking at these realty web pages. (At the same time, they will give you a sense of an agent's area of focus; *see "How to Choose an Agent, p. 68.*)

Finding these web pages isn't difficult. The major firms maintain gateway websites that can direct you to local offices. On-line member listings of regional real estate associations and boards provide links to sites. You can also access these sites through individual listings on MLS. As well, brokers promote their business through listings on independent commercial websites dedicated to the cottage property market.

The dead listings problem

When you examine the websites of individual real estate professionals, be prepared to encounter "dead" listings occasionally – properties that are either no longer for sale or ones where the listing agreement has, in fact,

TIP:
Look beyond MLS for private sales
Properties get on **MLS** by being listed by an agent who is a member of a real estate board or association that participates in **MLS**. That means properties that are put up for sale privately – known in the trade as "for sale by owner" or FSBO – are for the most part not found there. To locate FSBO properties, you'll have to check out independent commercial websites *(see the next page)* and local and regional newspapers and magazines.

• **Something evil this way comes.** It could be a new gravel quarry or a new resort that will change the nature of the area; or it could be the introduction of mandatory municipal sewage service, which will cost each property owner $30,000. Whatever it is, it's a real worrier: something that threatens a profound imminent change in the local character of the lake or community – and owners are bailing en masse, before property values crash or expenses become intolerable.

• **General decline.** There may be problems with water quality, or water levels. The lake may be fished out. Whatever it is, current owners know the best days have passed.

• **Hidden downside.** Some locations have high turnover because buyers weren't fully aware of some aspect of the area. (Heavy boat traffic is a common one.) The buyers viewed the cottage in the off-season, or on a quiet Tuesday. Then they take possession and discover they're vacationing on a major nautical freeway. Some areas are traps for unwary buyers who soon tire of the unanticipated problems and start looking for someone else to come along and view their property at the wrong time.

• **No good reason at all.** It just happens. A lake that usually has four or six properties for sale could suddenly have 16 in one season, for no good reason at all. Next year, it will go back to having four to six.

run out. Agents shouldn't be advertising properties for which they no longer have a listing agreement. But if an agent continues to list a property off MLS on a website of his own and someone contacts him about it, he has a reason to go back to the owner and say he has a lead for them. Besides, salespeople like to show off a lot of inventory, since it makes them look active, and dead listings increase the number of properties on the website. For a buyer, however, a dead listing is a time-waster if a property has already been sold or taken off the market or now listed exclusively with a different broker.

If you find a listing on an agent's website that isn't on MLS, ask why it's not. Maybe it's an exclusive listing; confirm that the agent actually has a listing agreement.

Their code of ethics requires agents to make their working relationship clear to you from the beginning. They're either working for the owner of the listed property or they're working for you – and if there's no listing agreement and no buyer agency agreement (*see p. 70*), they're not working for anyone other than themselves. Bad agents are the exception to the rule, but they do exist. Don't let one waste your time.

Independent commercial websites

If you search the Web, you'll find a variety of other commercial sites devoted to buying, selling, and renting real estate, with some of them specializing in the vacation property market. The quality of these sites varies widely, and they shouldn't be the starting point for getting a handle on a particular region's resale offerings. Some are more about promoting property rentals than sales. The number of for-sale-by-owner (FSBO) vacation properties on such sites for any given area is easily dwarfed by MLS listings. Nevertheless,

---

How to snag a property in an area where cottages rarely come up for sale

Your heart may be set on a place on Wahoo Bay, but there are only 18 properties on the entire bay, and they're all treasured family heirlooms. The rare changes of ownership are inside jobs – the properties are never listed and sell to relatives or close friends.

How do you deal with the heartbreak of Wahoo Bay? There are several strategies:

• **Be patient.** Make contact with real estate agents who know the area. Rest assured: They want a listing in Wahoo Bay as much as you want to own something there. Agents are constantly soliciting listings, even in areas with high sales turnover, and it's not unusual for demand to exceed supply. They will be keeping an ear close to the ground for news of any possible movement in Wahoo Bay's ownership ranks. An agent can also help you in adopting the next strategy: putting you in a property in another location with most if not all of the attractions that drew you to Wahoo Bay.

they are one of the most effective ways to find FSBO listings, once you know where it is you'd like to own a cottage.

Just don't be surprised if many of the properties for sale that seem to be private listings turn out to be represented by an agent: Agents will often place ads on private sites for some extra marketing push. Although it would be unfair to say these are all "problem" listings, odds are good that for whatever reason, they're properties that haven't found a buyer yet through MLS or the agent's own web page. If you find an agent-represented property on a third-party site, it wouldn't hurt to ask more pointed questions about it. You might find a highly motivated vendor – or a piece of property with troublesome baggage.

Print media

You can find real estate listings in a variety of print media – local weekly newspapers, big-city dailies, and regional magazines devoted to vacation country. They will turn up in classified ads, as well as in display ads placed by agents and by brokerage offices. There are also newsprint publications dedicated to vacation property listings. Keep a couple things in mind about print advertising:

• Timeliness is always an issue with print media. Lead times, especially for magazines, can be long. By the time you read an ad, the property may have been on the market for two months. This can mean you have room to negotiate on price – or that the place has already been sold.

• Agents and brokers generally like to spend as little money as possible advertising individual properties. Like any other business, they prefer to maxi-

---

• **Get over it.** Accept that a property is unlikely ever to come on the open market within your lifetime. Figure out what it is that you find so appealing about the spot, and look for those same characteristics in another area. Let Wahoo Bay inspire you, not discourage you – and a real estate agent who knows the area can help.

• **Bide your time.** Buy a cottage elsewhere, but let the local agents know you're still in the market for a place on Wahoo Bay. Stay in contact with them, remain on their mailing lists, and – above all – make sure you're on their active client lists. Position yourself as a ready buyer, and be prepared to move quickly when the opportunity finally does arise.

• **Be prepared to pounce.** Illness, death, or divorce can trigger a sale right out of the blue. A widow may decide that she can no longer enjoy the property the way she once did, and her adult children are living too far away to use it themselves. Or rather than leave the cottage to the kids, given capital gains tax issues or sibling hostilities, it just makes more sense to sell it and distribute the proceeds.

Such developments produce the unexpected phone calls to the local real estate agent. And if you're on the client list, you'll know about the opportunity long before anyone reading real estate ads ever will.

The "With Contents" Purchase

Cottages are often listed for sale with more extras than the typical home. That's because cottages tend to accumulate possessions that the owners don't need or want once they've sold the property. All kinds of "included with" items can be rolled into the price – everything from boats and motors to appliances, bunk beds, and the vintage fishing tackle in the boathouse.

Are all-inclusive deals good ones?

Whether a "with contents" purchase is advantageous depends not only on the garage-sale value of the extras, but also the cost and trouble of replacing and getting rid of them. With some cottages, particularly ones that have transportation complications (such as water access), moving everything off the property can be such a burden that the present owner would rather sell the place as is. You, the prospective buyer, are going to have to decide what your alternative costs would be – for the replacement furnishings and for getting them to the property.

If you do decide to strike a deal that includes all the extras, you should be ruthlessly honest about what you plan to do with them. If you're going to want to throw out the old dinette set and the beds and bureaus after the first summer, think carefully about how much you're willing to pay. After all, you'll most likely be paying for their disposal as well as for their replacements. If it's such an inconvenience for the present owners to get rid of old furnishings, you don't want to be essentially paying them to take on the responsibility yourself.

Retailers of economical, cottage-friendly furnishings such as IKEA, which sell assemble-it-yourself pieces in easy-to-transport flat packs, make it a lot simpler to move new furniture to the premises than it is to drag the old stuff away. Bottom line: If you really don't want something, don't agree to take it, even if it's almost as good as free. (*But see Tip, at right.*)

Don't expect your mortgage to cover the extras

When it comes to securing a mortgage, the financial institution cares only about the appraised value of the real estate, not the total price you've agreed to pay. Appraisals are at best ballpark estimates, so don't expect a second-hand refrigerator to make or break a mortgage application. But significant contents, such as boats and better quality furniture, *can* begin to add up – and create a possible discrepancy between the price you've agreed to pay for the property and the appraised value for mortgage purposes. While you might agree to pay $190,000 for a true turnkey getaway, complete with a ski boat and all the appliances and furnishings, the appraiser might set the value of the basic real estate package at $167,000. If you're working on the outer limits of your mortgage-based financing, you may have to find other sources of cash to close a deal if the appraised value won't stretch far enough to include the value of everything.

mize yields with minimum outlay, and will use less-expensive promotional resources before buying an ad. As a result, print advertising shows just a portion of the properties on the market.

• Display advertising in magazines is relatively expensive. Properties that end up being showcased this way either have a price tag that warrants the expense, or are really meant to advertise the broker. Such advertising is often meant to tell readers that the properties in the ad are typical of the kinds of buying opportunities available through the broker and can be a good way to find an agent who specializes in certain types of properties.

To be safe, approach the larger-ticket items with their own appraised value. If you're working with a real estate agent, he should be able to advise you what the property is worth from a strict appraisal perspective. Only then can you decide whether the additional contents are worth accepting as part of the deal. Anything that would cost at least a few hundred dollars to replace should probably be considered separately, as an out-of-pocket purchase. Power tools, chainsaws, the old snowmobile in the shed, and the pedal boat in the weeds should receive their own bargaining session.

Beware of boats rolled into the package

A powerboat with an inboard/outboard engine should never be agreed to as an all-inclusive item, or even a separate purchase, without a professional survey. Engine repairs can be hideously expensive, and boats can also have a serious flaw, such as structural damage, that is undetectable to the naked (and uneducated) eye. Given the cost of replacing them, even larger outboard motors deserve a careful look from a mechanic before you agree to buy a boat as part of a property sale. On the other hand, it's hard to go wrong if the boat being included is a basic aluminum runabout with a small outboard. As long as it floats, your worst-case scenario is that it might need a new engine (which, given its small size, will carry a much more modest price tag).

Sailboats are less of a purchase hazard, as most dinghies being used at cottage properties aren't going to have a total replacement cost (secondhand) of more than a few thousand dollars. But a sailboat should still be dealt with as a separate purchase if you're serious about wanting to use it. Some common designs, such as the Laser, Sunfish, and Albacore, are always available in the used market, and you shouldn't be agreeing to an inflated value of a boat that happens to be on the property when there are so many competing used examples around. That said, you *could* find a real bargain: Cottage owners aren't always aware of the used sailboat market – particularly if their boat has been kicking around the property for a few years and not actively used.

TIP: You can't always play hardball

In principle, you shouldn't have to agree to take any items you don't really want. But in a hot seller's market, the seller may be in the driver's seat, and you might be compelled to accept the property with all of its contents, useful and otherwise, in order to get the deal. You'll just have to learn to love that orange plaid sofa bed – or accept that you'll be paying tipping fees to dispose of it at the local dump.

Except for high-end properties, and private sales whose owners are looking for an edge in attracting buyers, the bulk of real estate print advertising is still being done at the local level, in a daily or weekly newspaper.

Perusing a copy of the local weekly while you're in cottage country is certainly a fun way to see what's available. But most of us aren't going to drive a couple hours to a vacation area just to grab the new issue of the *Lakeland Beavertail-Herald.*

For these reasons, the most potent marketing tool for real estate sales is the Internet.

How to choose an agent

Two bottom-line must-haves

Obviously, you want an agent who has experience in the business in general and is properly accredited, but when you're shopping for a cottage, two other factors are of utmost importance:

1. Local knowledge: Choose an agent who really knows the local real estate market. An experienced local realtor who has been working in the same area for many years will have a depth of knowledge that cannot be undervalued. Not only will such agents have a lock on local cottage values and comparable properties (they may have sold the very cottage you're interested in twice before), but they can also be a gold mine of insights on matters as diverse as taxation issues, hiccups with the area's official plan, and the success of a local lake trout stocking program. They'll know about setbacks and other restrictions that might get in the way of your plan to expand a deck or dock, and whether nearby cottages have kids or grandkids the same age as yours. They'll also have insights on local tradespeople if you need them after the purchase – as well as the best local spots to shop for sticky buns and fresh corn. Such local knowledge will save you a lot of time, money, and aggravation during your search. Use an out-of-town agent at your peril.

2. Compatability: You'll be spending a *lot* of time with your agent during your property search – more than during a typical city-property search (particularly if the cottage you're seeking is remote or unicorn-like in rarity). So find someone you (and your spouse) get along with and whose company you enjoy. (And certainly don't sign any buyer agency agreements until you find an agent you like; *see p. 70*.)

Understanding the agent's role

People generally understand that when they visit a car dealership, no matter how friendly and helpful the salesperson is, he is working for the dealership,

Coming to terms

real estate agent: a licensed real estate salesperson.

broker: can also be a salesperson, but has an upgraded license that allows administration and supervision of other agents.

realtor: a proprietary term; in the U.S., it designates a member of the National Association of Realtors; in Canada, a member of the Canadian Real Estate Association.

Let the real estate agent do the homework

Researching properties and locations is essential – and time consuming. But this is where an agent can help. What might take you considerable effort to learn is old news to a good local realtor. An experienced agent can be a real lifesaver, particularly if you're interested in empty lots or tear-downs that call for new construction, as he'll have knowledge of any zoning restrictions or other conditions that might interfere with your plans to build. Just be careful that difficult issues aren't sugar-coated in the name of getting you to buy. If you strike a formal buyer agency agreement *(see p. 70)*, you can also request that the agent represent you with respect to privately listed or "for sale by owner" (FSBO) properties. (Agents tend to keep a close watch on FSBOs, as they wait for the owner to tire of trying to sell the place himself.)

The real estate agent as matchmaker

Agents strive to develop two lists: one of properties for sale, the other of customers who are looking for them. Successful agents work especially hard at it, carving out a niche as a service provider where sellers and buyers converge. Their real estate territory is quite specific, and they develop mail and e-mail lists that keep prospective buyers apprised of their latest listings. That proprietary list of buyers is a strong incentive for sellers to bring their business to them. It also means that a lot of dealmaking can go on without an individual listing ever appearing in a traditional advertising environment – including making it onto MLS.

Many cottage owners are familiar with the solicitation mailings from agents who are seeking new listings. Sometimes this is a sign of simple desperation, a new agent trying to break into the business. But often, when they say they have buyers lined up, but nothing to sell them – a dilemma known as "low inventory" – it's absolutely true. And making yourself available as a buyer, through an agent, can end up being the cause of a property actually becoming available to you. As in the residential real estate market, plenty of people think of buying a new property, but are held back by the anxiety caused by the thought of trying to sell their current one. An agent coming along out of the blue and telling them that he has buyers already in hand may be all it takes to convince them to sell. It's easy to forget that the buyer, not the seller, represents the marketplace. By showing up, ready to buy, you create the marketplace, and some owners will respond by agreeing to sell.

not for the buyer. A good salesperson listens to your needs, and if he appreciates repeat business and referrals, he will try to get you a decent deal. But at the end of the day, it's his job to sell cars for the dealership, for as much as he can get.

This seems obvious – but when the same customers start shopping for real estate, they often don't understand who's working for whom. And unless you have a written agreement stating otherwise (we'll get to this in a minute), the situation in the North American real estate market is much the same: An agent is working for the seller – for the owner of the property listed for sale. *This is true even if you've approached the agent about finding you a property*, and even if the agent doesn't have the property you ultimately choose in his or her own listings.

Why is the seller the default client of an agent? Beyond the fact that the seller is the one with a written agreement with the agent, called the listing agreement, *the seller is the one paying the commission on a listed property*.

What working with a "seller agent" means

Real estate associations have codes of ethics that require members to deal fairly with all parties in a transaction, but unless explicitly spelled out otherwise, the agent's primary duty of care in a real estate transaction rests with the seller. No amount of fairness requires an agent to disclose to the buyer confidential information about the sellers, such as their motivation for sell-

TIP:

The best place to find experienced local agents is in the local paper

Long-time realtors usually trumpet their longevity in the local real estate market in their ads. And if you can follow a local paper for a few months, it's sometimes easy to see who consistently has the most listings – and whose name falls off the roster completely.

CAUTION:
Once more, with feeling
Never forget that unless it's explicitly spelled out otherwise, the agent's primary duty of care in a real estate transaction is to the seller. Nobody is representing you, the buyer, when an agent presents your offer for a listed property.

Getting the straight goods
Just because an agent's duty of responsibility is to the seller doesn't mean a property's dark secrets can be hidden from you. To learn about vendor disclosure documents and general obligations of sellers to disclose the condition of a property, see "Seller Disclosure: Telling It Like It Is," p. 125.

ing. (They're desperate for cash and will settle for anything, the lake turns into algae soup every July, the neighbors are a nightmare.) Nor does it prevent an agent from disclosing to the seller confidential information the prospective buyer injudiciously spills to the agent. (You're so desperate for a cottage on a particular lake, you'll pay anything to get one.)

Even in the case where "your" agent presents an offer to the listing agent, your agent is essentially acting as a subagent for the listing agent. He will be paid a percentage of the commission that flows from the seller to the listing agent. Unless there's paperwork indicating otherwise, nobody is representing you when an agent presents your offer for a listed property. (And there's an inherent contradiction here: If your agent is being paid on commission, the more money he saves you in negotiations, the less he makes. It's not a system with much incentive to hold down prices or find you a bargain.)

Increasingly, statutory laws on both sides of the border aren't leaving to chance the possibility of misunderstandings about who's working for whom and are requiring written agreements spelling out the terms of the relationship between client and real estate professional.

The birth of the buyer agent
In recent years, the general concerns of buyers about agent accountability and the lack of true buyer representation have been addressed by a relatively new concept: the buyer agent.

A buyer agent, even one working within the MLS system, is empowered by prospective buyers to represent them in purchases of all properties put up for sale, including FSBO ones, if they so choose. The two parties, buyer and agent, sign a document – called a buyer agency agreement (*see sample, p. 72*) – that sets out the relationship. The agreement can be exclusive or non-exclusive; a non-exclusive agreement is limited to a particular territory.

A buyer agency agreement creates a relationship where the agent is working for you, not the seller, and has your best interests in mind. If, for instance, a buyer agent has information about why a property is being sold, he is obligated to pass it along. From an agent's point of view, a buyer agency agreement also offers protection: It helps avoid situations where the agent does a lot of research and legwork, showing the buyer many properties, but the buyer then moves on to another agent, who makes the sale and reaps the rewards of the first agent's efforts. (Some top agents insist on having a buyer agency agreement in place if they're going to work with you.)

The emergence of the buyer agent is farther along in the U.S. than Canada, though it is beginning to emerge north of the border. However, in the vacation property market, there may simply be too few active agents in a given area to find one who can work effectively in the buyer agent role. If an agent or his office already has most of the local property listings, it becomes difficult for him to disengage himself from the interests of the sellers (though "dual agency" can be used in such situations; *see p. 76*).

Trying to solve the problem of a lack of suitable buyer agents in an area by securing one from a neighboring sales territory is not a good idea. What you gain in confidentiality, you lose in critical local knowledge.

Filling in the blanks on a buyer agency agreement

If you decide to sign a buyer agency agreement, among the variables you will have to consider are whether you wish to restrict the territory in which the agent will represent you (exclusivity) and how long you wish the agreement to be in effect.

A non-exclusive agreement can limit the buyer agent relationship to a particular territory, leaving you free to strike other non-exclusive arrangements with buyer agents in other vacation destinations you're considering. And they don't have to be separated by the Continental Divide: You can have a non-exclusive agreement for one lake area, and another one for the district right next door. This makes particular sense if agent expertise is very region-specific.

Don't consign a buyer agent more exclusive territory than he can reasonably handle. You always want local expertise, not a four-star real estate general overseeing a property search campaign throughout the entire Eastern Seaboard.

A six-month exclusivity agreement with someone you hardly know is probably asking for trouble. The shorter the time period the better – remember, the agreement can always be renewed. The time period becomes less critical if you make sure the agreement has a clear exit clause. Ideally, the clause should allow you to terminate the relationship unilaterally, at any time, for any reason. Keep in mind that such carte blanche power may not save you from a civil action if you're unethical enough to terminate the

TIP:

Don't let your search be tailored to the agent's advantage

Successful sales of their own listings, or of listings held by other agents in their own brokerage office, pay agents a higher commission than sales of properties listed on **MLS** by another office. (Arrangements for the way commissions are divvied up in the **MLS** system vary considerably.)

In the age of the Internet, it's easy to avoid having your search weighted towards certain listings. Both **MLS** and private listings are searchable on-line – so you can do plenty of market research in the comfort of your own home.

What a seller's agent is obligated to show you

Even though the seller is the agent's client by default if no agreement to the contrary has been signed, an agent is obligated (by the code of ethics of his real estate board or association) to inform potential buyers of any property listed on MLS that meets their criteria. In other words, the code says if you ask an agent to show you a particular style of property in a particular area in a particular price range, he can't restrict his sales pitches solely to the properties that he personally represents, or that are represented by other agents in his office or within the parent real estate company. He has to crack open the full slate of MLS properties that meet your criteria.

That said, he has *no* obligation to show you places listed *privately* for sale, or listed somewhere other than on MLS, such as a commercial website that showcases FSBO properties. Indeed, he has no incentive to do so – because there's no way within the seller agency system for him to be paid when the deal closes.

OREA Ontario Real Estate Association

Buyer Agency Agreement
Authority for Purchase or Lease

Form 300
for use in the Province of Ontario

TO:...(Broker)   Tel.No. (..........)..................................

ADDRESS:..

.... Fax.No. (..........)..................................

hereinafter referred to as the Broker.

I/We..., hereinafter referred to as the Buyer,

hereby give you the **exclusive authority** to act as our agent until 11:59 p.m. on the ....day of ....,20............,

{ Buyer acknowledges that the time period for this Agreement is negotiable between the Buyer and the Broker, however, in accordance with the Code of Ethics of the Real Estate Council of Ontario, **if the time period for this Agreement exceeds six months, the Broker must obtain the Buyer's informed consent and initials.** }

(Buyer's Initials)

for the purpose of locating a real property meeting the following general description:

Property Type (Use):...

....

Geographic Location:...

I hereby warrant that I am not a party to a buyer agency agreement with any other registered real estate broker for the purchase or lease of a real property of the general description indicated above.

1. **DEFINITIONS AND INTERPRETATIONS:** For the purposes of this Buyer Agency Agreement ("Authority" or "Agreement"), "Buyer" includes purchaser and tenant and a "seller" includes a vendor, a landlord or a prospective seller, vendor or landlord. A purchase shall be deemed to include the entering into of any agreement to exchange, or the obtaining of an option to purchase which is subsequently exercised, and a lease includes any rental agreement, sub-lease or renewal of a lease. This Agreement shall be read with all changes of gender or number required by the context.

2. **COMMISSION:** In consideration of the Broker undertaking to assist me, I agree to pay commission to the Broker as follows:
   If, during the currency of this Agreement, I enter into an agreement to purchase or lease a real property of the general description indicated above, I agree the Broker is entitled to receive and retain any commission offered by a listing broker or by the seller. I understand that the amount of commission offered by a listing broker or by the seller may be greater or less than the commission stated below. I understand that the Broker will inform me of the amount of commission to be paid to the Broker by the listing broker or the seller at the earliest practical opportunity. I acknowledge that the payment of any commission by the listing broker or the seller will not make the Broker either the agent or sub-agent of the listing broker or the seller.
   If, during the currency of this Agreement, I enter into an agreement to purchase or lease any property of the general description indicated above, I

   agree the Broker is entitled to be paid a commission of.....................% of the sale price of the property or ....

   ....
   I agree to pay directly to the Broker any deficiency between this amount and the amount, if any, to be paid to the Broker by a listing broker or by the seller. I understand that if the Broker is not to be paid any commission by a listing broker or by the seller, I will pay the Broker the full amount of commission indicated above.
   I agree to pay the Broker such commission if I enter into an agreement within ....days after the expiration of this Agreement **(Holdover Period)** to purchase or lease any real property shown or introduced to me from any source whatsoever during the term of this Agreement, provided, however, that if I enter into a new buyer agency agreement with another registered real estate broker after the expiration of this Agreement, my liability to pay commission to the Broker shall be reduced by the amount paid to the other broker under the new agreement.
   I agree to pay such commission as described above even if a transaction contemplated by an agreement to purchase or lease agreed to or accepted by me or anyone on my behalf is not completed, if such non-completion is owing or attributable to my default or neglect.
   Said commission, plus any applicable taxes, shall be payable on the date set for completion of the purchase of the property or, in the case of a lease or tenancy, the earlier of the date of occupancy by the tenant or the date set for commencement of the lease or tenancy.

3. **AGENCY:** I acknowledge that the Broker has provided me with written information explaining agency relationships, including information on Seller Agency, Sub-Agency, Buyer Agency, Dual Agency and Customer Service.
   The Broker shall assist the Buyer in locating real property of the general description indicated above and shall represent the Buyer in an endeavour to procure the acceptance of an agreement to purchase or lease such a property.
   I acknowledge that I may not be shown or offered all properties that may be of interest to me.
   I hereby agree that the terms of any buyer's offer or agreement to purchase or lease the property will not be disclosed to any other buyer.
   The Buyer hereby appoints the Broker as agent for the purpose of giving and receiving notices pursuant to any offer or agreement to purchase or lease a property negotiated by the Broker.

INITIALS OF BUYER(S):

Form 300   01/2004   **Page 1 of 2**

By signing a buyer agency agreement, you create a relationship where an agent is working for you, the buyer, not the seller. In the case of dual agency (see p. 2 of the agreement, opposite), it sets out the conditions that apply if your agent is also the property's listing agent and is thus representing both buyer and seller.

DUAL AGENCY: I hereby acknowledge that the Broker may be entering into listing agreements with sellers of properties I may be interested in buying or leasing. In the event that the Broker has entered into or enters into a listing agreement with the seller of a property I may be interested in buying or leasing, I hereby consent to the Broker acting as a Dual Agent for the transaction, however, the Broker is required to inform me in writing of a Dual Agency situation with the Buyer and seller at the earliest practical opportunity and in all cases prior to any offer to purchase or lease being submitted or presented.

I understand and acknowledge that in a Dual Agency situation the Broker must be impartial and equally protect the interests of the Buyer and the seller in the transaction. I understand and acknowledge that in a Dual Agency situation the Broker shall have a duty of full disclosure to both the Buyer and the seller, including a requirement to disclose all factual information about the property known to the Broker.

However, I further understand and acknowledge that the Broker shall not disclose:
- that the seller may or will accept less than the listed price, unless otherwise instructed in writing by the seller;
- that the Buyer may or will pay more than the offered price, unless otherwise instructed in writing by the Buyer;
- the motivation of or personal information about the Buyer or seller, unless otherwise instructed in writing by the party to which the information applies or unless failure to disclose would constitute fraudulent, unlawful or unethical practice;
- the price the Buyer should offer or the price the seller should accept; and
- the Broker shall not disclose to the Buyer the terms of any other offer.

However, it is understood that factual market information about comparable properties and information known to the Broker concerning potential uses for the property will be disclosed to both Buyer and seller to assist them to come to their own conclusions.
I further acknowledge that the Broker may be entering into buyer agency agreements with other buyers who may be interested in the same or similar properties that I may be interested in buying or leasing and I hereby consent to the Broker acting as an agent for more than on e buyer interested in the same property without any claim by me of conflict of interest.

4. **REFERRAL OF PROPERTIES:** I agree that during the currency of this Buyer Agency Agreement I will act in good faith and work exclusively with the Broker for the purchase or lease of a real property of the general description indicated above. I agree that, during the currency of this Agreement, I shall advise you immediately of any property of interest to me that came to my attention from any source whatsoever, and all offers to purchase or lease submitted by me shall be submitted through you to the seller. If I fail to advise you of any property of interest to me that came to my attention during the currency of this Agreement and I arrange a valid offer to purchase or lease the property during the currency of this Agreement or within the Holdover Period after expiration of this agreement, I agree to pay you the amount of commission set out above, payable within (5) days following your written demand therefor.

5. **INDEMNIFICATION:** The Broker and salespeople of the Broker are trained in dealing in real estate but are not qualified in determining the physical condition of the land or any improvements thereon. I agree that the Broker will not be liable for any defects, whether latent or patent, to the land or improvements thereon. All information supplied by the seller or landlord or the listing broker may not have been verified and is not warranted by the Broker as being accurate and will be relied on by the Buyer at the Buyer's own risk. The Buyer acknowledges having been advised to make their own enquiries to confirm the condition of the property.

6. **FINDERS FEE:** I acknowledge that the Broker may be receiving a finder's fee from a lender in the event that a new mortgage or an increase in financing is required for a transaction contemplated by this Agreement, and I consent to any such fee being retained by you in addition to the commission as described above.

7. **CONSUMER REPORTS: The Buyer is hereby notified that a Consumer Report containing credit and/or personal information may be referred to in connection with this Agreement and any subsequent transaction.**

8. **USE AND DISTRIBUTION OF INFORMATION:** The Buyer consents to the collection, use and disclosure of personal information by the Broker for such purposes that relate to the real estate services provided by the Broker to the Buyer including, but not limited to: locating, assessing and qualifying properties for the Buyer; advertising on behalf of the Buyer; providing information as needed to third parties retained by the Buyer to assist in a transaction (e.g. financial institutions, building inspectors, etc...); and such other use of the Buyer's information as is consistent with the services provided by the Broker in connection with the purchase or prospective purchase of the property.
The Buyer agrees that the sale and related information regarding any property purchased by the Buyer through the Broker may be retained and disclosed by the Broker and/or real estate board(s) (if the property is an MLS® Listing) for reporting, appraisal and statistical purposes.

9. **CONFLICT OR DISCREPANCY:** If there is any conflict or discrepancy between any provision added to this Agreement and any provision in the standard pre-set portion hereof, the added provision shall supersede the standard pre-set provision to the extent of such conflict or discrepancy. This Agreement, including any provisions added to this Agreement, shall constitute the entire Authority from the Buyer to the Broker. There is no representation, warranty, collateral agreement or condition, which affects this Agreement other than as expressed herein.

10. **ELECTRONIC COMMUNICATION:** This Buyer Agency Agreement and any agreements, notices or other communications contemplated thereby may be transmitted by means of electronic systems, in which case signatures shall be deemed to be original. The transmission of this Agreement by me by electronic means shall be deemed to confirm I have retained a true copy of the Agreement.

THIS AUTHORITY HAS BEEN READ AND FULLY UNDERSTOOD BY ME AND I ACKNOWLEDGE THIS DATE HAVING RECEIVED A TRUE COPY. Any representations and warranties contained herein are true to the best of my knowledge, information, and belief.

DATED at..this.................................. day of.., 20..................

SIGNED, SEALED AND DELIVERED in the presence of: IN WITNESS whereof I have hereunto set my hand and seal:

.... ⬤ DATE...........................
(Witness)   (Signature of Buyer)   (Seal)

.... ⬤ DATE...........................
(Witness)   (Signature of Buyer)   (Seal)

TIP:

Get a professional to read the fine print

Because real estate regulations vary between jurisdictions, you should have any buyer agency agreement vetted by a lawyer before you sign. (You're going to need a lawyer anyway to close the purchase. Getting the agreement between you and the agent right is a good way to start the lawyer-client relationship.)

agreement an hour before presenting an offer on a property your buyer agent has walked you through three times.

Who pays the buyer agent?

When buyer agents are already working within the traditional real estate system – the ones affiliated with an office that represents listed properties, such as you'd find throughout most of cottage country – the buyer agent is usually paid through the traditional commission system (i.e., he receives a portion of the commission that the listing agent receives from the seller). But in some jurisdictions, the law says that in the absence of any agreement stating otherwise, paying the buyer agent is the buyer's responsibility.

In any case, the details of payment need to be written down in the agreement, whether it's an agreed-on percentage split of the commission (paid by the vendor) between the listing agent and the buyer agent, or a set fee to be paid by the buyer. A fixed fee can work to the buyer's advantage if you feel the negotiating skills of the buyer agent are sufficient to lower the price enough to save you the fee.

Using a buyer agent to deal with private listings

One of the pluses of having a buyer agent is that he can represent you outside the MLS marketplace and negotiate purchases of private listings, which may very well be an important part of your search in vacation country. However, some buyers like to limit the agent's role to listed properties, and deal with FSBOs themselves. (Many buyer agents simply refuse this stipulation.)

One reason for excluding the buyer agent from FSBO negotiations is that the owners who are listing privately simply don't want to deal with an agent, period. If they wanted agents around and valued their judgment, they would have got one for themselves in the first place. The other reason they're suspicious is that they know buyer agents try to sell their value in FSBO purchases by saying they can whittle the price down far enough to cover the fee that the buyer has to pay them.

TIP: **The flip side: Why you might want to keep your options open**

In an emergency sale, motivated by divorce, death, or other extreme situation, the vendor often simply contacts a realtor, who then consults his client list for a possible buyer. In highly desirable locations, this means the property may never get listed on the MLS, much less advertised in the local paper.

This is a good reason not to be tied down to one agent through a buyer agency agreement, as your agent may never even get the chance to present an offer for you if a rival agent snares the listing and moves it quickly in the direction of his own clients. Keep as many local agents as you can informed of your interest.

Before excluding your buyer agent from FSBO sales, consider what you'd be missing out on. First, you may be surprised at how many properties your agent will know well. FSBOs sometimes come up for sale with a broker, and when no sale transpires, the owner decides to try selling it himself. By then, your agent may have been through an open house, or has otherwise become familiar with the property. He may know something you don't about why this owner has chosen the private-sale route, or about its past sales history. Tune out your buyer agent at your own risk.

Purchasers who try to cut their buyer agent out of FSBO negotiations are missing the point of buyer agency. The agent's job is to represent your best interests in making a sensible offer on a property that will make you happy. Whether or not the property is being sold privately or through an agency listing is irrelevant to the legwork required to assess the property's desirability and value and to identify pitfalls. If you think you need an agent to help you buy a property in the listed system, what gives you the confidence to do a deal on your own with an FSBO?

A horse of a different color: The exclusive buyer agent

You may have heard about something called "exclusive" or "independent" buyer agents, who work only on behalf of buyers. They're licensed real estate professionals, but they don't represent sellers at all. (They are not to be confused with "exclusive" or "non-exclusive" buyer agency agreements, which limit an agent to representing you in a particular territory.)

Exclusive buyer agents will tell you that buyer agents who are regular real estate agents working in the MLS system are too compromised by the day-to-day realities of working with sellers to be truly in your corner.

However, arguments about whether an exclusive buyer agent is better than what we might call "embedded" buyer agents (regular real estate agents who, for the purpose of working with you, have signed a buyer agency agreement) are going to be moot in most cottage areas: Exclusive buyer agents largely don't exist there. They are most common in thriving markets where a large inventory of properties creates a profitable niche for professionals who can specialize in representing buyers only. (In any case, the concept has been slow to migrate to Canada from the U.S.)

Choosing the agent relationship that's right for you

A good agent will explain the differences between buyer and seller agents upfront, so everybody knows where things stand. And any reasonable real estate professional will understand that, as a buyer, you won't commit to a contractual relationship on first meeting.

However, in some real estate firms, agents are expected to come to a clear understanding of their role with a prospective purchaser *from the very first meeting*. At the very least, they need to explain their default role as a seller agent with respect to listed properties. They should also ask upfront if

CAUTION:
You pay the agent if a property is FSBO

If a buyer agent is representing you in FSBO purchases, you have no choice but to pay him, since the seller, having chosen to list the property privately, is hardly interested in ponying up for your agent's commission. Buyer agents argue that they make their services worthwhile in FSBO purchases by negotiating the price down sufficiently to cover their fee. Again, put it all in writing.

THE BOTTOM LINE:
Local knowledge trumps everything else

Exclusive buyer agents working a low-density vacation area are going to have to service buyers over a large geographic area in order to make a go of it. And the more area they have to cover, the less specialized their knowledge may be.

In most cases, you're probably going to be far better off working with a local agent in a vacation area − even without a buyer agency agreement − than you will be hiring an exclusive buyer agent with an urban practice several hours away.

you are already represented by a buyer agent and present the option of being contracted to serve as one and work exclusively on your behalf. (That said, you may find agents who simply don't like the buyer agency arrangement and don't encourage property seekers to enter into one with them.)

If you want the agency experience to unfold on your terms, you need to have some kind of game plan. Going into the property search, you should have a good sense of whether you want to have a buyer agent. If you feel you do, then the early stages of your search process will be directed in part towards finding the right one. And unless you have a specific agent who comes to you with a solid personal recommendation from someone you know and trust, letting agents show off their proverbial wares is probably the best way to get a search at least started in a given area.

If the answer to the need for a buyer agent is "no," then you'll be dealing with agents on the same terms as you would any other kind of salesperson. As long as you understand that the agent squiring you around is always working for the seller, you're fine.

Dual and designated agents

Some agents are willing to proceed without a buyer agency agreement until you decide you'd like to make an offer on a property, at which point they'll require that a clear relationship with you needs to be spelled out with a buyer agency agreement. While this bit of legal housekeeping might seem okay, such last-minute switches in the agent's obligations can be problematic. The buyers had no confidentiality protection throughout the search process – and now they're supposed to have it? As for the seller: What happened to the confidentiality they thought they were enjoying all through the buyer's search process?

There are no clear-cut solutions to this problem, although "dual agency" is often used in situations where an agent is expected to represent

CAUTION: If you don't want to sign...don't sign

If you wander inside a real estate office and start chatting with an agent because some listings posted in the window caught your eye, you know nothing about the market knowledge, reliability, or credibility of that agent. It's just luck of the draw that you end up talking to him, rather than another agent. So if he proposes that you sign a buyer agency agreement, don't feel pressured into doing so right away. Take your time and make sure you feel comfortable contracting this person exclusively to work with you. You have the right to expect an agent to discuss the local market with you and show you some listings at the office. Some may agree to take you around to see a few of them. The process of being escorted around is a good way to judge if this person might be a good fit as a buyer agent. The wrong buyer agent can harm your search for the right property.

both the buyer and the seller. In a small cottage market with a limited number of agents, this option is not uncommon. Another solution is the "designated agent," in which a salesperson within the brokerage is designated to be working exclusively on the buyer's behalf, even while his brokerage holds the listing for the property for sale and continues to serve in the seller agent role.

Working effectively with your agent

Good agents are by nature dealmakers. They can't control market forces of supply and demand, and they're most interested in closing a deal sooner rather than later. It's a misconception that a seller agent is there to drag every nickel possible out of you, the buyer.

It's the number of properties an agent sells in a given period that determines how much he makes, rather than getting a maximum possible price for each one. Yes, an agent makes less in commission as the price of an individual property drops, but it's in his best interest to sell three properties listed at $220,000 for $200,000 each in one month than to defy market forces and try to sell one of them for $220,000.

It's also in the market's interest to have relatively short closing periods, as quick sales signify liquidity and give owners the confidence to list properties. One of the worst clients a seller agent can have, in fact, is one who professes not to be in a hurry to sell, and is obstinate about getting his asking price. Unfortunately for agents, this can happen more often with vacation properties than with primary residences, mainly because there usually isn't an imperative to drive a quick sale, such as a relocation or a closing date on a new home.

5. Taking a test drive

Figuring out how much you can afford to spend and how far you want to drive are logical decisions, ruled by the rational part of your brain. But taking your family to look at a specific property – one that on paper comes close to meeting all the requirements discussed in previous chapters – is in large part about how the place makes you feel.

That said, when you "test drive" a property that might be the one to provide a lifetime of memories, decisions still need to be tempered by common sense – not just ruled by your big old fallible heart.

In this chapter, we'll guide you through the common-sense part – some of the things to pay attention to when you visit a potential property. As Mom used to say: Have fun, but be careful!

Testing the location

Buying a cottage is about buying a piece of property. The structures are important but – unlike the landscape and the lake – they can be changed. The quality of the property trumps the quality of the building.

TIP:
Discretion is the better part of valor

Don't point out to the sellers – or discuss loudly while they're in earshot – all the changes you would make to their cottage once it's yours. Cottages generate strong emotional attachment – and more than one cottage deal has gone awry because the sellers decided they didn't want their place to pass into the hands of someone who was going to "ruin" it.

Is this where you want to be?

When you test drive a cottage, spend lots of time outside. Size up the view from the deck, not just what the deck is built from or its overall condition. Think about the type and size of the trees, and the landscape: Do they touch your soul? Sit on the dock and imagine yourself spending weeks at a time in this setting. If the price is right, the cottage behind you can be renovated or even replaced. But you won't be able to replace the view, or the quality of the swimming, boating, or fishing, once you've bought it.

Kitchens can be gutted, guest cabins can be added, docks can be replaced. The rocks, the old pine trees, the shore, the view of the sunset: They're close to permanent. So don't be distracted by the bathroom fixtures or the off-putting shag rug in the living area. Stand outside and ask yourself: Is this where I want to be? If it isn't, all the money in the world isn't going to put you in a cottage on this property that will truly make you happy.

Where does the sun set?

There's no question that "western view" is considered a prime asset in many cottage areas, and even more prime if that view is also over the water. Because the sun sets (more or less) in the west, watching the big blazing red orb melt into the horizon at the end of the day is one of those quintessential cottage experiences for property owners graced with this view.

But to each his or her own. Some of us would prefer to be able to greet the sunrise from the front deck or the dock. Others would welcome the day-long presence of the sun that a southern view affords. Then again, if the cottage faces a little west of north, you might be able to avoid direct sun heating up the interior, then round off the day with a glimpse of the setting sun – provided the neighboring property or tree cover isn't in the way.

Just remember that the sun's path changes daily as we move through the seasons. And it changes enough that, depending on the property, the dock that's drenched in late-day sunlight on the June afternoon you visit

TIP: Love the property, but the cottage doesn't cut it?

Kudos to those who can look beyond the state of the present cottage and envision the possibilities. Too rundown? Tear it down and build a new one. Too cramped? Add a wing, a screened-in porch, a bunkie, or a boathouse with accommodations. Too rustic? Bring the utilities into at least the late 20th century. Too ambitious? Maybe.

If your enthusiasm for a property is based overwhelmingly on the terrain and the waterfront, and not what's already standing on it, you need to start doing research, well in advance of making an offer to purchase, on what structural changes are feasible from a regulatory standpoint. Do the bylaws leave room to grow? Cottage country is not the anything-goes Wild West that it used to be. See Chapters 6 and 8 for information on possible legal roadblocks to modifying a property, and the nitty-gritty of buying a tear-down.

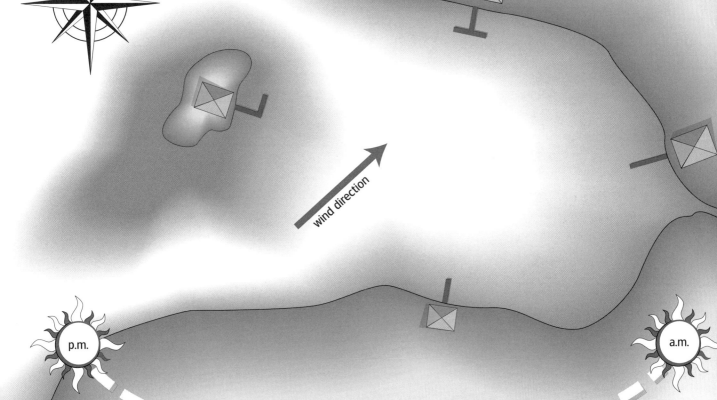

might be in complete shade by late summer. And the sunset you saw on the property in March, framed perfectly by two jack pines, won't be there in June. It will have moved on, perhaps to somewhere even nicer – or perhaps behind a neighbor's cottage, boathouse, or point of land where you can't see it at all.

If it's really important to you, do a little research on the sun's path for the latitude in which the cottage is located, and ask questions. While a property facing west is not suddenly going to be completely denied a sunset, the point is that you can't judge a property's relationship to the sun without considering its unique characteristics at different times of the year.

Consider how the sun's path will affect the cottage. Will you have morning sun on the dock? A view of the sunset from the deck? And what's the prevailing wind direction? It can affect how easy it will be to launch a canoe or moor a powerboat.

Which way does the wind blow?

Wind and the waves it produces can affect your enjoyment of a property. Especially on a rocky shore, they can complicate launching, landing, and mooring boats, as well as swimming.

The shoreline downwind of the prevailing winds can also become the resting place for whatever finds its way into the water, both man-made debris and nature's detritus: driftwood, weeds, and algae.

Case study:

Off-season buying requires more detective work

Karen was in the market for a modern, low-maintenance, drive-to cottage with all the amenities. When her agent told her a place meeting her criteria had just been listed on a lake on her shortlist, she dropped everything and headed north for a look. She liked what she saw, made an offer, and the place was hers.

The only problem was her visit was in December – when the shoreline was frozen and already snow-covered. Although she knew the lake, she wasn't familiar with the particular bay the cottage was on. And when she arrived in spring, she had a surprise: Her shoreline was awash in rotting leaves. Her bay, she discovered, faced into the prevailing winds, and the shallow water immediately offshore of her property was the final resting place for seemingly every leaf that had fallen from every tree on the lake the previous fall.

Her neighbors were already busy raking – which certainly didn't fit her definition of "low-maintenance cottaging"…especially when she discovered she also got weed blown onto her shore all summer long.

It could have been lots worse. Buying in the off-season is tricky: Yes, the price can be right and the competition less, but the waterfront is under wraps. Not only can't you tell what the swimming off the property is like, but you also can't get a first-hand picture of lake use: Is it a lake of kayakers or wakeboarders? How much boat traffic is there?

In late fall and winter, you'll also have a more difficult time gauging everything from how much sunlight the deck gets to how gregarious the neighbors are to what kind of ground cover the property has. Off-season buying requires more detective work: You need to ask more questions, look at more photos, do more research.

Karen's story, meanwhile, had a happy ending: She put the cottage up for sale that first summer – with an in-season price tag. Even after her agent's commission, she made a tidy profit – enough to buy another cottage on another part of the same lake. No rake required.

Wind, of course, will also carry sound. The lake you're considering might have a resort at one end. Before buying, you might only see the cottage on a Saturday afternoon, or in a shoulder season. You may have no idea that the prevailing southwesterly blows the sound of the resort's every-Saturday-night-in-summer karaoke contest your way. (And as the wind dies, calm conditions allow the sound to travel across the water with pin-drop clarity.)

Wind also helps drive near-shore currents, causing changes in water temperature. In large water bodies such as Georgian Bay and the Great Lakes, heating doesn't extend much deeper than the first few feet of the upper surface, so wind and wave action can cause mixing that plunges water temperatures over a very short period. One weekend, there can be lovely swimming in water of 78°F, and in a matter of days, high winds and wave action can dredge up deep, cold water that drops the temperature at the dock to 65°. (Small, high-sided lakes are largely immune to this process.)

None of these wind effects are necessarily deal-breakers, but better to know about them now than get an unwelcome surprise later on.

How close are the neighbors?

To many city dwellers, any lot wider than 40 feet can sound estate-like. Certainly a property advertised with 80 to 200 feet of waterfront can strike prospective buyers as a sprawling paradise, compared to what they're used to at home. But it's remarkable how small a property can feel once you're actually standing on it.

One reason is that waterfront lots 80 feet wide aren't necessarily very private...especially when the cottages on them can be 60 feet wide. City homes tend to be longer than they are wide, to maximize square footage of living space within the available frontage. With cottages, there's little incentive to build on the "bowling alley" plan of city lots, with a narrow structure extending back along the lots. Cottages are built "sideways" compared to most city homes, emphasizing their width along the waterfront, to maximize the view from inside and the size of the front deck. This means that

TIP:

Two noisy questions a knowledgeable realtor should be able to answer:

1. Is there a potential source of unwelcome noise in an area? It could be a highway, railway, resort, kids' camp, or a marina that acts as a seaplane base.

2. When is it most likely to be the loudest, and how often does it occur?

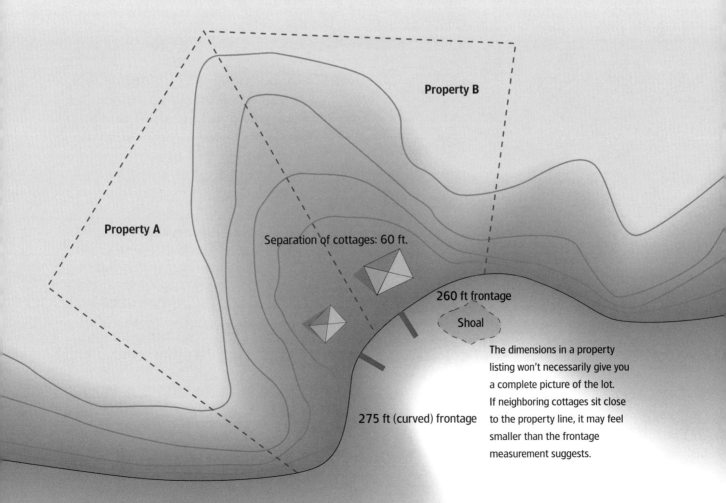

Property B

Property A

Separation of cottages: 60 ft.

260 ft frontage

Shoal

275 ft (curved) frontage

The dimensions in a property listing won't necessarily give you a complete picture of the lot. If neighboring cottages sit close to the property line, it may feel smaller than the frontage measurement suggests.

neighboring lots with relatively modest cottages on them can have structures almost as close together as homes on much-smaller city lots. So don't get too excited about the lot's dimensions until you've actually been there.

Another reason that a cottage lot might not seem as big as you'd imagined is the realtor didn't measure the frontage the way you'd imagined. There's an important difference between the width of a lot and its frontage. Assuming a lot has parallel sides, the width is measured at right angles to them. But that doesn't mean the actual waterfront runs at right angles to the sides. It may well be angled so that the frontage is 110 linear feet, while most of the lot is only 80 feet wide.

If the waterfront also has a few curves in it, the seller may try to claim a frontage measurement that follows each and every curve, which could increase the linear measurement considerably. While there may be 135 feet of measurable waterfront for a particular property, if the lot itself is 80 feet wide, the neighboring cottages are going to be much closer than the advertised amount of waterfront would suggest. If a property is distant or otherwise difficult to access, you would be well served to see a copy of the survey before going to the trouble of making a visit. (*See Chapter 6 for info on what a survey can tell you.*)

How do you get to the property?
One if by land: Road access
There are vacation areas with road systems as nice as anything you'll find in suburbia: paved, assumed by the local municipality or district, and complete with curbside trash pickup. And there are still many, many vacation areas where the road to the cottage is privately owned and maintained by an individual property owner, or owned communally by a group of cottagers.

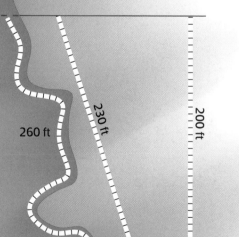

260 ft

230 ft

200 ft

Since frontage is measured in actual linear distance, a lot that has **260** feet of waterfront when every curve is taken into account may actually have only **230** feet of straight-line waterfront. And the width of the lot (assuming it has parallel sides) may be only **200** feet. So don't be surprised if a lot feels smaller than you expected when you actually set foot on it.

Such private roads can range from a glorified trail through the bush to a regularly graveled, plowed-in-winter thoroughfare.

The differences in the type, and quality, of the road access can affect your plans for the property. Communal roads, paid for and maintained by private owners, can be a vexing complication. Access to the property you're considering may be on a communal road shared by 10 other cottages. You may envision using the property as a year-round retreat, but that doesn't mean the rest of the road users do. As the new kid on the block, you can quickly find your ambitions seriously compromised by neighbors who don't see a need to gravel a dirt road or share in the cost of regular winter plowing.

There are, of course, other options for winter access. Some cottagers who only visit occasionally in the winter already have a routine of parking at the end of the municipal road and continuing to the cottage along the communal road by snowmobile, or even on skis or snowshoes.

Conversely, you might not be happy paying for the costs of year-round maintenance if you only plan to use your cottage during the summer months. In either case, be sure you understand what the present pattern of road use is, what the annual costs are and, if your personal ambitions for the property are leaning towards the year-round, what the road is like in winter. (Just because a road is plowed doesn't mean easy driving for all vehicles.)

(*For legal aspects of communal roads, see Chapter 6. For road access and retirement living, see Chapter 13.*)

Questions to ask about a property's road access:

☐ Is the road assumed by a municipality or district, or is it private?

☐ If the road is private, does it belong exclusively to the property, or is it a communal road shared by cottage neighbors?

☐ Where the road crosses other properties, is right of access properly deeded? (*See Chapter 6, p. 109.*)

☐ What is the arrangement for sharing costs of maintenance on a private communal road?

☐ Is the road kept open year-round?

☐ Is the laneway or driveway from the cottage to the road private or shared with cottage neighbors?

☐ Does it cross another property? Does the parking area? If so, is there legal, deeded access?

☐ Do your plans for use of the property agree with the present arrangement for maintenance of the communal road or the nature of the municipal road – particularly if you're considering the property for year-round retirement living? (*See Chapter 13.*)

Two if by sea: Water-access

In Chapter 2, we discussed the general aspects of water-access properties in terms of seasonal versus year-round use and the challenges that coming and going by boat can pose to weekend use and rental potential. But "water-access" can mean a sheltered two-minute ride from the marina – or a 30-minute trip across exposed waters. Now it's time to take a hard look at what it means for the property you're considering.

This may not seem difficult since viewing the property requires you to actually make the trip. But a test-drive showing can be a distracting experience. You will most likely be a passenger in a boat driven by an owner or a

Questions to ask about a property's water access:

☐ What is the length of the boat trip in both distance and time?

☐ Is it sheltered or does it traverse open water?

☐ How much "local knowledge" is required to navigate the route? Is there an official buoyage system, or private marks maintained by the local cottagers' association?

☐ Is the cottage a getaway for experienced boaters, or can a novice boater comfortably manage the route?

☐ Can you make the trip with your family and your possessions (groceries, belongings) safely and comfortably?

☐ Will a different boat be required to satisfy the above point? Can you budget for such a boat?

☐ If a larger boat is required, can the route's fluctuating water levels and the cottage's existing dock accommodate it?

☐ If a larger dock is required, is there space for one, with adequate depth alongside it and on the approach? Can a larger dock be installed without running afoul of local bylaws or navigation rights? (*See Chapter 6.*)

☐ Where will you keep the boat and park the car? How much do local marinas charge for these services?

☐ Will you need a second boat to accommodate cottage activities (such as fishing or wakeboarding) and/or orchestrate cottage comings and goings?

☐ Is the route manageable in inclement weather? After dark? If not, does it agree with your planned patterns of cottage use?

☐ If a couple is involved in the purchase, are both willing to master the necessary boating skills to make the trip, so that getting to or from the cottage (particularly in an emergency) doesn't depend on a single person who might not always be present?

☐ Do you plan to have frequent guest visits? Are you prepared to make the boat trips to pick them up and drop them off? Will guests feel comfortable making the trip?

real estate agent; the boat you're riding in may not be the one that you're going to have to make the trip in yourself. Being ferried to a property by an agent in a 24-foot runabout with full canvas enclosure is a lot different than making the same trip yourself in the 16-foot fishing boat that comes with the cottage. (Sure, you can always upgrade to a bigger boat; just make sure you earmark sufficient funds for the purchase.)

And, with any luck, you're seeing the property on a glorious day. Sunny skies make for pleasant boating, but on your test drive you need to imagine what the same trip might be like in wind, rain, or darkness. Unless the water-access route is a very quick and entirely sheltered one, cottages that depend on boats to reach them are best suited to people who are comfortable with boating. That may seem an obvious statement, but it can lead to a real crisis in enjoyment of the property if, say, only one family member has the necessary skills – and confidence – to drive the boat to and from the cottage.

Testing the neighborhood

For some buyers, fast boats, personal watercraft, and waterskiing are what make a cottage fun for the family. For others, a quiet lake with light power-boat traffic or even the tranquility of a no-motor lake is their definition of heaven. Some are looking to socialize, some are looking for quiet retreat. As we stressed in Chapter 3, part of the key to cottage happiness is finding a lake whose residents share your vision of cottaging. Otherwise, like trying to pound a square peg into a round hole, you will simply not fit in.

Who are the neighbors?

The ability to enjoy any kind of property depends so much on how one gets along with the folks next door. But the potential for poor relations is probably even higher in vacation country than at home, since so much time is spent out of doors within sight and sound of each other. And that includes more than immediate next-door neighbors: Since sound travels so easily over water, you have to consider the cottagers on the other side of the bay, and even the other side of the lake, your neighbors, too. Add to that the predilection for some people in vacation mode to cut a little too loose a little too loudly, and you have a recipe for everything from mild frustration to unending conflict.

If you choose a cottage on a lake that has restrictions on boat type or horsepower limits (*see Chapter 3, p. 53*), the other cottagers, to some extent, will be like-minded. However, since most cottage lakes don't have such legal restrictions, the onus is on you to get a good match.

The most obvious cause of sparks between neighbors is incompatible lifestyles. Stereotypically, there will be a quiet couple with a canoe on one property, and a crowd of twentysomething party animals with late-night

CAUTION:
Water-access adds to building costs

Thinking of a reno? Want to add a bunkie or build a whole new cottage? You need to factor in the additional cost of bringing in all your building materials by boat and barge. A ballpark estimate is that a water-access building project can cost at least 20% more than a similar project at a road-access place. Keep in mind that tradespeople may charge for the additional travel time, too.

bonfires and a cranked-up boom box on the other. We don't need such extremes to have sour relations, but the stereotype nevertheless tends to hold. One cottager is at the lake for peace and quiet, the other to play and party hard.

Eyeball neighboring properties and ask questions

There's no simple way to find out what the neighbors are like. At the very least, you should cast your eyes over their place: Take note of how many high-performance water toys are jammed around the dock and the number of cases of unreturned beer empties stacked by the back door. Look for other lifestyle clues, such as prominent lights, which might signal nighttime activity and annoying (to some) light pollution.

You can ask the sellers or their agent, but they are under no legal obligation to confess to poor relations with the folks next door, or to tell you what they're like.

A real estate agent also isn't obligated to reveal his client's reason for selling the property (beyond areas covered by vendor disclosure documents; *see Chapter 7, p. 125*). But that doesn't mean you can't and shouldn't ask. You can work around to the specifics of their reason for selling by asking if they're investing in a new property elsewhere. And the questions can certainly include guileless inquiries about the neighbors. If you have kids or grandkids, it's more than fair to wonder aloud if the neighbors have some of the same age, how often they're at the place, if they're enrolled in the local sailing school.

Talk to the seller or the neighbor more than the agent. And when you talk, ask questions, listen carefully, and don't talk too much. People generally love to talk, and by leaving a void in the conversation, most people will jump at the chance to fill it. The less willing the seller or agent is to say anything about the neighbors, the more cause you have for concern. Anyone dumb enough to say, "I'd rather not talk about them," has already said more than you need to know.

Listing agents' client confidentiality and tight-lipped behavior by sellers are reasons to have an agent working for you under a buyer agency agreement. (*See Chapter 4.*) If the agent really knows the area, he or she can fill you in on the local scuttlebutt.

Do the neighbors rent out their cottage?

One thing you definitely want to find out is how often the neighboring properties are rented out. People routinely rent out their cottages for a week or two when they're not there. But this is altogether different from a cottage that exists purely as an income property. As property values soar in prime vacation areas, taking rental rates with them, more and more cottages are purchased purely as investments by what are essentially absentee landlords back in the city, and then rented out all season long.

TIP:

Be a weekend warrior

To get a sense of how the neighbors behave when things are in full swing, visit the property you're considering (by land or water) on a weekend during peak season. A Thursday afternoon in early June isn't going to give you much of a picture of either boat traffic or the neighbors' style of relaxation.

Owning a cottage next to a full-time rental property is a bit of neighbor roulette: Every week, there's a new cast of characters next door. Some will be splendid people, others a pain. And you probably don't want to be spending a lot of your relaxation time trying to get in touch with an absentee owner, to complain about the behavior of renters.

What is the boat traffic like?

As you size up a property's waterfront, the volume and nature of passing boat traffic are important considerations, and visiting the property on a nice summer weekend is a good way to get a feel for them. Here are some things to think about:

• how boat traffic will affect swimming or the safe use of canoes, kayaks, pedal boats, sailboats, and other floating toys, especially where children are concerned

• how much boat wake will be sent your way, causing your own boat to bounce against the dock and accelerating shoreline erosion

• how much noise is produced by the type of boats you're seeing.

As discussed in Chapter 3, a lake may have legal restrictions that affect boating. But all the rules and regulations in the world won't guarantee your everlasting happiness. However, by knowing the style of boating that takes place on a particular water body and understanding the rules and regulations that do exist, you'll be able to choose a lake or river that agrees with your version of boating.

Speed limits: What the law permits

In the U.S., individual states and municipalities can impose restrictions on boat speed. In Canada, however, a federal speed limit applies to all bodies of navigable fresh water from Ontario west: Within 30 meters (100 feet) of shore, a speed limit of 10 km/h – about six mph – is in effect.

But this does not create a blanket zone of snail-pace boating along the entire shoreline of cottage country. The law permits water-ski boats to exceed the limit while moving perpendicular to the shore – in other words, when getting a skier up on his boards from a sitting position on the end of the dock. The really critical exception is that the restriction does not apply to channels marked by federal aids to navigation within that 30-meter buffer zone. The speed limit was not meant to impede orderly traffic flow in those channels.

If you're considering buying shoreline property on a busy waterway, you need to realize that boats in a buoyed channel are not within the 30-meter restriction zone, even when the channel is within 30 meters of shore. This does not permit them to roar by recklessly and cause property damage with their wake, but a speed limit on this channel can only be imposed by the Canadian Coast Guard. Traditionally, such restrictions have only been set in response to a demonstrated need to protect swimmers, canoeists, and other non-motorized boaters from high-speed craft; however, the Coast Guard has recently begun considering shoreline property damage as legitimate cause for granting such an application.

While this is good news for property owners along busy waterways (often made busy by cottagers themselves), planning to launch a bid for a speed restriction isn't an effective way to ensure you end up with the sort of waterfront property you desire. The process, overseen by the Coast Guard, involves thorough consultation with all affected parties: not only your cottage neighbors, but also area residents who do their boating out of a local marina or from a public launch ramp, and transient recreational boaters, who pass through while cruising.

In some areas, an unfortunate amount of antagonism has developed between recreational boaters and cottage owners over attempts to bring in a boating restriction. You're much better off choosing a suitable area than trying to change the area to suit. (After all, you wouldn't buy a home beside an airport and expect them to stop landing planes.)

Is the water used by transient boaters? Or anglers?

The right of navigation in effect in both Canada and the U.S. includes the right to anchor and operate a vessel as close to the shoreline as is feasible. Boaters can't land on your property (except in an emergency), but they may get closer than you'd prefer. Some limitations exist, particularly in states or municipalities where laws set minimum distances a motorized vessel can approach a swimmer, or where a water lot lease could be cited as a ban on anchoring by transient boaters. But by and large, navigable waterways are public spaces and boaters big or small are free to go anywhere they choose.

TIP: How to get a handle on boat traffic

- Be sure to assess any property fronting on a navigable waterway or other water with a high volume of traffic or with high-speed traffic during the regular summer vacation period, and not in the off-season. Know what you might be getting into.

- Check whether a speed restriction is already in place. While this will assure you that boat speeds – when properly observed – will be low in these areas, it will also indicate areas where high volumes of traffic exist. Ask locally, or in Canada, check the Boating Restriction Regulations (available on the Dept. of Justice website: laws.justice.gc.ca; search under "regulations" for boating restrictions). In the U.S., you'll need to check with the appropriate individual state and municipal authorities; some restrictions are statewide; others apply to a specific body of water or just a portion of it.

The picturesque bay in front of a cottage you're thinking of buying is not going to be "your bay" in any legal sense. You own the land within the perimeter of your survey (*see Chapter 6*) – not the water in front of it. If there's a chance that it's going to be used regularly by other people, you need to understand that before proceeding with a purchase, and be comfortable with the way it's used.

If your potential cottage is on a lake, bay, or river that is part of a popular cruising route, you may find cruising boaters dropping anchor right in front of your shoreline – particularly if you are blessed with a property on a spectacular scenic cove. Some buyers don't mind this sort of thing, but for others, a fleet of total strangers out front – even well-behaved, considerate ones – defeats the whole point of having a cottage to get away from it all.

If you're considering property in a popular cruising area, do your homework on where those cruisers (which can include rental houseboats) like to hang out. (*See Tip, at right.*) Editors of cruising guides and boating magazines are constantly reminding boaters to respect private property and the privacy of the owners – and cruisers are looking for their own private piece of heaven every bit as much as cottagers are – and to respect the environment. But all the mutual goodwill in the world isn't going to change the fact that, in some locations, a small bay is going to be host to a dozen or more cruising boats on a typical weekend.

Fish, too, have a way of choosing habitats close to shore, and some highly desirable species prefer the shadows cast by trees, docks, and boathouses. Trolling and spin-casting anglers, particularly on "tournament-quality" lakes, are known to work their gear up and down the sides of cottage docks and even poke their noses into the open bays of boathouses.

Don't wait to be surprised: Figure out how likely you are to have overnight guests out front – and how you feel about it – before you decide to buy.

TIP:
Do some book learning
Popular boating areas are covered by cruising guides, comprehensive map/tour books designed expressly for boaters. Buy one and see where the authors have stuck the little anchorage symbols on the maps and photos. They will likely represent anchoring hotspots you may wish to avoid.

Testing the cottage

In Chapter 7 we'll look at hiring a professional to inspect the cottage and its systems. But before you go as far as that, you'll want to look at the nitty-gritty of the place yourself, with an eye to how well it lives up to the criteria you've set for a cottage. The inspector will tell you if the structure is sound and the systems are in good working order; your job first is to evaluate whether the structure and the systems are the right ones for you.

How does the cottage get its power?

Among the things you'll want to know is whether the cottage's electrical supply comes from a utility. If it doesn't – and this is still the case in plenty of vacation areas – you'll have to generate your own power, which can be

TIP:

Add this to your record collection

The well record, a document created by a licensed driller and then submitted to the cottage owner, is an invaluable resource for a potential buyer. It will accurately date the well and give information about its depth and the type of casing used, the composition of the soil or rock it runs through, and the flow rate attained when it was drilled. Owners can tell you anything they want about the well and the quantity and quality of water it produces, but without a well record, you'll have to trust the accuracy of their information.

The bad news is that most owners never have a copy of their well record. The good news is that most reputable well drilling companies do, some of them dating back to the dawn of time. First, find out who drilled your well. If the owner can't provide this information, simply call around to local well drilling companies. (There are usually only a few and most have been in business for many years.) With a bit of information like the lot and concession number of the subject property, there's a good chance they'll be able to dig up a copy of the well record.

done via a diesel, propane, or gas generator, or by harnessing wind energy or solar power, or some combination of the three.

If you're "off the grid," it's a basic law of energy self-sufficiency that in the name of conservation, the fewer things you have that require electricity, the better. This doesn't mean you can't run a television and an XBox from a battery bank replenished by a wind generator, or crank up a generator to pump water, but you need to match your power appetite to the capability of the system – or vice versa. You also have to adjust your attitudes about power usage. In the city, it's rare to have to think about whether a home is capable of supporting a particular device or appliance. The electricity bill might skyrocket, but you won't be left without any juice for the refrigerator because of the draw of the surround-sound home entertainment system.

If you're considering a property with anything other than standard 100- or 200-amp service provided by a utility, think about the following:

• Alternative power-generating systems are often beyond the expertise of a professional home inspector; if a qualified technician isn't available to assess the efficacy of the system before you close a deal, can the seller satisfy your concerns about its working order and give you enough information to judge whether it will meet your needs?

• A do-it-yourselfer's mentality is useful when you're generating your own power, since components will have to be repaired and replaced, and systems upgraded, from time to time. Are you willing to learn the theory and practice of the technology?

• Off-grid power requires discipline. A few injudiciously selected appliances can make a major dent in your power supply. Appliances that generate heat – such as ovens, dishwashers, space heaters, water heaters, and clothes dryers – consume the most energy.

• Compressor motors in refrigerators and freezers use enormous amounts of energy, especially at start-up. Microwave ovens are also energy hogs.

• Air conditioning? Forget about it.

If your list of desired cottage appliances includes most of the basic urban amenities, then you probably want a cottage whose electricity is supplied by a utility.

Where does the cottage get its drinking water?

Potable water is available one of four ways: directly from a public utility (where a vacation area is sufficiently urbanized), from a private or communal well, from the lake, or from bottles – lugged up from home or bought from the store. If you are responsible for your own water, you will need to ensure that its quantity, quality, and supply system are up to snuff. (*See "Questions to Ask," next page.*)

How does the cottage treat sewage?

Getting rid of sewage (black water) and water from washing dishes, clothes, and people (gray water) should be of special interest when you scope out a cottage. If a cottage has a private system consisting of a septic tank and a leaching bed, as most do, you'll want to make sure it's functioning properly before you close the deal, since a new system can easily cost $5,000–$10,000

Questions to ask if your water...

...comes from a well

☐ How old is the well?

☐ Is it a drilled well, a dug well, or a sand point?

☐ How deep is the well?

☐ Is the "well record," a document created by the driller attesting to depth, construction type, and flow rate, available? (*See Tip, facing page.*)

☐ When was the well water last tested and is the report available?

☐ How old is the water system (the pump, pressure tank, and water heater)?

☐ How does the water taste? Is a secondary filter necessary to improve the look and taste?

...comes from the lake

☐ All surface water should be treated (purified) before drinking. Is there a purification system in place?

☐ When was the purified water last tested and is the report available?

☐ Does the purification system supply the entire cottage or just one dedicated tap?

☐ Does the system produce water with an acceptable taste?

☐ Is the water system winterized?

☐ Who performs work on the water system? Does the owner do it or is someone hired?

☐ How old is the water system (the pump, pressure tank, water heater, and purification system)?

...comes from a public utility

☐ What are the costs associated with municipal water supply?

☐ Where is the treatment plant?

☐ Does the municipality have a history of water problems or "boil water" advisories?

☐ How does the water taste? Do local residents use a secondary filter to improve the look and taste?

or more, depending on size and site access. Asking some general questions – see the list, below – can give you a heads-up on the system at this stage. If you proceed to an offer, you'll want to know more. (*See Chapter 7 for info on septic-system inspection.*)

If you're looking at an older cottage on a tiny, rocky lot, it may have a holding tank for sewage instead of a septic system. In the past, such tanks were allowed on lots where the terrain or size didn't permit a leaching bed. Today, however, approvals for new tanks of this type are rarely granted. (*See Caution, p. 96.*)

Perhaps the cottage has neither a septic system nor a holding tank. The other options for getting rid of black water are an outhouse or an alternative toilet that works by composting or incinerating wastes. An outhouse is as low-tech and reliable as it gets – keep it clean and well-screened and it will serve you well for decades. But like alternative power systems, alternative toilets require a certain commitment from their owners – you can't just flush and forget. Regular maintenance procedures are required, the frequency and type varying with the toilet.

Questions to ask if the cottage has...

...a septic system

☐ How old are the septic tank and leaching bed and where are they located?

☐ When was the last time the tank was pumped out or inspected by a licensed installer?

☐ Are maintenance records available? A recent inspection report?

☐ Have any toilets, showers, sinks, or a dishwasher been added to the cottage after the septic system was installed? (If so, the system may already be too small.)

☐ Do you plan to modify the cottage to include more toilets, sinks, etc.? (If so, the system may need upgrading.)

☐ Is the main waste pipe winterized?

...a holding tank

☐ How old is the tank and where is it located?

☐ How large is the tank and how often does it need to be pumped out? Who performs this service and how much does it cost?

☐ Does the tank feature an alarm that warns you when it is getting full?

☐ Have any toilets, showers, sinks, or a dishwasher been added to the cottage after the holding tank was installed? (If so, the tank may already be too small.)

If there isn't a septic system on the property, you also need to determine how gray water – waste water from washing clothes, dishes, and bodies – is disposed. Sending it to a leaching pit is the most common solution when a cottage is seasonal and has a non-flushing toilet.

What sort of communications systems are available at the cottage?

The first thing you need to think about when it comes to cottage communications is how important telephone, Internet, and cellular services are to you and your family. Some cottage properties don't have land-line service. Do you care? In many areas, cellphone service negates the need for wires and poles. In other areas, a cellphone is utterly useless. If land-line service is available, how much will it cost to have it hooked up to your property?

Basic telephone service is one thing, but the speed of the dial-up Internet connection usually available on such services will seem pretty slow to anyone who is accustomed to urban bandwidth. For cottage buyers who consider wireless communications (web-enabled cellphones and PDAs, text

Look up, way up: Satellite service can put cottages on-line

If the cottage area you're considering only allows dial-up access and high-speed is one of your cottage necessities, take heart: A new service is making cost-effective, high-speed Internet access possible in rural areas – via satellite (Anik F2, launched by Teleset Canada). You'll need a satellite modem plus a small dish. Visit www.telesat.ca, or WildBlue Communications, its U.S. service partner, at www.wildblue.com.

☐ Do you plan to modify the cottage to include more toilets, sinks, etc.? (If so, the tank may need to be upgraded or replaced.)

☐ If a new tank is necessary, is it even possible to gain government approval for it, or will it need to be replaced by a different type of system?

☐ Where is the sewage pump that delivers waste to the tank?

☐ How old is it and when was it last inspected?

☐ Does gray water go to the holding tank? If not, how is it disposed of?

...an alternative toilet

☐ What type of toilet is in use?

☐ Is the company that manufactured it still in business?

☐ What sort of regular maintenance does it require? How frequently?

☐ Is the original owner's manual available?

☐ How is gray water from sinks and showers disposed of?

...an outhouse

☐ How long has the outhouse been used in its present location?

☐ How is gray water disposed of?

CAUTION: Change isn't always a good thing

If you find a cottage waste-disposal system doesn't meet your needs, don't assume you can simply increase its size or change to another type of system. Because faulty, undersized, or improperly installed systems create environmental damage in waterfront locations, most municipalities have tightened their regulations concerning size and placement of waste systems. In the past, for example, some cottages on islands or tiny, rocky lots were allowed to use holding tanks to contain waste water that was then pumped out when the tank got full. Today, approvals for new tanks of this type are rarely granted. Similarly, a cottage that uses some form of alternative toilet may not meet the size and setback requirements necessary for the installation of a traditional septic system. These requirements vary from jurisdiction to jurisdiction, so it's imperative to check with the local municipality to see what systems and upgrades are permissible.

TIP:

Dial-up doesn't have to be doom and gloom

If the cottage has a phone connection, low-speed (56K) dial-up service may be available, and that may be sufficient for your cottage needs. But check with your regular Internet service provider to see whether a dial-up connection from the cottage will require a long-distance telephone call. Depending on the scope of their service area, many providers will be able to provide you with a local dial-up number at no cost. Alternatively, many cottage-country Internet providers can set you up with an account for a month or two, just for the periods you plan to spend at the lake.

messaging, paging) an absolute must, vacation country does present its challenges. Much of the cottage market is still in "fringe" areas of coverage for various wireless services, or in areas that have no coverage at all. You should consult the coverage maps of service providers, but there's often no way to tell if a particular wireless service works in a given location without actually trying it while you're there.

Many vacation communities, as they become more developed, do boast the availability of high-speed Internet through cable service providers, but usually only for properties quite close to town. Similarly, high-speed service via telephone line is generally unavailable because phone companies usually don't offer it to customers who are more than about 1 mile/1.6 km from a central switch. *(For another high-speed option, see sidebar, previous page.)*

Is the cottage suitable for year-round use?

This question is not concerned with whether you can get to the cottage in winter *(see "How Do You Get to the Property?," p. 84, for that)*, but rather with how comfortable the place itself will be when you arrive. And to answer that question, you need to answer two others:

How is the cottage insulated?

Insulation, the stuff that keeps heat in and cold out, is rarely seen as a cottage "system" and often overlooked. Bad mistake. Poorly or non-insulated places might be fine for summer-only use or the occasional shoulder-season visit, but if you're planning regular stays beyond the summer months, you'll want to know how well the cottage is insulated. Many times, the owners won't have much of a clue – so you need to do a bit of sleuthing.

• Is the cottage insulated at all?

• If it is insulated, was it converted from a summer-only place?

• Are all the floors, walls, and attic spaces insulated?

• Are soffits and attic spaces ventilated? (Proper ventilation is crucial to a good insulation job.)

• Is this the original insulation or has the cottage recently been renovated?

• If renovated, was the work done by the owner or a licensed tradesperson?

• Do the owners use the cottage year-round? If so, what is the length of their longest winter stay?

• Are the windows double-glazed thermal panes, single-pane glass with storm windows, or just single-pane glass?

• Does every bed feature an electric blanket or a down duvet?

How is the cottage heated?

Like regular homes, cottages can be heated in any number of ways, often combining a variety of systems as a result of additions or renovations.

• What is the annual cost of heating the cottage?

• If heated by natural gas, oil, or propane, what is the age of the furnace and when was it last serviced?

• Does the owner have a service contract with a heating company?

• If heated by propane or oil, where are the tanks and how often do they need to be refilled? Can the truck access the property in winter?

• If electrically heated, when were the heaters installed? Are they protected by the right size of wire and breakers or fuses?

• Are the heaters controlled by a central thermostat or are they individually operated?

• If heated with wood, what is the age of the woodstove or furnace and when was it last cleaned and inspected? Does it bear a UL, ULC, or CSA stamp of approval?

• Do flue gases exit through modern, insulated stovepipe, older single-wall pipe, or a traditional brick or stone chimney? When was the chimney last cleaned and inspected?

• Is heat provided by an open fireplace or an efficient stove or insert?

• Where is the wood stored and how easy is it to access?

• Where does the current owner get his wood and how much does it cost?

(See Chapter 7, "Inspecting the Cottage," for more information on the topics covered in this chapter under "Testing the Cottage.")

SELLER'S TIP:
Learn to love disclosure documents

Vendor disclosures, documents that warrant the basic condition of the property and its systems, are sometimes viewed by sellers as a burden. But if you want an advantage in a busy market, you should embrace them, including as much accurate information as possible. Assemble them in a sales package that gets presented to potential buyers even before they ask for the information. *(See Chapter 12, p. 200, for more.)*

6. The property survey

Y ou've seen the property, toured it with the family, and fallen in love. Before you proceed further, it's time to find out exactly what, from a legal perspective, you are about to buy.

It is not uncommon for a property to have changed hands many times, each transaction relying solely on the description in the deed, with the same incorrect information being passed on to the next buyer. This can get tricky, because on many recreational properties, portions have been set aside by the Crown (in Canada) or the municipal government as "not part of the deal," things such as registered and unregistered easements (for example, a hydro right of way), concession road allowances that run intermittently at right angles to the water, and (primarily in Ontario) shoreline road allowances that reserve a 66-foot swath of land at the water's edge. A proscriptive easement could give a local trapper the right to cross your property because he's been doing it for 30 years, while a Crown reservation could withhold a strip of land on your property for a road allowance.

Stories abound of vendors selling lots they didn't own, and cottages being built on the wrong lot. In one case, a cottager thought he had deeded title to the land, only to find the cottage had been built at the exact inter-

SELLER'S TIP:
A recent survey can give you a leg up

Your property will be all the more marketable if you can produce a current survey. Peace of mind is a valuable selling feature: An up-to-date survey assures purchasers that the property is unencumbered by problems such as encroachments, and makes them aware of significant property details such as road allowances and easements.

If a recent survey does not exist, it's definitely in your best interest to have one done.

section of a road allowance and a concession road. In the end, he owned nothing. But don't be put off by these tales of terror: Every one of them could have been avoided by obtaining an up-to-date survey.

Survey basics
Different types, different levels of information

When you're considering a survey, it's important to note that there are several variations on the theme, and that the language describing them (and what they constitute) can vary from state to state and province to province.

Unless you're buying a substantial chunk of land, your purchase will involve a lot, which at some point was legally subdivided from a larger property for development. The most basic lot description is known in Canada as a *lot plan, reference plan,* or *plan of survey*; in the U.S. you are most likely to see it called a *plat*. It basically defines in a drawing what a deed describes (commonly called the "metes and bounds") with words, outlining a property's boundaries in relation to the neighbors. It will also include things such as concession road allowances, shoreline road allowances, Crown reservations (in Canada), utility easements, and the like.

Another type of survey, the *plot plan* or *real property report,* is more detailed. In addition to all the information found in a lot plan or plat, a real property report also shows the main building and "improvements" (anything constructed) on the property. Not all jurisdictions require the same level of detail in a real property report, but the best ones include things

How recent is recent?

When realtors and lawyers use the word survey, it is usually prefaced by "recent," as in, "A recent survey will guarantee that your cottage is not sitting on your neighbor's property." But how recent is recent?

Generally, "recent" is taken to mean a survey executed close to, or at the time of, a real estate transaction. Theoretically, a survey is accurate forever as long as no changes have been made to the property. But as soon as you build a shed or move the outhouse, that survey is no longer recent. In one case, a survey became incorrect and out of date over the course of a weekend when a vendor with an encroaching garage tore the structure down just after it had been plotted on a real property report.

It's often tempting to go with an old survey just to save a few bucks, but even if the property hasn't changed, surveying has. Modern surveys are more accurate due to better equipment, and have higher standards regarding details such as septic beds, driveways, and municipal zoning requirements than were required in the past. If the survey in question is simply a lot plan (*see text, above*) and doesn't show all improvements on the property, it would be wise to get a new one done. If it's a real property report and you can be absolutely certain that no changes or improvements have been made to the property, have a surveyor look it over for zoning discrepancies. Then consider it recent.

TIP: Stakes can be suspect

When you tour a property, an owner or real estate agent may show you the stakes that mark the perimeter of the lot. But those wooden stakes, or laths, *aren't* the legal property boundaries. They only indicate the location of the actual markers, the monuments, usually square steel bars that are buried in the ground. On older lots, the monuments may be lengths of rebar or metal pipe that have been hammered into the ground, and you may have to dig down a few inches to locate them. (Monuments can also be incised into boulders. In really old surveys, a tree may be cited as a monument.) Sometimes you'll encounter stakes that don't even locate monuments; they've been placed to help sight a property line. Over the years, the wooden stakes may have been disturbed by construction, repositioned by kids, or knocked flying by snow blowers and lawn tractors and then stuck back in the ground any old place, so don't rely on them. Dig down and find the actual monument. And if a monument itself somehow becomes disturbed, only a licensed surveyor can reposition it.

such as decks, docks, carports, septic beds, driveways, footpaths – even the humble outhouse – and places them precisely on the lot. This information is vital because while a lot plan, plat, or a basic property description might show the property and outline the various and sundry road allowances and reservations on it, only a real property report can show whether your buildings and improvements encroach on those areas. More importantly, a real property report helps avoid future encroachments due to municipal rezoning requirements by showing, without a doubt, that if you build a deck, it will go over the sidelot setback or that a proposed septic bed will run onto a neighbor's property.

If all this isn't enough to convince you of a survey's worth, remember that in cottage country, each municipality will have its own specific requirements concerning things such as sidelot setbacks, height restrictions, and permitted distances between septic systems and water sources. What might be legal in one municipality might be strictly forbidden in the next. The peace of mind offered by a formal survey can't be understated: Rather than forcing prospective purchasers to become experts in municipal zoning laws, it is the surveyor's job to know all of these pertinent bylaws and reveal them in a real property report. Keep in mind also that these municipal bylaws are constantly changing, with some areas having unique requirements. For example, in some parts of Ontario, bylaws state that you can only build on 10% of the area lying within 200 feet of the high-water line. So the only way to know whether the cottage of your dreams will even be permissible is to have a survey done.

The second component of a survey – beyond the paper part – is what's physically staked out in the ground. A *boundary survey* confirms the location of the perimeter markers of a lot, which are called monuments. Not all real property reports are meant to be used as boundary surveys. (Some might

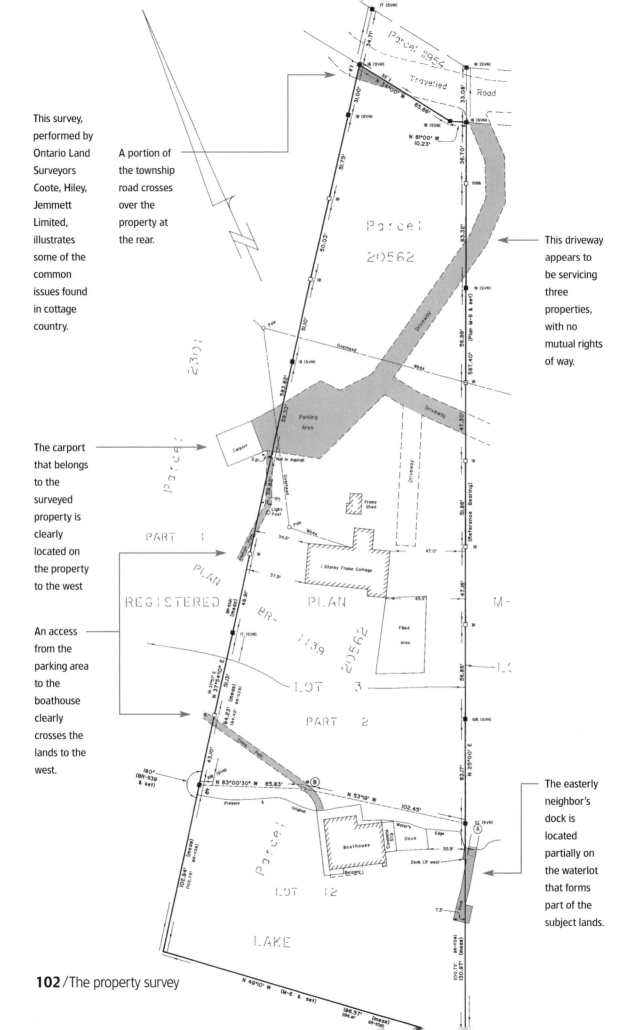

This survey, performed by Ontario Land Surveyors Coote, Hiley, Jemmett Limited, illustrates some of the common issues found in cottage country.

A portion of the township road crosses over the property at the rear.

This driveway appears to be servicing three properties, with no mutual rights of way.

The carport that belongs to the surveyed property is clearly located on the property to the west

An access from the parking area to the boathouse clearly crosses the lands to the west.

The easterly neighbor's dock is located partially on the waterlot that forms part of the subject lands.

CAUTION: **Is there a grandfather clause?**

Many cottages were built before there was an organized municipality with zoning regulations.

These cottages may well have been "grandfathered" at the time zoning was introduced, and

are described as being "legally nonconforming," so that they are not considered to be in violation of current restrictions

on new construction, such as sidelot and waterfront setback allowances.

If a cottage is grandfathered, you need to know what rights you will enjoy as its owner to renovate or expand the

existing building. Legal nonconforming status might allow you to have a boathouse, in breach of current municipal law,

but should that structure need to be replaced, current zoning might prevent you from doing so.

only confirm that the monuments are there, but not that they are located exactly where they should be, based on the reference points provided in the metes and bounds.) In Ontario, for instance, you might encounter a *building location survey*, which, just like it sounds, locates buildings on a property. But it is only required to reference one monument. Whatever sort of survey you accept or commission, it's vital that it confirm the locations of *all* monuments for a lot.

Who pays for the survey?

While it is definitely in the best interest of a vendor to be able to offer a recent survey, many times one is not available and the vendor is unwilling to pay to have it done. A purchaser shouldn't have to foot the bill for a survey, but closing a deal without one just isn't a good idea.

If you really like a property, you might pay for the survey yourself, and include a condition in the offer to purchase that lets you walk away from the deal if that survey is not satisfactory (at your sole and absolute discretion). And when it's your turn to sell, your property will be all the more marketable if you can produce a current survey.

Expect to pay $1,500–$2,500 for a real property report on a standard 1 1/2-acre cottage property. But keep in mind that the more time the survey crew spends on site and the more time a draftsman spends on the drawing, the more you'll have to pay. A small, cleared property with few improvements will cost substantially less to survey than a 300-acre family compound with swamps and cliffs and four sets of cottages.

Survey issues

Encroachments and boundary disputes

Don't be surprised if a new survey turns up problems in the boundary between the property you're buying and the neighboring ones. Beyond the predilection for people over the years to have built things without paying a whole lot of attention to where their property ended and the vacant lot next door began, lakefront lots in many states and provinces were laid out in the 19th century, and the process of dragging rods and chains through the woods inevitably introduced some margin of error. And the metes and bounds may have included measurement instructions that lacked precision (for instance, distances calculated from the water's edge, or from the big oak tree on the Johnson farm, which was chopped down 60 years ago when the Johnson farm was turned into a subdivision). It is entirely possible for two modern surveyors to stake out neighboring properties and come up with a different property line between them.

If the overlapping claims are minor and mostly involve natural landscape, there may not be much reason for concern. But where there has been an "improvement" to one of the properties – any type of construction, from a fence to a boathouse to an outhouse to a garden shed to a septic bed – the resulting infringement on the neighboring land is known as an encroachment. Encroachments can be minor, or they might be so serious that you might not want to proceed with a purchase: Finding out that half a septic bed or a substantial part of the cottage itself is on the wrong side of a

CAUTION: Title insurance is no substitute for doing your homework

Title insurance provides protection, or indemnification, against loss suffered by an owner or lender when title turns out not to be what it was insured as at a particular point in time. For instance, a new survey done post-purchase indicates that the property is smaller than the deed described. Title insurance will compensate the owner for the diminution in value of the undersized lot. Or the person selling the property turns out not to have clear title: Estranged spouses and offspring have been known to dispose of property when they have no right to do so.

Unfortunately, there is a growing trend towards substituting title insurance, which is relatively inexpensive, for the security of a property survey. This is a bad mistake. Professionals such as surveyors and lawyers stress that title insurance shouldn't be thought of as a cheap substitute for the proper verification of deeds and title that a survey provides. As one prominent cottage-country surveyor puts it, title insurance doesn't cover the stress you'll experience in the courts trying to rectify, say, a boundary line that runs right through the cottage you just bought, a situation that could have been avoided altogether with an up-to-date real property report. Indeed, some have argued that the growing popularity of title insurance is resulting in a slackening of due diligence by lawyers in vetting deals, since the insurance safety net is supposedly on hand to address problems after closing.

If you choose to secure title insurance, make sure that the purchase is still thoroughly assessed by professionals. Title insurance is no excuse for not securing a proper survey or doing a thorough title search. There's no guarantee that a claim on the policy will be successful or will deal with the post-closing problem to your complete satisfaction.

property line can seem an insurmountable problem. But even many worst-case situations can be addressed to the satisfaction of both property owners.

• If the encroachment is minor and doesn't affect your enjoyment of the property, you just might want to live and let live. Bring it to the attention of the neighbor, but let it slide in the name of good relations. But don't be recklessly good-natured. A neighbor's tool shed could encroach on your property only a few inches, but its proximity to your cottage could represent a fire hazard, particularly if it's where he likes to do his small-engine repairs and stores the gasoline.

• If your survey indicates an encroachment by the neighbor, be prepared for the neighbor to hire his own surveyor and arrive at a different conclusion. When two different up-to-date surveys commissioned disagree on where a property line exists, neither survey may ever be proven "right" because of the difficulty of working from the 19th-century description of the lots. Filing a lawsuit to get your way can be expensive and unproductive. It probably makes more sense to mediate a new property line with the neighbor, and have it legally described. (Neighboring countries have to do it all the time, and it beats going to war.)

• If a new survey of an old property disagrees with how that property has actually been laid out and used over time, a court may decide to follow evidence of historic use rather than the modern survey to fix the property lines. The location of an old stone wall that predates the U.S. Civil War, for example, could be accepted as the "real" property line, even if the modern survey disagrees.

• As an imminent purchaser, you may discover through a real property report that a neighbor's outbuilding, such as a shed, is on your side of the property line. If it doesn't have foundations, relocating it may not be difficult, either by dismantling and reassembling it, or by using a small forklift.

Addressing the problem can be handled in two ways. Ideally, you can make it a condition of purchase that the vendor arrange to have the encroachment resolved before the closing date, so you don't inherit the problem. (It's one more reason for the seller to have performed "vendor due diligence" – *see Chapter 12, p. 200* – which would have addressed the problem before the property even went on the market.)

But it may not be possible, because of the work involved or the time left until closing. Rare is the person who deliberately encroaches on a neighbor's property, and if you want to keep relations with your new neighbor friendly, work out an agreed schedule for getting the encroachment removed. Depending on what's involved, it might require only a week or two to get it done (and offer to help, if necessary). But if winter's coming, the work might have to wait until the following spring. Before you close, try to get something in writing, in the way of an undertaking from the neighbor that acknowledges the encroachment and agrees to remove it by a particular date.

• Some encroachments are just too burdensome to remove. An entire fence can be on the wrong side of a property line by a few inches. Ditto for a driveway, a garage, a septic bed, or a boathouse. And having the neighbors address even a minor encroachment may create more trouble for them than you'd like. For example, suppose they have a boathouse, a garage, and a toolshed. If the toolshed is on the wrong side of the property line, they may be agreeable to relocating it, but doing so may open up a legal can of worms for them. The municipality may have introduced zoning since they built the shed that now limits properties to two outbuildings. Your request to have it moved could amount to an order to tear it down.

You can instead allow the encroachment to continue without implicitly surrendering any claim to your property by having a lawyer draw up a license of occupation or an easement whose rights are restricted to the current owner of the neighboring property. Such rights can also be limited to the lifespan of the offending structure. For example, you can put up with the present septic bed encroaching on your property, but a license can make it clear that when it comes time for the bed to be replaced, the neighbor must relocate it. The same goes for the tool shed that is violating current zoning restrictions on the number of outbuildings.

The shoreline road allowance

When you examine the survey for an Ontario cottage property, you might notice a strip of land about 66 feet deep along its waterfront, ominously labeled "road allowance" or "shoreline road allowance." Some people own cottages literally for years without being aware of this allowance, and don't discover it until they apply for a building permit. Which is reason enough to inspect a survey well in advance of making a purchase.

Does such an allowance mean the local municipality is going to build a public road between your cottage and the dock? No. But it does mean that you don't own your waterfront, and that your dock and your boathouse – and maybe even your cottage – are encroaching on public land.

Shoreline road allowances are overwhelmingly an Ontario phenomenon. They date back to the time when water was the most logical way of getting around, and unfettered right of access to the shoreline along many lakes and rivers was guaranteed by the Crown to allow for safe and economically productive transportation. Many are artifacts of 19th-century Crown grants to individuals or land companies.

These road allowances are often misunderstood to be a kind of easement, a right-of-way spelled out in a restrictive covenant (*see p. 109*) that grants a right of transit. That's not the case: The adjoining lot owner does not own the road allowance. It's public land.

(see p. 109)

Working on the chain gang

Why are most shoreline road allowances 66 feet? At the time when the "fabric" of the land was first being plotted, surveyors measured distances using a series of linked metal rods known as a "chain." One chain equals 66 feet.

Good for the fish, good for your wallet

Thanks to Ontario's network of dams built to control water levels, many of the province's lakes are at higher levels now than they were when shoreline road allowances were first surveyed. This is a bonus if you wish to purchase your shoreline road allowance, because all or part of the originally surveyed area may now be under water – and these road allowances are sold by the square foot from above the current high-water mark. Another reason to get a new survey.

While log rafts, canoes laden with beaver pelts, and barges carrying cattle no longer form part of the landscape in cottage country, these allowances nonetheless have endured, even after provincial governments granted municipalities the right to sell (or, literally, to close) them to the adjoining lot owners.

One reason that not all road allowances have disappeared is that many cottage owners haven't acted on the opportunity to purchase them. Because municipalities will only sell an allowance to the adjoining property's owner, cottagers have often been reluctant to spend the money because they are in no danger of a third party purchasing the allowance and cutting off their water access. Another reason some allowances have endured is that, particularly along river courses, opposition grew to their elimination because they were still being used by recreational paddlers and campers. Finally, some road allowances have been tied up in larger native land claims and thus can't be sold.

Acquiring your road allowance

Unless such a legal complication exists, an application to purchase a road allowance will seldom be denied, since they're such a ready source of cash for the municipality. (One possible stumbling block is the designation of the waterfront as primary fish habitat. In this case, the road allowance may still be available, but the property owner will be required to enter into a site-planning agreement with the municipality, to ensure that no construction affects the habitat.)

In fact, you may be compelled to purchase the allowance in order to clear up the deed of ownership, as cottages have often been built in whole or in part on the road allowance, compromising clear title. A township may offer an alternative to outright acquisition, called a license of occupation, which is essentially a lease. For $50 a year for 20 years, say, the encroachment problem created by your cottage, boathouse, or dock might be taken care of.

But a simple lease is not always the solution. For example, a lot normally cannot be severed without the road allowance first being acquired. Another reason for wanting to purchase a road allowance is a cottage renovation. It may turn out when application is made for a building permit that the existing structure, or the envisioned addition, exceeds the zoned limits of developable land within a prescribed distance of the high-water mark. The owner may want to purchase the allowance to increase the total area of the land holding, in order to have a large addition approved.

TIP:

All together now...

One way to reduce the cost of purchasing a shoreline road allowance is for several neighbors to band together and have their allowances closed at the same time. This will reduce the costs associated with surveying, lawyering, and registration of plans.

Sample cost calculation for a road-allowance closure

Lake of Bays (in the heart of Ontario's cottage country) provides an "average" cost structure in its application form for a shoreline road allowance 150 feet wide and 66 feet deep, exclusive of tax:

Application fee (refundable if the application is denied)	$400
Registration costs (payable to the township)	400
Survey and registration of plan	1,500
Lawyer, including disbursements	1,450
Land acquisition costs	1,980–5,940
Total	**$5,730–$9,690**

Before buying a cottage with an outstanding road allowance, check into its availability and the need to acquire it. Acquisition can be expensive. The land costs are generally calculated on a price per square foot, and vary considerably. (In 2004, the top rate per square foot for a property on a larger lake in the township of Lake of Bays, in the heart of Ontario's cottage country, was posted at 60 cents, while on Lake Muskoka, next door in the township of Bracebridge, it was 48 cents, with other properties in the same area as low as 28 cents.) A purchaser also faces application and administration fees, as well as all legal and survey costs, which in total can easily exceed the cost of the land.

Other road allowances

Not all road allowances are shoreline road allowances. For example, a concession or sidelot road allowance leads back from the water, along the edge of the lot. If such an allowance does or can provide water access from prop-

Cottages on leased land

You may come across cottages for sale that are unusually well priced. Chances are, they're resting on leased land. Often these properties are part of a native reserve or are on publicly owned lands such as those in federal and provincial and state parks. Sometimes the main property on which a cottage is located is privately owned, but a critical section of adjoining land, such as beach waterfront, is leasehold.

On the plus side: The price is right

Even where there are no obvious problems with the current lease, buildings on leased land are invariably worth less than comparable structures on privately owned land. Owning a building that sits on rented property carries a reasonable risk of serious devaluation, since if the lease cannot be renewed, the structure (unless it can be relocated intact) isn't worth much more than its salvage value.

Properties on leasehold land (sometimes called a ground lease) aren't an altogether bad thing. They can be extremely affordable, in part due to the leasehold's suppression of speculation in long-term appreciation, and in part because most cottages on leasehold tend to be modest, as owners aren't willing to create grandiose structures that may have to be torn down. And banks will consider issuing a conventional mortgage on a leasehold property, provided the term of the mortgage is less than that of the lease. Retirement communities – also called "manufactured communities" – are being built on a leasehold basis by real estate investment trusts, the developers enticing the 55-plus market with promises of lease costs indexed to the consumer price index that are less than the property taxes on comparable homes. (Rather morbidly, leaseholders aren't supposed to worry about the lease expiring in 30 years, as their life expectancy will make renewal concerns moot.)

On the minus side: No guarantee the term will be extended

Ground leases on cottage properties vary widely in their terms, but generally fall somewhere between 20 and 30 years – not the 99 years of a condo tower. Purchasers of condo apartments generally have a "not in my lifetime" peace of mind when it comes to worrying about what becomes of their real property when the building ground lease expires. But with cottages, lease terms can present the very real prospect of having to tear down any build-

erties or roads to the rear of your lot, the municipality may not be willing to close it. (Bracebridge, Ontario, for one, will not sell a sidelot allowance that does or can provide public access to the water.) If there's an encroachment problem with a side allowance that can't be closed, it may be addressed with a license of occupancy.

Restrictive covenants and easements

Be sure to ask your real estate agent, the seller, or your lawyer: "Are there any restrictive covenants that apply to the property?" A covenant is a legal promise, and in real estate, covenants are part of a property deed. The body of law surrounding covenants is complex, but for anyone looking to buy a cottage, the most important ones are covenants that are said under common law to "run with the land." These are promises that are binding on all future owners of the property. The covenant may be attached to a single property or affect all properties in an entire subdivision.

ings at the end of the lease, should the term not be extended. Cottagers in Ontario's Algonquin Park, for example, know that the provincial government will not renew their leases after 2017, and all buildings must be torn down – at the owner's expense – by then.

Another problem with cottages on leased land is that ongoing debate over the appropriate use of public lands can leave leasehold cottagers on tenterhooks, constantly unsure of their fate. In Rondeau Provincial Park on Lake Erie, cottagers were granted lease extensions in 1986 that let them stay until 2017. In 2001, activists lobbied against a cottage presence within the park. The cottagers lobbied back, calling on the government to extend the leases for 99 years, and the lobbying continues on both sides.

Needless to say, invest in cottage properties located on ground leases at your own risk, with plenty of research and legal advice. Determining a fair market value for a building on a ground lease that may not be renewable is not for the faint-hearted, and the value will depend considerably on the number of years left on the lease, the prospects for renewal, how annual lease payments are indexed, and what – if any – compensation the lessor will make for the value of the lessee's structures should the lease not be extended.

Word to the wise: An unhappy ending

The downside of leasehold property was vividly illustrated by the fates of some 40 cottage owners on British Columbia's Pitt Lake in 2003. The second largest freshwater tidal lake in the world, Pitt Lake is located only an hour's drive from Vancouver. In 1978, the Katzie First Nation opted to lease lands on the lake to cottagers for a 25-year term. Not every member of the Katzie band was happy with the lease decision, and unhappiness grew when a resort that had been promised for some of that land was never built. In 1999, the band voted not to renew the cottage lot leases when they expired on December 31, 2003. Under the terms of the lease, cottage owners had to remove every scrap of property by that time. Some cottagers salvaged what they could from their modest retreats over the summer of 2003. Others simply burned them to the ground.

CAUTION:
Get it in writing

If your lake or road access is across another person's property, make sure your right of access is clearly defined in a concise easement document before you purchase the property.

SELLER'S TIP:
Spell it out in a vendor disclosure document

To ensure that prospective buyers are fully aware of any legal promises they'll be required to keep if they become the new owners of the property, covenants should be clearly spelled out in a vendor disclosure document. *(See Chapter 12 for more on this document.)*

A property can have a covenant attached to it for many reasons. The covenant may place restrictions on the property's use or the conduct of its owners (which is often the case with "mutual" covenants that are in force in a planned subdivision overseen by an owners' association). Because covenants routinely place some limitation on how a property can be used or developed, they are typically known as "restrictive" or "protective" covenants.

Many prescriptions limiting use and development of a property, and the behavior of owners, exist within a municipality's zoning regulations (such as required setbacks of buildings from the sidelot lines and noise restrictions). Covenants differ in being attached in the form of a legally binding promise to a *specific property*. And unlike zoning regulations, they can't be changed with a local bylaw. While the application of covenants in some circumstances can be waived with the consent of all affected parties, they're generally considered to exist in perpetuity.

Some of the more common covenants attached to individual properties are restrictions on the number of residential units and disallowance of commercial activities. Mutual covenants can include everything from a ban on clotheslines to a restriction on the sort of vehicles permitted in the drive. In vacation country, they are frequently used to ensure protection of the waterfront. For example, a common mutual covenant requires the property owner to maintain a specified amount of shoreline vegetation.

For cottagers, easements rank among the most important covenants that can appear in a title deed. An easement is a right of access extended to another property owner or owners. They don't surrender actual title to the part of the property specified in the easement, but they do extend a kind of right of trespass. And remember that an easement is different from a sidelot or shoreline road allowance, which is actual public property. An easement might grant an adjoining or neighboring property owner the right to transit your property to reach a shoreline. Or it might give you the right to cross your neighbor's. Or it might provide for the right to use a private road, driveway, or parking area that crosses another property.

Without the easement being spelled out in a covenant, a property owner has no legal right to use the portion of a private road that crosses another property. All the properties serviced by this road should have a mutual covenant in place that is said to be "concurrent": All the easements are being performed at the same time.

Covenants can be densely worded, and some have landed the affected parties in court because of a lack of clarity. A key issue in interpreting the validity of a restrictive covenant is whether the covenant "runs with the land," meaning it is binding on all future owners, or is "personal" in nature, ceasing to exist with the death or dissolution of the original landowner. In either case, you may need a lawyer to decipher their meaning.

With or without a covenant, several other legal principles can come into play. Through historic use or the importance of maintaining public access to the shoreline under the public trust doctrine, transit of private property by the public may be upheld by the courts.

Ownership beneath and on the lake

Waterfront property ownership almost never extends beneath the waves. With few exceptions, lake and river bottoms belong to the state or province, and this public ownership can affect your plans for the shoreline. If you choose a property and envision changes along its waterfront, you need to be aware of restrictions that may apply.

Docks: You can't always get what you want

Whether floating or fixed to the bottom, docks almost always intrude on public space or a public right. They have been permitted historically because in allowing access of citi-

Where does the waterfront end and the lake begin?

There are inevitably differences between what's fixed in a survey (or described in a deed) as waterfront and where that waterfront happens to be physically at any given time: The boundary between land and water changes, of course, with fluctuations in water level and as a result of erosion or human meddling. Deeds of ownership may use vague language such as "to the water's edge" or "to the shoreline," but they have no strict legal meaning since those locations are moving targets.

In the common law of both Canada and the U.S., the furthermost limit of private shoreline property is considered to be the high-water mark (though some title deeds describe ownership extending to "the water's edge" or "the low-water mark"). Local regulations, for instance, may require a setback from the water's edge measured in relation to the high-water mark. And how is the high-water mark determined? From historic data drawn from observed water heights or, lacking that, by inspecting the shoreline for physical signs.

For some waterfront property owners – those with a wide swath of beach in front – a more pressing issue is the often testy one of who has access to the shoreline between the high-water mark and the actual water's edge. The "public trust doctrine," which dates back to the Emperor Justinian in Rome, considers access to the shoreline a public right. (The public trust doctrine is enshrined in U.S. legal principles; it has not yet been thoroughly tested in a Canadian court.) Even if a property deed specifies ownership to "the water's edge" or "the low-water mark," it can be overriden by the public-trust doctrine, which may well permit usage of some of the beach by the public.

This is a highly contentious and far from clear-cut area. (In Tiny Township on southern Georgian Bay, waterfront property owners, residents of backlot properties, and other beach users have been fighting it out in the courts for well over a decade.) When you're looking at waterfront property, particularly beachfront lots, it's important to know what the permitted public uses are of the shoreline in front of private property in your area before you purchase – rather than suddenly discover afterwards that you are swamped by "trespassers." Emperor Justinian could have decided they had a right to be there long before you bought the property.

zens to public waters, they are considered to support activities in the broad public interest. But that doesn't mean limitations won't be imposed.

Control over their construction often falls under local zoning bylaws. Provincial and state natural resources and/or environmental authorities can have a hand in regulating dock construction too, particularly where fish habitat is involved. And in restricted waterways, higher levels of government might also impose rules, in order to ensure a structure doesn't interfere with safe navigation. (Swim platforms and mooring rigs affixed to the lake bottom likewise cannot interfere with navigation.)

To avoid disappointment, don't assume you can double the size of an existing dock, change its orientation, or replace it with a dock of another type (particularly a fixed dock) without checking with the appropriate authorities. Many waterfront structures predate regulations that now curtail or forbid their construction. Docks, concrete piers, berms, breakwalls, and the like can result in permanent changes to the shoreline and near-shore waters; if they affect protected wildlife habitats, such as fish-spawning habitat, they may not be permitted at all.

Boathouses

In some higher-end cottage areas, boathouses have become more concerned with incorporating second-storey living quarters than housing boats. In the past, such boathouses have helped vacation property owners overcome the restrictions local zoning imposed on expanding the land-based cottage. Not so any longer, as governments now take a greater interest.

If the property you're looking at has a boathouse, find out if your jurisdiction demands a waterfront lot lease, as some do, for the use of the lake bottom. Contact your local municipality to find out what zoning rules apply: Is it grandfathered in under older legislation? Are there regulations governing its repair or replacement? And if the cottage doesn't have a boathouse, don't get your heart set on adding one until you've checked on zoning and other permissions.

Aboriginal land claims

While few and far between, land disputes between native bands and governments do exist – and can go on for years. While some claims arise from disputed treaties dating back centuries, others are based on more recent events, such as "temporary" expropriations of treaty land during wartime that the government never got around to returning, or expropriations permitted for railroad construction that never came to pass, in both cases with the land then sold off for private real estate development.

In some cases, the dispute doesn't involve the present property owner directly, and is unlikely to result in an eviction – a band might instead be compensated by the government for the historic loss. Still, you should be well aware of any claims in the area where you're considering buying.

7. Inspecting the cottage

So far, so good. You've fallen in love with the cottage, the property is spectacular, the lake is a shimmering jewel, the neighbors seem nice, and an up-to-date survey says that all the information on the deed is exactly as stated. The financing is in order (*see Chapter 9*), and you've made a successful offer. Now it's time to bring in an inspector to take a closer look at the structure and systems of the cottage itself before you close the deal.

While all real estate purchases benefit from a professional inspection as a condition of closing, cottage purchases demand them more than any other kind of residential property deal. Although you might be tempted to forego an inspection because a particular cottage is less expensive than your home and therefore doesn't seem as financially risky, that less-expensive property can be harboring a host of problems with serious financial consequences. Those problems can lead you to reconsider the asking price or demand repairs as a condition of closing the deal.

Even if a professional inspection turns up some minor deficiencies, at least you'll know what you're getting into and can budget accordingly. As the old saying goes, "Forewarned is forearmed."

Why inspect?

Cottages are particularly strong candidates for professional inspection for a number of reasons:

• **The do-it-yourselfer factor.** Many resale cottages are not professionally built. They were erected by their original owners as weekend carpentry projects, and their construction and design may have had little or no guidance from a building code, a professional designer, or a municipal inspector. And over the years, repairs and additions were also likely tackled by the owner, often without a building permit.

• **Nonstandard designs.** It's an issue directly related to the do-it-yourselfer factor. Most buyers aren't familiar with buildings that don't have a full basement, and many cottages exist entirely above ground, set on pilings or masonry blocks. They are also often built on ground that doesn't commonly crop up in cities or suburbia. Soil can range from very sandy to wet clay or solid rock. Lot grades can be steeper than those of urban and suburban properties, too. These factors require special considerations for foundations and create the potential for shifting and settling; if grading and perimeter drainage weren't properly addressed, basement flooding (if a basement exists) can become an issue as well. And with cottage designs ranging from A-frames to geodesic domes, the building itself can be unconventional.

• **The harsh environment.** A cottage by definition is closer to nature than an urban home. (You probably haven't seen a lot of houses in the city that have been gnawed by porcupines.) Given their location and their construction, cottages are candidates for rot and insect infestation. And many cottage areas are in the "snow belt." Snow loading on roofs can be high, and if the supporting structure hasn't been built to withstand that immense weight, structural damage can accumulate over the years.

• **Infrequent occupation.** When you're in a home daily, potential problems often come to your attention quickly, and you can deal with them right away. A cottage that is used mostly on weekends, and then left unoccupied for months on end in the off-season, can develop problems that owners might not notice as soon as they would have liked. And the repairs they choose to make (which often tend to be do-it-yourself) may be quick fixes that don't really address more serious underlying issues. The potential for long-term neglect, masked by inadequate or cosmetic repairs, is probably higher in a cottage than a home.

• **A completely different set of mechanical systems.** Urban homes have relatively predictable systems. Drinking water, sewage, and electricity are taken care of by municipal utilities. At a typical cottage, on the other hand, at least some of the mechanical systems are not hooked into a utility. Cottages usually operate their own water and waste systems. A cottage may be "off-grid," relying on solar or wind power, or using propane for cooking and refrigeration. All these can and do run wonderfully, but the average cottage buyer from an urban environment with little or no experience of them will need a useful opinion on the shape they're in. The same applies even if cottage electricity is supplied by a utility: It may not be typical 100- or 200-amp service, and sometimes the equipment is so old that it's considered hazardous by modern standards.

• **Outbuildings and other outdoor structures.** Cottage properties usually also feature structures not found in the urban landscape – things such as docks, boathouses, seawalls, workshops, old icehouses, and sleeping cabins.

When to inspect

While it would be ideal to hire an inspector to crawl through every property you are considering, the expense would be prohibitive and the logistics impractical – which means no formal inspection actually takes place until after you have successfully made an offer for a particular property. As with residential homes, a professional inspection is generally a "closing" condition. An offer is accepted, and an agreement of purchase and sale is drawn up, with the closing subject to a satisfactory inspection. (*See "Inspections and Options for Closing," p. 128, for how the inspection process should be incorporated into the agreement.*)

Goals of an inspection

An inspection – and it may require more than one professional – should help you answer the following questions:

• Am I prepared to close a deal on this property in its present condition, at the agreed price, without any remedial action from the seller?

TIP: Once more, with feeling: Make sure there's a survey

David Hellyer of Hellyer Engineering Ltd. in Mississauga, Ontario, is one of Ontario's most experienced cottage inspectors, regularly called as an expert witness in litigation cases. "Many properties don't have a survey and have never seen a building inspector," he says. "I'll have cases where the septic system or the cottage is on someone else's lot." While his job does entail things such as inspecting the electrical panel and the furnace, he says he can't stress enough the importance of making sure you don't end up buying a "nonviable building" – one that extends over the property line, or is on a property where it's virtually impossible to build anything new (including a new septic system) that will adhere to current zoning regulations. "I often see people who have overbuilt" – the cottage is too large for the lot – "and have an order to comply, and can't."

• If there are deficiencies in the property, can I have them remedied before closing at the seller's expense?

• Is there anything about this property that would make me reconsider purchasing it altogether?

• How much do I need to budget, above and beyond the agreed price, to make repairs and improvements over the short to medium term?

• Do I adequately understand the various systems – heating, plumbing, electrical – of this property? As the new owner, what should I watch for in the way of potential problems as systems and structures age?

There's a point at which the purchase must become a leap of faith. You can't know everything. Home inspectors generally take care to distinguish between things that are *defective*, which is a principal area of concern, and things that are *just getting old*. Things that are defective don't work. Things that are just getting old are still working, and could go on working for years. Other things getting old, such as roofing materials, have a relatively predictable lifespan, and a good inspector can advise you on how many more years might be left in them.

Who inspects cottages?

While various cottage systems can demand different experts, the general assessment of a property's condition is usually handled by a home and property inspector. Such inspectors can flag areas of concern that someone with more specific expertise can then address if necessary, and by explaining to you what they do and do not address, you'll know better what gaps you might wish to fill elsewhere.

Anyone in North America can set up shop as a home inspector. It's a trade that has generated much consumer anxiety. Someone calling himself an inspector could be a home handyman looking for work – telling you all the things you need to have him fix for you – or could be working on commission for a roofer.

That said, professional associations do exist that can help guide your choice of inspector. In Canada, provincial associations have training and certification programs and codes of ethics and standards for home inspectors. A national umbrella organization, the Canadian Association of Home and Property Inspectors (CAHPI), has been striving to create a national certification standard, and the Canada Mortgage and Housing Corporation recommends CAHPI and the provincial associations as sources for hiring an inspector. However, no federal authority imposes professional licensing standards, and at the time of writing, Ontario was the only province with a legislated, self-regulating professional body.

In the U.S., inspector licensing exists at the state level. There is one major national association for the trade, the American Society of Home Inspectors, whose standards of practice were adopted by CAHPI. The standards of practice lay out what they do – and do not – require their members to do.

Finding a cottage inspector

Although they are mainly trade organizations, these professional associations in Canada and the U.S. are a good place to start. (And stick with known associations: Anyone could launch an Internet site tomorrow, charge money for "inspectors" to pass a 20-minute on-line exam, and accredit them as members of a new organization.)

Be aware that in the U.S. the licensing levels for practitioners vary. It's also possible to belong to a particular inspection association without actually being fully certified by that association. In Ontario, for example, inspectors can become listed as associates of the provincial association after completing course work, but they still have to complete a minimum number of inspections before being fully certified as a Registered Home Inspector.

Whomever you approach, ask for three references, as you would for any other tradesperson. Also ask how many years they have been a fully certified or registered inspector, and how many properties – and, specifically, cottages – they see a year. If they haven't been in business long, ask what they were doing before they became an inspector. Inspection certification is generally done by correspondence course, which means pretty well anybody can be certified to some degree without ever having actually inspected a building. As important as certification is, there's no substitute for experience in the field – or by the lake.

A good place to start is, of course, the Yellow Pages for your area of cottage country. Look under "Home Inspection Services," then check back with the relevant professional association to make sure your local inspector is properly accredited. The websites of the professional associations also have on-line tools to help you locate inspectors in a particular area. Or ask your real estate agent for a list of local inspectors. (*See Caution, below.*) The inspec-

TIP:

Hire an inspector who knows cottages

Though they don't call themselves "cottage inspectors," look for home inspectors who are experienced with cottage properties and familiar with the specific issues they present. An inspector from the city who has limited experience with things such as pump-driven water systems, septic tanks and leaching beds, or pier construction won't be able to offer as accurate an assessment as someone who regularly deals with cottage properties.

CAUTION: Get a list from the agent, not a single name

You should never turn to the real estate agent handling the property you are interested in purchasing for an inspector recommendation. If you do ask your agent, he should provide you with a list of all the local certified inspectors, and not a single name – unless, of course, that name happens to be the only one in the area. It's a conflict of interest for an agent representing a seller to recommend to the buyer an inspector whose report has the potential to cause the price to be adjusted downward or the deal to fall apart. Even if you have a buyer agent working for you, make sure you get more than one name.

tor's job is to give you a report on the condition of the cottage, and in some cases to oversee the repair process that the buyer and seller agree to. He has nothing to do with determining the value of the property, nor is he involved in post-inspection price negotiations.

What an inspector does not (or might not) do

Although the go/no-go list varies from inspector to inspector, there are certain aspects of a property that a home inspector does not address. Some areas (such as producing a legal property survey) are out of bounds because the inspector lacks certification that rests with another profession. Other items may be ruled out in their association's standards of practice but, in fact, individual inspectors may choose to include them – because they are comfortable with rendering an opinion that is not in any way a warranty, because they have additional training and certification, or because they feel it's part of the job. For example, the CAHPI and ASHI codes don't require the inspector to provide an opinion on the adequacy of any structural system or component. That doesn't mean an individual inspector won't choose to render that opinion. Some not-required tasks approach the trivial and time-consuming (inspecting window screens), while others, such as the condition of docks and outbuildings, are of interest to cottagers and may be tackled by a particular inspector.

Before hiring an inspector, ask what is included, and what could be included, in an inspection.

No-nos for home inspectors

- A home inspector should never behave like a scout for local tradespeople. Inspectors can be an excellent source of recommendations, if you're the one asking, and they may also share with you helpful information on products and systems that they've seen in use. But they shouldn't walk through an inspection dropping contacts in your lap. And they should never provide you with quotes on work themselves. Home inspection associations don't permit their certified members to be associated with related trades or to accept commissions.

- The inspector should have nothing to do with the real estate deal. Inspectors are not there to appraise the value. Their job is to describe the condition of the property and provide guidance on what should or must be repaired.

- The inspector should not exceed the bounds of his authority. You can glean a lot of useful information from an inspection on things such as water and waste-treatment systems, but home inspectors can't certify that the water is potable or that the septic system meets regulatory standards, without additional qualifications. They can, however, be of major assistance in determining those facts.

- A good home inspector never does an inspection at night. It's a daylight-only job.

TIP: **The good book for buyers and sellers**

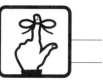

Buyers should ask for, and wise sellers should prepare, an informal "cottage manual" that outlines the major cottage systems and provides advice on those subtle nuances of operation that only an experienced owner could know about. It doesn't have to be fancy: Information such as the location of wells and septic beds is helpful, as are any super-secret tips on getting the water system running smoothly in the spring (e.g., "Remember to close hidden valve under the north side of the screened porch," or "Cleanout plug in kitchen sink has been removed – replace before using taps!"). As well, general info such as, "We buy firewood from Mr. Abbott on Spruce Rd.," will be much appreciated.

A cottage manual is a great tool for sellers because it makes a clear statement that they want to be helpful, open, and honest. A manual that includes records of major repairs, receipts for equipment upgrades, and instruction manuals would be a buyer's dream. *(See "The Owner's Best Friend: How to Build a Cottage Operating Manual," p. 208, for more.)*

Pay attention to items that fall under "not required to inspect." In some cases you may not be able to find any certified inspector who is prepared to include items of concern to you in a report. But you should find out what a particular inspector is willing to include and then bring in specialists as needed. *(See "Got 'em Covered?," p. 120.)*

The inspection process

Arrange to go along

A typical inspection takes two to three hours, longer if you also arrange a proper inspection of the fireplace or woodstove and chimney. *(See p. 127.)* Inspectors like to have the buyers tag along rather than just send them the report because seeing is believing, and the buyers benefit greatly from having the inspector walk them through the property.

Most first-time cottage buyers from the city will have virtually no experience with the mechanical systems of cottage country, and it's the inspector who will give them an educated tour. While the seller can show you how to operate the water pump, an experienced inspector will have seen plenty of similar systems and be able to tell you if this particular one is a Rube Goldberg nightmare. And in cases where serious shortcomings are discovered, the buyer can go over them then and there.

It's important that the cottage be inspected while it's in use. This doesn't mean it has to be occupied, but the systems do have to be running. Inspection professionals' standards absolve them from having to activate any system that's turned off in order to assess it. (An inspector doesn't want to be responsible for the consequences of firing up a dormant water system or furnace.) This is one more reason for not buying a cottage in the off-

SELLER'S TIP:

What you need to do before the inspector arrives

• Have the place up and running with all mechanical systems activated.

• If the cottage is set on poured concrete or masonry-block pilings, make sure the crawl space is clear and easily accessible so that the foundations can be inspected.

season. Even if it's a four-season cottage in full operation, snow cover can make it impossible to inspect a roof or foundations.

If you are really determined to buy a property in the off-season without being able to have a full inspection done, and if the vendor is sufficiently motivated to sell, you can make a purchase offer that includes a holdback pending the successful inspection of, say, the roof once the snow has melted. You might also want to include a mechanism for remedying a substantial problem that the subsequent inspection uncovers. For example, an agreement could state that the vendor and purchaser will mutually agree on an inspector who will recommend and oversee repairs, and that both parties will share in the repair costs.

What an inspector is looking for

Beyond verifying the operation of basic systems, an experienced inspector will be looking for two categories of problems: He will detect where past repairs have been made, and if those repairs have solved the problem. And he will detect current problems that require remedies of their own.

The first category, detecting and assessing past repairs, is critical. Water damage in a ceiling may have been patched, but has the underlying problem – a leaky roof – been repaired as well? An inspector may notice taped

Got 'em covered?

Before closing, you should make sure these items have been addressed, either by a home inspector or a more specialized professional.

• **Survey:** Make sure there's a recent survey. *See Chapter 6.*

• **Septic system:** Have the system inspected by a licensed septic system installer or, at an absolute minimum, have the seller provide records attesting to the state of the system: its age, location, size, and condition; when it was last serviced and inspected; and if it is currently certified. *See "Septic Smarts," p. 124.*

• **Fireplaces and woodstoves:** Make sure these systems have been inspected for safety (not efficiency). *See "Getting the Green Light on Woodstoves," p. 127.*

• **Electrical system:** Many older cottages have some oddball electrical schemes. For the most part, they're usually safe and have been used without trouble for years. If the cottage inspection comes out clean, you're fine. But if your cottage inspector notes any truly flagrant electrical hazards such as a grossly undersized panel or too many smaller "pony panels" patched into the main panel, seriously degraded wiring, old-style "knob-and-tube" wiring, or a service mast that brings power from the pole to the cottage that is coming loose from the building, it would be in your best interest – for safety and savings – to have a full-blown electrical inspection performed by the local electrical safety authority.

Unlike a cottage inspector who gives advice, the verdict of the governing electrical safety authority is legally binding: Deficiencies are noted on a work order and must be performed within a certain time period

and plastered drywall cracks. The cracks may have been caused by normal drying and shrinkage – or they may have been caused by the structure shifting. An inspection should address the question of whether that shifting has in fact stopped, or whether the building has a significant ongoing problem with its foundations.

This is where a good inspector earns his keep. Properties put up for sale can go through a rash of quick fixes to make them more presentable. The average buyer probably won't understand that the drywall repairs in the corners of the ceiling and walls (which might even be hidden under fresh paint) could open up again as the building continues to shift as a result of poor soil drainage or as support pillars keep on tilting downhill.

Evaluating the inspection report

No cottage is going to be perfect, and a home inspector will provide you with a lengthy written report filled with information on major problems – if there are any – as well as countless small details such as cracked window

– or the power gets shut off. The electrical inspection can be made part of the offer to purchase. A vendor can choose either to correct the deficiencies, subject to re-inspection, or get quotes for the work and adjust the closing price accordingly.

- **Hazardous building-code violations:** Remember, an older cottage may have been built when a local building code didn't exist, and a current building code is not applied retroactively to older buildings. Inspectors are capable of pointing out the likelihood of egregious code violations, such as the absence of railings around home-built decks. Often this ability to spot likely code violations is most useful as a tip-off that some construction was performed without a building permit. If you want an airtight opinion on how a structural deficiency may affect you as the new owner, the municipal building inspector can help.

- **Water quality.** An inspector can give you a report in which the basic water system is described, and can tell you if the pump is running, but he can't certify that the water flowing through it is safe to drink. Basic water-quality tests are available through the local public health unit, but to get a complete handle on your water, spend about $150 for a thorough laboratory analysis of a sample. The results will run to several pages and will cover not only items related to safe drinking standards (such as coliforms), but a host of others that range from aesthetic (color) to practical (hardness, which can affect plumbing). This will help you decide on possible treatment measures, and save you from spending a bundle on water softener and filtration systems you may not need.

    Some cottages have treatment systems in place to soften water or remove specific minerals. These can be older technological orphans, without a manual to guide you or a qualified service person within the same time zone. While the efficacy of such systems may not be a deal breaker, try to determine if they're in fact working properly before you close. If you're not sure, hire a mechanical contractor with expertise in this area.

panes and blocked downspouts. These little items are good to know about so you can address them in the future if the deal goes through, but don't sweat the small stuff.

It's most important to understand the condition of the cottage's *major* systems, since deficiencies in these could cost thousands to remedy once you've bought the place. Even if there are some big deficiencies, if you know about them ahead of time, the cost of correcting them can either be factored into the price or the vendor may agree to have them remedied to your satisfaction to see that the deal closes.

The following checklist addresses the big items – the *potential* deal breakers – that could bite you in the wallet. Note that it doesn't address items that may just be old or inefficient, such as single-pane windows, the hand pump in the kitchen, a lack of insulation, or ugly vinyl siding.

Structural

• **Roof:** What is its age, composition, and condition? What is its remaining expected lifespan? How much will it cost to have it replaced?

• **Foundation:** What kind of foundation does the cottage have (if it even has one)? What is its general condition? Are there any faults such as major cracks or extreme spalling (crumbling or flaking) that point to a structural problem? Has the building shifted due to inadequate foundation work? Assuming these problems can be repaired, how much would it cost?

• **General framing:** Are the visible framing members adequate for the loads they carry? Are there any signs of advanced rot or insect damage? How much would it cost to fix?

• **Outdoor framing:** Are decks, railings, and stairs sound and built to code or a reasonable equivalent? Are elevated portions adequately supported? How much would it cost to replace the inadequately constructed portions?

TIP: **Is the cottage bugged?**

Although wood-boring insects do turn up in urban and suburban locations, cottages can be good candidates for infestation, particularly if they're built of logs, or stand on wooden piers, or have sill plates in direct contact with the soil. Termites are the most destructive (they actually *eat* wood, rather than just living in it), and checking for evidence of their presence and any resulting structural damage is an important item on an inspection checklist. A good inspector will also look for signs of other wood borers, such as carpenter ants, which don't eat wood but merely excavate for their colonies. (They only attack moisture-laden wood, so their presence is a tip-off to moisture.)

But don't despair if you learn you're sharing your future cottage with such pests. In most vacation areas, pests are just that − pests − a problem that can be dealt with, not a reason to forego the place of your dreams.

Q & A:

Uh-oh: Structural problem discovered. Is it time to walk away?

Q: I've found an older cottage that I truly love and have called in an inspector. I'm pretty handy, so many of the little items in an inspector's report, like cracked windows and loose caulking, aren't a big deal to me. But how should I proceed if the inspector finds some serious problems, say with the cottage's roof or foundation? Are big (expensive) repairs like these usually considered deal killers?

A: Even if there are significant problems with the roof or foundation (or both), money technically can fix almost anything. The specific costs shouldn't actually matter – as long as the problems are identified and built into the final price, or dealt with under the terms of the agreement of purchase and sale. Your agreement of purchase and sale should contain a mechanism for you to have either the closing price adjusted or the costs of repairs on accepted deficiencies addressed by the seller after the inspection. (*See "Inspections & Options for Closing," p. 128.*)

That said, it's possible to end up at loggerheads over a few hundred dollars. The vendor's willingness to offer an abatement to the closing price or pay for the repairs directly is going to depend on the state of the market and whether buyer and seller agree that the cost of fixing the problem hasn't been reflected already in the closing price.

• **Boathouses, bunkies, and other ancillary structures:** Outhouses and potting sheds don't count, but if the property has major outbuildings – say, a double boathouse with living quarters on top or extensive dockwork – make sure they get inspected, too. Although problems in an outbuilding or dock usually don't result in buyers walking away from a property, knowing if they hold any problems can help negotiations – and allow you to plan your future to-do lists.

Mechanical
• **Electrical:** Is the electrical panel sized properly and in good condition? Replacing a panel isn't actually that expensive, but if the cottage's wiring itself is inadequate (knob and tube), poorly distributed (one circuit runs the entire cottage), or lacks ground wires, the labor costs of rewiring can be astronomical. Check with your insurance company: Some underwriters may refuse coverage if you have a small old-style panel or knob-and-tube or aluminum wires. If you're planning to add additional appliances, how much expansion can the system support?

Pumps and plumbing
Water supply: Water pumps, pressure tanks, and hot-water tanks are critical items, but the cost to replace them isn't high enough to make these components deal breakers. Even a nonfunctioning water purifier or other

SELLER'S TIP:
A proactive approach pays off
Mandatory vendor disclosure documents aside *(see box, p.125)*, it makes good strategic sense for vendors to go even further with their due diligence, probing their property for weak spots and remedying them before being required to. When properly done, such due diligence can pay for itself with stronger buyer interest and a faster sale. *See Chapter 12, p. 202, for a vendor due diligence checklist.*

water-treatment system isn't necessarily a major deficiency (although replacement can reach four figures). Replacing wells and septic systems, on the other hand, can require a call to your bank manager.

Wells (*report from licensed well installer*): What type of well is present (drilled, dug, or sand point)? How old is the well? What is the well's flow rate? Are there any indications that the well is inadequate (low flow rate), damaged, or contaminated? Are there any ways to rehabilitate the well without installing a new one, such as "hydro-fracturing" a drilled well? How much would it cost to install a new well, if necessary? Is the well the approved distance from the septic tank and leaching bed?

Septic systems (*report from licensed septic system installer*): What are the age, size, and style of the septic tank and leaching bed? Where are they located? Is the system large enough to accommodate the existing cottage? Can it accommodate additional bathroom facilities in the future? Is the system in

Septic smarts: The snowball effect

A proper septic system inspection should be made a condition of the agreement of purchase and sale. In addition to having a certified septic system installer determine the size and condition of the system, you'll also need to contact the building department to see if it conforms with the lot limitations and is sized correctly for the square footage of the cottage and the number of bathrooms it serves. Since owners are not legally required to provide this information (though it's in their best interest to do so), it's up to you.

Why should you ensure the septic system has a proper inspection before you purchase? For starters, because a new system can cost $5,000–$10,000 or more, depending on the property. Beyond simple replacement cost, however, problems can multiply if the old septic system, the cottage itself, the survey, and the local zoning aren't in concordance.

Here's how it works: Say a succession of owners, all do-it-yourselfers, gradually renovate and add to an old cottage. None of them bothers to secure a building permit. Gradually, the cottage grows in size and an extra bathroom is added, exceeding the legal capacity of the existing septic tank and leaching bed.

The system works fine for years until, under new owners, it fails and needs to be replaced. To their dismay, the current owners learn that under today's standards, in order to match its square footage and plumbing requirements, the cottage needs a larger leaching bed – but the leaching bed can't be made any larger because the lot's dimensions won't permit it. On what are known colloquially as "spaghetti lots" – long with narrow frontages – it may simply be impossible to accommodate a septic system that meets current standards along with a cottage that will adhere to the setbacks that the zoning regulations now require. Whoops.

While a traditional leaching bed might be out of the question due to the property's shape and size, other alternatives do exist – engineered beds that take up less physical space – but they usually come with a premium price tag. Or an extreme worst-case scenario might leave you unable to have a septic bed of any kind. The point is that you don't want to find yourself in this position unknowingly. Which is why you should determine if there are any problems *before* you close the deal. In addition, if you're borrowing money, the lender may require that the system have a certificate of compliance (proving it was installed according to regulations) or undergo a site inspection.

TIP: **Maintenance records are a clue to lifespan**

A septic system has a finite lifespan: At best, a system might last about 20 years, but lifespan is a function of how frequently the cottage is used — and how well the system is maintained. (It also assumes the system is correctly sized for the cottage; *see "Septic Smarts," opposite.*)

That's why it's important to know not only the age of the system at the cottage you're buying, but also whether the tank has been regularly pumped out — which should be done at least every three years. If it has not had regular pumpouts, sludge gradually fills the tank, leaving less space for incoming sewage, and therefore less time for solid wastes to settle out before the sewage moves into the leaching bed. The result? A prematurely plugged leaching bed, and a shortened lifespan for the system.

good condition and functioning properly? Has the tank been regularly and recently pumped? Are there maintenance records? (*See Tip, above.*) What is its expected remaining lifespan and how much would it cost to have the system replaced in your cottage area and at your particular location? (If the property is rocky or hard to access, costs will increase.) Does the property have sufficient space for a new leaching bed that meets current regulations? (*See "Septic Smarts," facing page.*)

Seller disclosure: Telling it like it is

Increasingly, property sellers are being required by law to provide the buyer with what is generically known as a vendor disclosure document. It requires the sellers to go through their property, feature by feature, and formally certify its condition to the best of their knowledge. This is a far more complex document than standard warranties regarding the absence of liens, asbestos, and urea formaldehyde insulation.

The point of a disclosure document is to have the vendor make a signed statement about the condition of the property. Civil law already exposes to litigation anyone involved in a sale who not only knowingly makes a false statement with regard to a serious defect, but who deliberately fails to reveal it. For example, a cottage might have a roof with a cracked ridge beam. The owner knows about it, because he's noticed a slight dip in the roofline, and has called in a contractor to give him a quote on the repair. Rather than fix it, however, he decided to sell the property to an unsuspecting buyer. While caveat emptor – buyer beware – is a basic consumer principle, it doesn't let this seller off the hook. A naive buyer who fails to ask about the condition of the roof, or who doesn't hire an inspector to look at it, still has an actionable case if after closing the deal he discovers that the previous owner knew about the problem and failed to voluntarily disclose it. In other words, this seller didn't have to lie about the condition of the roof in a disclosure document in order to bring about an actionable case. If the seller has been deceitful, the buyer has legal recourse.

But while getting stuck with a cottage with a bad roof may give you an actionable case, as a buyer you'd much prefer not to end up in a tangle of lawyers. For this reason, a disclosure document is an ideal solution. It causes both you and the seller to focus on significant potential problem areas, and deal with them to everyone's satisfaction before a sale is finalized.

Continued on next page

Heating systems

Furnace: if the cottage has an oil, wood, liquid propane, or natural gas furnace, what is its age and condition? Old age is a fact of furnace life, but if its main components are in really bad shape, you'll need to budget for its replacement down the road. If the cottage has a wood-fired furnace, check with your proposed insurer.

Woodstoves, zero-clearance fireplaces, fireplace inserts (*report from a certified woodstove installer*)**:** Is the wood-heating appliance the primary heat source? Is it certified by Underwriters Laboratories (UL), Underwriters Laboratories of Canada (ULC), or the Canadian Standards Association (CSA)? What is the stove's age and condition? Was the stove installed correctly, observing correct clearances to combustible materials? (*See also "Getting the Green Light on Woodstoves," facing page.*)

Chimneys (*report from a certified woodstove installer*)**:** What is the age and style of the chimney (single-wall steel, insulated stainless steel, or masonry)? Was the chimney installed correctly, observing correct clearances to combustible materials? Again, check your insurance: Many underwriters will refuse coverage based on the age and style of the appliance and its chimney, or provide coverage only if the cottage is used on a seasonal basis. (*Also see facing page.*)

Seller disclosure *continued from previous page*

But there are a couple of things to keep in mind with these disclosure documents. It is unfair to expect a seller to complete one in good conscience to the level of detail of a professional home inspection report. A seller can't be expected to reply to questions that are beyond his scope of knowledge. That's why you need to bring in a home inspector, as they often turn up problems that the present owner didn't know about or understand properly. Owners can only disclose as much as they understand, and can hardly advise you on potential repair costs.

Also keep in mind that many problems with homes are unforeseeable. A seller can't honestly know the condition of every aspect of the property and when it might require a significant repair. He can state that the well is in good working order, but what happens if the pump seizes up two months after the deal closes? Is the buyer going to come back at him, demanding he pay to have it replaced?

As the buyer, you should expect a disclosure document to testify to the *present condition* of the property, to the best of the knowledge of the vendor. It should not contain any deliberately false or misleading statements. But neither should it serve as a bottomless cornucopia of loopholes, allowing you to go back to the vendor and demand that he pay for a carpenter to fix a sticky cutlery drawer that he "failed" to disclose. (*See Chapter 12, p. 200, for more on vendor disclosure documents.*)

If a vendor declines to provide a vendor disclosure document (in locales where they are not legally mandatory or where real estate boards don't require them as a condition of listing the cottage), a buyer could still require the vendor to provide specific warranties in the offer to purchase. These can address a specific aspect of the property, such as the septic system being in good working order and meeting current regulations. Like a vendor disclosure document, a warranty does not make forward-looking guarantees. It is specific to the date of the warranty, not a guarantee that the purchaser will have trouble-free ownership to some future date.

Getting the green light on woodstoves

Woodstoves and other wood-burning appliances are certified for safety of construction and operation by either Underwriters Laboratories (UL), Underwriters Laboratories of Canada (ULC), or the Canadian Standards Association (CSA). Their efficiency, a rating based on how much heat they produce from a given amount of fuel and the level of emissions that come out of the chimney, is also rated, by either the CSA or the Environmental Protection Agency in the U.S. As a cottage buyer, while a clean-burning, high-efficiency unit is a bonus, your real concern when closing a deal is that the appliance is safe (UL, ULC, or CSA certified) and properly installed.

The majority of woodstove-related fires are due to faulty installation, the specifics of which are under the purview of the building code. (Specific local bylaws may also govern the installation and use of wood-burning appliances.) That said, having a verified installation that meets local code doesn't prevent insurers and lenders from having their own higher standards. (They might, for example, refuse coverage if your appliance isn't CSA or EPA certified.)

There can be problems with older non-certified stoves (which may not in and of themselves be forbidden in a particular jurisdiction) complying with the installation requirements of the building code. In Colorado, for instance, where woodstoves are very popular, it can be impossible to sell a property or secure fire insurance without verification that a non-certified stove was installed according to the code. And if the verification isn't in the present owner's hands or can't be found in state or provincial building inspection office files, there's no way for authorities to certify the installation retroactively. Many jurisdictions have similar problems where a non-certified stove was installed by a homeowner and there's no formal verification of code compliance.

Some insurance companies and lenders will accept an inspection by a certified home inspector or chimney sweep as verification of code compliance. In Canada, inspection of woodstoves and chimneys is limited to specialists certified according to the Wood Energy Technology Training (WETT) standard: This is a separate inspection from the general home inspection, requiring about an hour. The U.S. counterpart to WETT is the National Fireplace Institute.

The chain of compliance goes roughly like this:

• Just because a stove is certified for safety doesn't mean its installation is accepted by a local municipality under either its bylaws or its building code.

• Just because a particular installation satisfies a particular building code doesn't mean that an insurer or mortgage lender will accept it.

• Just because one insurer or lender won't touch a property with a particular stove and installation doesn't mean that another insurer or lender won't as well.

Confusing? Here's the bottom line: If you're considering purchasing a cottage with a wood-burning appliance, even one with a conventional fireplace, you should:

• talk to your insurance agent and (if pertinent) finance company to determine what their expectations are with respect to wood-burning installations

• expect the seller to be able to verify that the particular installation at least meets local standards

• expect the seller to provide proof of a recent professional inspection of the appliance or fireplace and the chimney.

Due to the many concerns surrounding woodstoves and fireplaces, it is not unreasonable for buyers to demand that sellers have their wood-burning systems inspected and verified before the property is put on the market.

Inspections and options for closing

You have the inspector's report and it contains items you feel need to be addressed before you can proceed with the closing. Where do you go from here?

To begin, before you get to this point, the agreement of purchase and sale should prepare for this outcome. An agreement of purchase and sale that includes the condition of a professional inspection should also deal with the outcome of the inspection. The two main issues to be addressed are:

• The right of the buyer or the vendor to walk away from the agreement.

• The right of the vendor to remedy the deficiencies.

From the buyer's point of view, the agreement should be worded so that you can terminate the offer unilaterally. In other words, the original agreement, at the price stated, in the present condition of the property, is dead. Vendors, on the other hand, may want the agreement to give them the right to challenge the conclusions of the inspector.

The purchase price in the agreement can be maintained if the offer provides a mechanism for dealing with deficiencies. One strategy is to include a maximum dollar amount of repairs that that vendor agrees to undertake as a result of the inspector's report. Should the estimate of those costs exceed the capped outlay, the agreement can permit the buyer to terminate the agreement, have the vendor assume the additional costs, or agree to share those additional costs.

In the absence of such a forward-thinking clause in the agreement of purchase and sale, buyer and seller are left to haggle over how to proceed with the closing. If the agreement has been worded so that the buyer has the right to terminate the offer on the basis of the inspection, he can walk. This is especially true if the inspection turns up a truly daunting problem with the property, and no amount of remediation will change his mind about closing. Similarly, the seller has the right to say "take it or leave it" if the buyer is balking at paying the price specified in the agreement without any adjustment for the inspector's recommended repairs.

Getting the repairs done

But if the buyer and seller are both motivated to get the deal done, they will try to come to an understanding on how to proceed. One method is for both sides to get quotes on the cost of repairs and then agree on how they're to be handled. They may share the cost, or the seller may have to underwrite them, either by paying for them out-of-pocket or offering an abatement in the selling price.

TIP:

Be prepared for a joint decision

If an agreement of purchase and sale for a property specifies that an inspector's report is going to be the basis of agreed-upon repairs, this also usually means the inspector will vet those repairs and authorize the release of a holdback payment under the agreement. In such cases, you may be required to hire an inspector jointly with the seller, or at least secure the seller's approval of the individual.

The most hazardous outcomes for the buyer are if the seller tries to effect the repairs himself, or if both parties agree for the repairs to be performed after the deal closes.

Do-it-yourself repairs by the seller run a fair risk of not being up to a buyer's expectations. Stories abound of shoddy, done-on-the-cheap owner repairs: plumbing leaks "fixed" with tape, loose siding reattached with roofing nails.

Ideally, repairs should all be taken care of before you actually close. But if your inspection turns up problems only a few days before the closing date, there's unlikely to be time for the repairs to be done before you assume ownership if the agreement of purchase and sale is to be honored. It can also happen that the required tradespeople may not be available to complete the work before the closing, even when there's a month or two between inspection and closing. This means you have to come up with some way of ensuring that the repairs are made to your satisfaction after you've closed the deal.

One way for the buyer to ensure that all repairs are up to snuff is to require they pass muster with the inspection professional who produced the report that flagged them. If the work is to occur after closing, the agreement must address:

– a time frame for completion.

– a holdback until the work is pronounced satisfactory.

– the responsibility for determining the nature of the repair work and for declaring it to be properly completed (ideally, the original inspector in both cases).

– what will occur if all of the prescribed work is not completed properly or on time.

8. Buying a lot or tear-down

In your search for the perfect vacation getaway, the most appealing property may turn out to be an undeveloped lot, or a lot with an existing cottage that cries out for a major renovation or a total replacement – a "tear-down." Or you may be starting your property search with an empty lot or a reno/tear-down in mind, keen to create something new and distinctive. Or you may simply like the idea of purchasing vacant land at a lower cost than a resale property, and building something yourself.

Whatever your motivation, properties other than resale cottages abound. They also abound with idiosyncratic considerations.

"Non–resale" options

Properties other than resale cottages fall into three general categories:

1. Vacant land. This runs the full gamut from a new property severed from an existing one to a piece of remote moose pasture being disposed of by a state or province. The issues vary accordingly.

CAUTION:
Your cottage on wheels might not be welcome

Don't assume you can create a cottage on the cheap by purchasing vacant land and putting inexpensive accommodation such as a trailer or mobile home on it. Zoning may not permit their use, except as temporary quarters while construction of a permanent dwelling is underway. Check with your local building department before you buy that Airstream.

2. Tear-downs and major renovations. A cottage exists, but is either in such poor condition or so modest in scope that you plan either to extensively renovate/rebuild it or to replace it altogether.

3. Planned subdivisions. The real estate business has become more attuned to the potential of creating subdivisions and planned communities in vacation country. Already a well-established phenomenon in the Sunbelt, they've also been cropping up in northern lake areas, particularly as the retirement-property market thrives. Some of these developments are high-end "gated" communities, with their own golf courses and marinas. Others aren't much different from a developer's suburban subdivision.

Vacant land
Pluses:
– Initial cost of land may be considerably less than a resale property.
– Opportunity to do the building yourself (in whole or in part).
– Opportunity to create a cottage exactly to your specifications.
– An ideal way to secure a property with true privacy, especially in less-developed or undeveloped areas.
– Can be a rare chance to create a new cottage in an established area.

Minuses:
– Site topography might make building impossible or significantly increase costs if extensive site alterations are necessary (for example, blasting, excavation, or trucking in massive amounts of fill).

Q & A:
Can you rebuild a tear-down that breaks current rules?

Q: I've heard that if I build my cottage on the same "footprint" as the one I'm tearing down, I won't run afoul of new setback regulations that were enacted after the existing cottage was built. Is this true?

A: Plenty of older cottages don't comply with regulations created after their construction that enforce minimum side lots, shoreline setbacks, and other standards. While these cottages are protected in their present state by grandfathering clauses – they're known as "legal nonconforming" – renovating or rebuilding them, never mind expanding them, is often not allowed or will require a number of expensive and time-consuming zoning variance approvals to make them legal.

A general rule is that aggressive renovations that amount to a whole new building are most feasible when they employ the original foundations, but this is hardly a certainty. Zoning regulations are particularly sensitive about septic systems and how they may be affected by expansion of living space. You don't need to add designated bedrooms or bathrooms to run afoul of local regulators in this regard: You can be denied a building permit for a four-season sunroom because it is deemed to increase living space beyond the septic system's capacity.

– If the lot is unfinished, utility services such as electricity or natural gas may be difficult, expensive, or impossible to secure. Municipal services and public or private roads may not exist.

– Construction costs can be high, due to shortages of available skilled labor and transportation costs of materials. With a remote property, you may even have to provide on-site accommodations for workers.

– Limitations on permitted development in a particular area may inhibit plans to build what you want.

– Financing of vacant land is less flexible and more expensive than with a resale property. (*See Chapter 9.*)

– You cannot use your main home (in U.S.) or principal residence (in Canada) capital gains tax exemption until there is a building on the land, which may affect your tax planning. (*See "Tax Tips," p. 138 and 140.*)

Tear-down/renovation
Pluses:

– Opportunity to own a location you truly love, even if the existing structures aren't satisfactory.

– Opportunity to build what you want with many of the "start-up" considerations and expenses already taken care of.

– Property is most likely to satisfy the need for a finished lot, already having the desired utilities and municipal services and other infrastructure, such as roads. Existing property systems (water, sewage) may be adequate or adaptable to new construction.

– Can provide an opportunity to build in a highly desirable location, such as an established cottage community, where vacant lots are either not available or of less-desirable quality.

– If present cottage is habitable, it can meet certain financing and tax-related standards that vacant land cannot.

Minuses:

– A "tear-down" is often in the eye of the beholder. Where lots are essentially of the same quality, a habitable cottage will cost more than vacant land, and it may be more expensive in the long run to buy an existing cottage and replace it than it would be to begin with a vacant finished lot.

– Many cottages that invite being torn down or largely rebuilt were erected before a local building code and an official plan governing development were in place. While the present cottage may be permitted under a "grandfathering" clause, replacing it could be a major regulatory challenge.

Planned subdivisions
Pluses:

– You know exactly what you'll be moving to and what the neighboring properties are going to be like.

TIP:
"Prefab" doesn't mean cheap

Because of the logistical challenges of building in cottage country, prefabricated and packaged custom homes are popular solutions, though not necessarily less expensive than traditional construction, depending on the site. Manufactured homes, whether they are called "modular," "panelized," or "precut," can be of very high quality, attracting buyers not with absolute cost savings but because they offer cost certainties and a high quality of construction and materials. They can also offer a more predictable timetable: The more prefabricated the building, the fewer delays or complications likely in the final assembly due to weather or the scheduling of tradespeople.

If you have an idea that the prefab route is the secret to affordability, contact a builder or visit a local dealer or contractor and determine what the actual costs are.

Variation on a theme
A relatively new trend is the planned development that offers part, or fractional, ownership in a newly built cottage. *For information on fractional ownership, see Chapter 10, p. 170.*

– Green spaces will be carefully considered and the development will probably include details such as walking and bicycle paths and even local recreation facilities for the exclusive use of residents. There is also often a high degree of control of the area's character, through a cottagers' or owners' association that funds amenities.

– There are no mysteries about the availability of utilities and municipal services. While these organized communities may still require their own waste management (septic system) and their own water (drawn from the lake or a well), it's the developer's responsibility to ensure that these services are provided according to local regulations.

– Because these properties are meant to qualify for conventional mortgages, they are, for all intents and purposes, as sophisticated as any residential home.

Minuses:

– Planned developments, even where site planning is sensitive to the natural environment, can be more "suburban" than a classic cottage area.

– When it comes to architectural options, you will be restricted to what the developer is offering. Planned communities can be highly regulated, down to restrictions on the available colors of brick, siding, and shingles. There may also be restrictive covenants controlling landscaping, the construction of outbuildings, and the presence of boat trailers, camper trailers, or motor homes on the property – and more. While many of these restrictions can be found in typical municipal bylaws, they are far more prevalent and more controlling in a planned community. Overall, there is much less individual freedom for the property owner.

– With sophistication comes cost, and you can end up paying for facilities and services that you don't really want. Some planned communities, for instance, feature security gating and private facilities such as golf courses and marinas. The subdivision's residents' association may be responsible for the ongoing costs of these amenities.

Heading off headaches

While it's impossible to anticipate and solve all the issues that may crop up while you're undertaking massive renovations or building from scratch, you can lessen the potential of problems by working through these questions and to-do lists:

Will you be allowed to build?

Just because land is for sale in cottage country doesn't mean you can actually build something on it. When buying through or from an agent, make sure the vendor disclosure process identifies any significant limitations to

Cottage builders: Not necessarily ready when you are

Given the ongoing demand for vacation and retirement properties in cottage country, local builders and subcontractors are often exceedingly busy, and it is not uncommon for the best general contractors to be booked solid more than 12 months in advance. Once you've settled on building from scratch – when you have a site and a rough budget – contact some local contractors to get an idea of how much lead time they will require in order to take on your project. If you call a builder in March, clutching a set of blueprints, and expect to move in by the first weekend in July, expect laughter on the other end of the line.

construction on empty lots. If you buy privately, you should expect less-informed guidance from the seller. Whatever the case, you need to know for certain what the local zoning regulations, including restrictive covenants, will permit.

Many cottage areas have properties built decades ago that would not be permitted today because of changes in regulations intended to limit density and prevent overstressing the lake environment. Some areas have been overbuilt, and their governing municipalities (and residents) are determined to hold the line on further growth.

What to do before buying a property for new construction or major renovation

• Have a lot survey performed or, if you have an existing lot plan, ask a local surveyor to give you some advice on its accuracy. Survey in hand, contact the local building department to see if there are any zoning issues that might affect your construction plans. (This task is pretty much impossible without a survey, as building officials are understandably hesitant to offer specific advice on a property if they can't see its precise dimensions and layout.) Things to consider include:

– Minimum lot dimensions required for residential development
– Minimum side-lot and shoreline setbacks
– Restrictions linked to the capacity of septic systems
– Height restrictions on buildings
– Environmentally sensitive areas where construction is either restricted or forbidden.

• Pay particular attention to flood-plain designations. You may not be able to build, or rebuild, in such areas. (*See Chapter 3 for more.*)

• Zoning regulations typically specify setbacks from watercourses. If there's any kind of stream, even one that only carries spring meltwater and runoff from heavy rains, you need to be clear if the local authority will require a setback from it. Some properties that are cleaved by small watercourses can be virtually impossible to build on because of setback requirements. Again, a survey will help building officials make a decision.

TIP:
Don't let the neighbors be your guide

Don't use what other cottages in your area look like as a guide to what you can erect on your own vacant lot. For starters, the other cottages may be "legally nonconforming" because they predate the zoning bylaws. But beyond that, other factors can come into play. Perhaps, for instance, your lot is a bit smaller than the neighboring one: In addition to regulating setbacks from the property lines, the zoning bylaws can also specify the percentage of a lot that can be covered by buildings.

As well, bylaws can differ from area to area and even from lot to lot in the same municipality.

To be safe, check with the municipal zoning office before you get your heart set on a cottage like the one next door.

TIP:

How large is that lot? The taxman will want to know

If you're a Canadian taxpayer buying vacant land to build on – or even an existing cottage on a large lot – be aware that when you sell (or hand down) the cottage, the CRA will allow the capital gains tax exemption for a principal residence *only* on property to a maximum of a half-hectare. Any land beyond that half-hectare limit is subject to capital gains. Some exceptions are permitted. *See Caution, p. 227, for more.*

• An increase in living area may require an increase in lot size that can sometimes be satisfied in Canada by purchasing an adjoining shoreline road allowance. (*See Chapter 6 for more.*)

• Don't imagine significant changes to the shoreline, including new docks, boathouses, or breakwalls without first looking into local and state or provincial measures to protect shoreline habitat. Control over such construction may fall under both local zoning bylaws (contact the municipal office) and provincial or state regulations. (Contact the department or ministry of natural resources and/or environment.)

• Be sensitive to adjoining property owners. If you're planning a new building or a major renovation that significantly changes the character of the property, you might be in for a legal fight with the neighbors. As shoreline property values soar and the original cottage stock ages, tear-downs are inevitable and often desirable, helping to revitalize an area. That doesn't mean you can purchase a tear-down property with 100 feet of frontage in an area of 40-year-old, single-bedroom cabins and not expect a fight when you try to secure a building permit for a multi-storey getaway that's built to the very limit of all setbacks and blocks the neighbors' view.

• In a similar vein, if resale value is any concern, make sure what you build is appropriate to the property area. (*See Chapter 9 for more.*)

How much will it cost?

The lure of inexpensive land can produce sticker shock when it comes time to actually put up a cottage. Invariably, an inverse relationship exists between land cost and construction cost in vacation country. Highly serviced, accessible lots are more expensive than ones that can only be reached by boat or along an unassumed bush road. At the same time, construction costs are going to be less per square foot for a lot that is easy to drive to and presents no complications for delivery of materials and access for tradespeople and their equipment.

With a water-access property, everything from septic tanks to topsoil to lumber to shingles must be barged in – creating a significant spike in construction costs. And even when you can find tradespeople able to work on the site, transit times to and from the site will eat into each day's productivity (not to mention that it is standard practice for workers to charge for the time spent going to and fro).

Expenses to-do list

• Determine whether a lot is "finished." This means some degree of utility service – electricity, water, sewage, land-line telephone – is directly available to the site. Often, it can also mean it is located on an assumed public road.

• If a road doesn't exist and utilities are not already available to the site, first of all determine whether it is even possible to connect to these services. (On some remote sites, hydro, municipal water and sewer, and telephone service are simply not available.) Then decide which ones you absolutely want and determine how much you will be charged to hook up (if you can hook up at all). An electrical utility may provide free connection within a certain distance of the road, but then start charging hefty rates for the linear distance to the building afterwards. (When additional utility poles are required to bridge the distance, costs can be astronomical.)

• If utilities are not available or are prohibitively expensive, figure out what you're going to need to provide on your own (such as power, potable water, and a septic bed and tank). Check requirements with the appropriate authorities (for instance, the necessary size and setbacks of your septic system) and get estimates from local professionals on the costs involved. Water and waste can be big-ticket items. Spending $10,000–$15,000 on a drilled well is not out of the ordinary, and a septic system, depending on the size, style, and the site, can easily top $10,000.

• Get a grip on your design costs. Most organized cottage municipalities have zoning regulations and building codes in place, so you can't just toss together anything that strikes your fancy without a permit. If you're not working from scratch with an architect and intend to use stock plans, you still have to buy them and then ensure, either on your own or through your contractor, that the specifications satisfy the local code.

• If you intend to have someone build the cottage for you, round up the local contractors, get references, and ask for a general estimate of building costs, based on what you envision in terms of square footage, winterizing, and foundations. You don't need a finished set of plans. A good contractor will be able to tell you the sort of ballpark costs per square foot your dream getaway will command, before you get to a specific quote bid.

• Even if you are determined to build the property yourself, you may want tradespeople for certain phases to speed the work along. Hiring framers is a common strategy for getting together at least the shell of the building. Find out who's available locally and what they'll charge. Be prepared to rely on hired help more than you anticipated. Getting the basic structure up and enclosed is a major hurdle, especially before winter sets in. Once you have a roof, windows, doors, and walls, you can work on finishing the interior yourself.

• While it's true that square footage drives cost, budgets for an individual project will vary tremendously according to labor (how much of the job the owner can take on, the logistics involved for tradespeople to access and work on the site) and materials.

• Consider managing costs by building in increments. A basic cottage can be designed and built, with an add-on wing planned for a few years later. Just be sure that your expansion can be accommodated by the applicable zoning regulations.

Tax tips for Americans buying land and building a cottage

Interest deductibility for American taxpayers has particular wrinkles in the realm of vacation property, and can become complex when dealing with vacant land and tear-downs.

The basic issues of interest deductibility on mortgages and home-equity loans for main and second homes are addressed in Chapter 9. You might want to read it first, to be clear on the lingo before diving into this discussion. Otherwise, take a deep breath and put your accountant on standby.

Deducting interest charges on purchases of vacant land

When it comes to deductions of interest on money used for home acquisition, the Internal Revenue Service thinks of qualifying properties foremost as something you can live in. As is discussed in Chapter 9, eligible residences include not only traditional homes, but any sort of accommodations with some kind of kitchen, toilet, and sleeping facilities. That means things such as boats, trailers, mobiles homes, and RVs qualify. Cottages naturally qualify as well.

The IRS permits you to claim the home-acquisition deduction for interest costs on loans secured by a qualifying main or second home, provided that what you're using that loan to buy will qualify as either the main or second home. With residential real estate, the underlying property is considered part and parcel of the residence from the perspective of deduction-eligible borrowing costs. But it's possible, of course, to buy land that doesn't have a fixed residence on it.

To claim interest costs associated with the purchase of land, there must be something that qualifies as a fixed residence (not a trailer or a mobile home) on the property. If you put a trailer on the vacant land, you can claim the loan interest on the trailer, if it qualifies as a second home and the loan is properly secured, but not the land itself. Similarly, if you build a dock on the vacant land and use it to moor a boat with accommodations that you list as a main or second residence, the interest on whatever properly secured loan you used to buy the boat is deduction-eligible, but not the interest on a loan you used to buy the land.

Undeveloped land as an investment property

Although no home-acquisition loan deduction is permitted for the underlying land if there is no main or second home on it, you may be able to treat the undeveloped land as an investment property and claim the interest on any money you borrowed to acquire it as an investment expense. There's another loophole to keep in mind: The IRS will let you borrow money against a home other than your first or second home, and claim the interest if it is used for investment purposes. So if you have another property that qualifies as a home, such as that boat or trailer, it's possible that you could borrow against it, use the funds to buy land, and claim the interest as an investment expense.

Deductions for a home under construction

The tax code allows you to claim a property as a first or second home for up to 24 months while it is still under construction, counting back from the date of completion. On completion, it must qualify as one of your two homes. This means you can't fool around with power tools on a cottage project for two years, then walk away for a year and still designate the property as a qualifying home for that construction period.

During that period of up to 24 months, claiming construction loan interest is permitted under the home acquisition category. You can also claim interest on a mortgage secured either while this cottage is under construction, or up to 90 days after its completion.

Let's say you own a parcel of land. You begin building a cottage on it on April 1, funding the work yourself. Your total construction cost is $100,000. On August 1, with work still to be completed, you secure a mortgage of $75,000. The cottage is completed and ready to be occupied on November 1. You can list the cottage as your second home as of April 1, the date construction began, and claim the interest costs on the mortgage from the date it was secured, August 1. Should you decide instead to secure a mortgage after all the power tools have stopped shrieking, you have until the following January 29 – 90 days after completion – to arrange that mortgage and have it qualify as a home acquisition loan. The cottage is still claimable as your second home from April 1, when construction began.

Be aware as well that the value of empty land, which does not qualify for a home-acquisition deduction if financed on its own, can be financed in a claimable way later, when a qualified home is built on it. After completing construction of the home, you can secure a mortgage on the entire property, land and building included, within the 90-day period and claim the mortgage interest as a home acquisition loan. In this way you can consolidate a series of borrowings – first to buy the land, then to finance the construction – into one claimable mortgage. The interest on such a debt becomes tax deductible from the point at which you are able to have the property qualify as a first or second home.

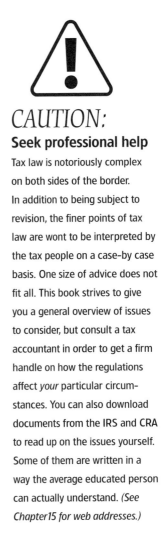

CAUTION:
Seek professional help

Tax law is notoriously complex on both sides of the border. In addition to being subject to revision, the finer points of tax law are wont to be interpreted by the tax people on a case-by case basis. One size of advice does not fit all. This book strives to give you a general overview of issues to consider, but consult a tax accountant in order to get a firm handle on how the regulations affect *your* particular circumstances. You can also download documents from the IRS and CRA to read up on the issues yourself. Some of them are written in a way the average educated person can actually understand. *(See Chapter15 for web addresses.)*

Tax tips for Canadians: Vacant land can carry a nasty capital gains tax bite

While Canadian taxpayers do not enjoy mortgage interest deductibility like their American neighbors do, they are essentially exempt from paying tax on capital gains on their designated principal residence. *(See Chapter 14 for information on designating a cottage a principal residence and avoiding and reducing capital gains tax in Canada and the U.S.)*

Like the IRS, the Canada Revenue Agency extends its definition of "residence" to things such as trailers and houseboats. But whatever the residence is, it has to have accommodations – and empty land doesn't. Therefore, buying land and then building on it demands a bit of foresight in order to avoid a potentially unhappy tax situation down the road.

If you're a Canadian taxpayer who doesn't currently own a property that can be designated as your principal residence (for example, you're renting an apartment in the city, or have sold a principal residence to fund the purchase of a vacation property), you can only start calculating your capital gains exemption on a land acquisition from the year in which you have a habitable building on it that can qualify as your principal residence. Until that time, wherever you're living is your principal residence, even if you don't own it. Any appreciation in the value of the land during the years in which it remains undeveloped is ineligible for the capital gains exemption. In addition, because of the way the exemption is calculated, this period also affects how much of the capital gains you'll end up paying tax on when you do dispose of a qualifying residence.

That's because (bear with me) the basic calculation used to determine the capital gains exemption on a principal residence uses the number of years a property is owned, *starting from the year in which the vacant land was acquired.* If the number of years in which a property is a principal residence is small in comparison to the total years a property is owned, the available capital gains exemption is proportionately small.

The calculation looks like this:

CGE = A x B/C

CGE = the taxpayer's capital gains exemption on the principal residence

A = the adjusted cost base of the property (market value at time of disposition less the eligible costs, such as acquisition, construction etc.)

B = the number of tax years in which the property qualified as the principal residence, calculated as 1 + number of years inclusive. (For example, a property that qualified as a principal residence in May 2001 and was disposed of in October 2004 would work out to be 1+4 = 5.)

C = the number of tax years the property has been owned, with or without a residence of any kind standing on it

The calculation can be punishing if there are significant differences between the appreciation of the property when it wasn't your principal residence, and when it was. You might buy empty land on which you plan to build a principal residence, but leave it undeveloped for half of your years of ownership. The land might not appreciate much, but once a cottage is built, market forces could cause the property to soar in value. Eighty percent of the capital gain might occur during the principal residence years, but if half of the years of ownership fell into the vacant land period, a disproportionate amount of the property's appreciation is going to be denied a legitimate

---

Case study:

Ka-ching, ka-ching: Reducing the buy-now, build-later tax hit

Joe and Jean purchased a parcel of vacant land for $100,000 in 1996, planning to eventually build a cottage on it and retire there. For the first five years, the property remained empty and the value of the lot increased a modest $20,000. In Year Six, 2001, they spent $200,000 to have a cottage built on the property and relocated there, moving out of an apartment in the city.

Three years later, in 2004, they decided to sell the property, which had served as their principal residence, and move closer to their children. Property values on their lake had recently soared, and the sale realized $450,000. Their total capital gain was $150,000 ($450,000–$200,000–$100,000=$150,000).

At this point, they got a nasty surprise. Because nothing stood on the property for the first five years, only half the number of years they owned the land and the cottage qualified for principal residence status. (1 + the number of tax years inclusive from year of designation as principal residence to year of disposition. *See complete calculation on facing page.*) And so, using the CRA's basic calculation, their capital gains exemption was only half of their total gain: $75,000. With an inclusion rate for taxation purposes of 50 percent, Joe and Jean were having to show an additional $37,500 of income on their tax return.

Fortunately, Joe and Jean had an accountant who was on the ball and advised them to use the optional calculation the CRA permits to isolate the periods of capital gains. To do so, they just needed to have a fair market value for the empty lot for the last taxation year in which the property was not the principal residence, and then determine the taxable capital gain for the vacant-lot period alone. By hiring a professional appraiser, they were able to establish that the total capital gain on the lot indeed was only $20,000 as of 2000, before they built the residence on it. All of the capital gain that followed thus could be sheltered using the principal residence exemption. The additional income they had to show from the sale of the property thus plunged from $37,500 to $10,000.

---

exemption from capital gains taxes. Similarly, you might buy vacant land, leave it undeveloped for a number of years, then build a cottage on it. But while you plan to retire to it, you can't designate it as your principal residence for a few years at least. Again, the amount of capital gains you are going to be able to avoid, using the above calculation, is limited to the proportion of years during which the property qualified as a principal residence, even if a disproportionate amount of the capital gains was incurred during the principal residence years.

Fortunately, however, there is a way around this. CRA permits you to employ an optional calculation in which you determine the capital gains for the individual periods of ownership. You can figure out the gains for the period when the property was an empty lot (or when it was an empty lot and then had a cottage on it but wasn't designated your principal residence), and report that gain if it turns out to be less than the gain arrived at by the basic fractional calculation shown above.

To do this, you need an additional fair market value, for the last taxation year before the property qualified as your principal residence. You can secure one in hindsight by hiring a professional appraiser to research the value at a particular date. But if you're developing a property with an eye to it becoming your principal residence, you can exercise some foresight and secure an appraisal at the time the cottage is about to become your principal residence, then keep it on file for the day you dispose of the property and need to work out the capital gains obligation. (*See the case study, p. 232, for an example of how this is done.*)

9. Financing the cottage purchase

I f you're like most cottage purchasers, you'll need to finance at least part of your vacation property. And in order to do that to your best advantage, it's helpful to understand how the brains of those in the money-renting business work.

The mortgage products and lending programs of financial institutions are constantly changing, but what doesn't change is the underlying logic. Get a handle on that logic, and you can get past all the marketing labels, slick packaging, and sometimes confusing conditions.

Risk assessment in cottage real estate

Think of the financial institution that you're asking to put up some or most of the money to pay for your vacation property as an investor. If the risk is perceived to be low, you will be offered the most favorable terms possible; the "investor" is willing to accept a lower return because of the higher cer-

TIP:

Deal with a banker who understands the local cottage market

We made this point way back in Chapter 2, but it's worth reiterating in the context of how lenders assess risk. A banker based in the area where you're contemplating a purchase will most likely have a better feel for the local real estate market than a banker based in the city. And this can work in your favor when it comes to the type, size, and cost of the loan he or she is willing to offer.

tainty of receiving that return. And if the risk is perceived to be high, the lender is going to set terms that deliver a higher return and also limit its risk exposure.

Assessing risk on a real estate loan has a couple of components. One, obviously, is based on the borrower's ability to service the debt by making uninterrupted payments. The second, the one particularly relevant to potential cottage buyers, is the nature of the security or collateral. If the borrower defaults on the loan, how easily can the lender sell the underlying security, receive at least its appraised value in return, and recover its money?

Lenders see traditional residential property as a fairly low-risk lending area because property in general appreciates over time. As a result, the appraised value grows steadily larger while the outstanding balance of the loan drops as payments are made. Cottage properties, on the other hand, are sometimes viewed as more of a risk, depending on the location of the property and the style and construction of the cottage itself. For example, should a borrower default on a loan for a more rustic vacation retreat in a remote and less-populated area, it could be difficult for the lender to recoup its investment. *(See p. 148 for the types of cottages that concern lenders.)*

Where trouble lies: How big a mortgage will you need?

Lenders see danger in the following two situations:

1. The borrowers have such a high-ratio mortgage (mortgage ratio refers to the amount of the loan in relation to the value of the property) that when they get into trouble making payments early in the life of the mortgage, there's very little equity in the property for them to cash out, and the bank finds itself having to step in and assume ownership of the property. This is where mortgage insurance addresses the lender's risk. In Canada, high-ratio mortgages (those with a loan-to-value ratio of 75 percent or higher) are required by law to be insured. In the U.S., the ratio set by state authorities as requiring insurance is usually around 80 percent.

2. The borrowers find themselves with an "upside down" mortgage – where the outstanding balance of the loan exceeds the market value of the property. This is fundamentally caused by market volatility. If the market experiences large price swings, an appraised value made during a peak can create an upside-down mortgage in a trough – and the possibility of this happening increases with higher-ratio mortgages.

Volatility can be caused by two main factors, and both can be found in the cottage market:

• **Low turnover:** Specialized properties that have a small number of buyers and sellers are subject to wild changes in valuation, since supply-and-demand is so precarious. Without a sufficient volume of deals in a particular property area, it's hard to judge a "fair" price. You may be willing to spend $150,000 for an island retreat that requires a seaplane to reach, but if you or your bank is forced to sell the property in a few years, what are the odds of enough interested buyers coming forward to sustain that price and realize a reasonably quick sale?

The problem can be exacerbated by the type of building erected on a property. If it's too distinctive and too pricey, and the property is too remote, the resale market may be so small that an aggressive buyer could negotiate its purchase for far below replacement cost.

• **Overspeculation:** While real estate in general has trended upwards in value, pricing cycles are inevitable. Prices can fall because an overheated market drives values to unsustainable levels.

If a vacation area suddenly becomes hot, the rush of capital into the region can create an investment bubble. Vacation property bubbles are more prone to bursting than ones in the residential market because they are nonessential investments that people can unload if money becomes dear. If someone is having a hard time meeting the payments both on their house in the city and the cottage at the lake, common sense says they will dispose of the cottage first.

(It's worth noting, however, that sometimes common sense loses out to the emotional attachment a cottage property can have: In the past, many cottagers chose to sell their primary residences in the city, rather than lose their little bit of lakeside heaven.)

But if too many people put too many pricey properties on the market at the same time, particularly in an unfavorable economic climate, a price collapse results. In the early 1990s, for example, property values in some Canadian cottage areas took a hit when American money withdrew as a recession took hold.

Such corrections may be temporary, but they only have to last a few years to cause a lender pain. The possibility of such corrections increases in times of low interest rates. When money is cheap, people are more inclined to borrow large sums because of the low carrying costs – not just by borrowing to purchase property, but by using the equity in their property to secure loans that can be used for all kinds of spending. If rates then rise enough to create painful monthly payments, and owners have no refinancing options, they're going to sell into what may be a crowded market with more expensive money. A shift in the supply-and-demand, combined with increased borrowing costs, can trigger significant price drops.

Minimizing lending risk: Who gets the best financing deals?

Overall, however, lenders recognize that the vacation property market has huge potential, thanks to the purchasing muscle of the ubiquitous boomers. But because banks are by nature cautious about financing property deals that can't guarantee the long-term price stability of thriving urban centers and main residences, they're still warming to the idea of treating vacation properties as rock-solid collateral. Protecting themselves from unhappy surprises means minimizing the lending risk, using the following guidelines:

1. As with all real estate, the best financing deals are reserved for the properties with the highest collateral security. That security comes from stability in appraised value of the collateral and from its liquidity – the ability to be converted from something illiquid, like property, into cash. For this reason, you can expect to find far more variety in the nature of mortgages and loans within the vacation property market than there is in the residential real estate market, precisely because the collateral used in vacation properties is so varied.

2. The lower the ratio of debt to equity in any mortgage or loan, the better it is for the financial institution, because the borrower is in a better position to absorb losses from price drops. By the same token, the less confident a lender is of a property's ability to avoid significant price drops, the more equity it wants to see the borrower hold.

The degree of risk being assumed by the financial institution ends up being expressed in four fundamental ways. Other issues will crop up, but these are the main ones:

– The kind of loan product it is willing to offer
– What percentage of the property's value it will agree to finance
– The interest rate charged
– The borrowing period

Types of loan products available for cottages

What can make the lending waters murky is that many different loan and mortgage products are on offer – and they're changing all the time. The following are some generalities about the types; not all the features listed below are necessarily going to be offered in every loan product that falls within these categories, or in every banking jurisdiction.

Conventional mortgages

• Property serves as a principal or main residence.

• Loan-to-value ratio is at or below 75 percent of lending value in Canada. (The ratio can be higher in some states in the U.S.) Mortgage insurance is not required.

• Can be transferred to another qualifying property without penalty.

• Can be assigned to or assumed by another lender or borrower.

Cross-border financing: American buyers and Canadian banks

If you're an American shopping for a vacation property in Canada and are thinking of dealing with a Canadian bank, you need to be aware of an important consequence of going that route. U.S. tax law requires American citizens to withhold a percentage of any income they provide to foreign entities and remit it to the IRS on their behalf as a tax payment. Among the forms of income that the IRS says require remittance are interest payments on loans from foreign banks. The current schedule requires a withholding of 10 percent on interest paid on such loans to Canadian banks. There are also restrictions on Canadian banks lending to nonresidents.

Some Canadian banks, however, do specialize in catering to American purchasers of Canadian real estate, and are well versed in the regulations and can explain them to you.

• Cannot be terminated without penalty (which often consists of several month's payments).

• Is eligible for the bank's best loan interest rates.

• Has a fixed amortization period. Cannot be paid off in full or in part without penalty.

Insured mortgages

• Essentially the same as a conventional mortgage, except that the property has a high loan-to-value ratio (or other conditions that the lender feels could affect resale). Mortgage programs are constantly changing with market conditions but, generally speaking, financial institutions now approve mortgages on prime vacation properties with a loan-to-value ratio (LVR) of 75 percent or even higher (*see Tip, at right*), which is the same as what's available for resale homes. You may encounter a cutoff for this higher-ratio mortgage. (For instance, a bank might provide a mortgage with an LVR of 75 percent for up to, say, $300,000, then reduce it to 60 percent beyond that.)

• When the financing is more than 75 percent of the value (sometimes lower) in Canada, more than 80 percent in the U.S., mortgage insurance is required.

• Won't necessarily attract the best lending rates.

Collateralized mortgages

• While called a mortgage, this is really a kind of loan, collateralized by the property itself – when the nature of the property doesn't make it eligible for a conventional mortgage. Conventional mortgages are seldom offered on cottages unless they meet the minimum standards of the conventional

TIP:

Minimizing your down payment: How low can you go?

It wasn't long ago that securing a mortgage on a cottage with less than 25 percent owner equity was a major challenge. Today, while the 25 percent threshold is still typical, it's possible with some vacation properties to secure a mortgage with only a 10 or 15 percent down payment. Theoretically, if the property can qualify as a principal residence, it can also qualify for mortgage insurance backed by the Canadian Mortgage and Housing Corporation (CMHC) in Canada. In the U.S., buyers looking to mortgage more than 80 percent of the market value need to turn to private mortgage insurance.

residential home market. Even those that do can be disqualified because of other factors. (*See "Conditions that Concern Banks," below.*)

- Cannot be transferred to another property.

- Cannot be assigned to or assumed by another lender or borrower.

- Has higher interest rates than a conventional mortgage.

- Is considered an "open" loan, and can be paid off in full or in part by the borrower without penalty.

Conditions that concern banks

A number of conditions will make a bank decline to consider a vacation property for a conventional mortgage or collateralized mortgage, or lead it to offer less-favorable interest rates, loan terms, acceptable loan-to-value ratios, and requirements for mortgage insurance.

- **Lack of four-season road access.** It's hard for a bank to think of a property in the same financial terms as a main residence when you can't drive to it in February. Seasonal access can almost single-handedly disqualify vacation properties from consideration for a conventional mortgage. Nevertheless, the property can collateralize its own loan if it meets other criteria.

- **Water access only.** See above. Actually, see above for any kind of access that doesn't accommodate a Toyota Echo in the middle of winter.

- **Leased land.** Banks won't issue conventional mortgages on any property where the land is leased (such as when the cottage is on public land or an

CAUTION: Make sure the building suits the property

Generally speaking, conventional mortgages aren't a good bet for properties where the structures are out of character with the setting. A luxury home that looks perfect in the city, or even in some lakeside locations, is out of place, resale-wise, if plunked down in the middle of nowhere. Even if you're not looking for a conventional mortgage, keep this in mind if you're planning to build in a rural or remote setting: If you build something too high-end, you may have trouble finding a buyer at a price that recoups your costs if you decide to sell someday.

Another warning flag is a property in a location or neighborhood that's going downhill. This usually applies to urban locations, but it can crop up in vacation country. You might try to get ahead of the renovation or tear-down wave in a down-on-its-luck waterfront community, but the bank might not be convinced that the rest of the neighborhood is ready to join you, making it tough to have faith in resale value.

aboriginal reserve) if the mortgage term exceeds the life of the lease. And for good reason. If the mortgage runs 25 years but the lease expires in 20, it's possible that the lessor won't agree to extend the lease and will force the mortgaged building's owner to remove or tear it down. (*See Chapter 6, p. 108.*)

• **Inferior construction.** This runs the gamut from crumbling foundations to sagging floors and rooflines to archaic styling to aesthetic disaster.

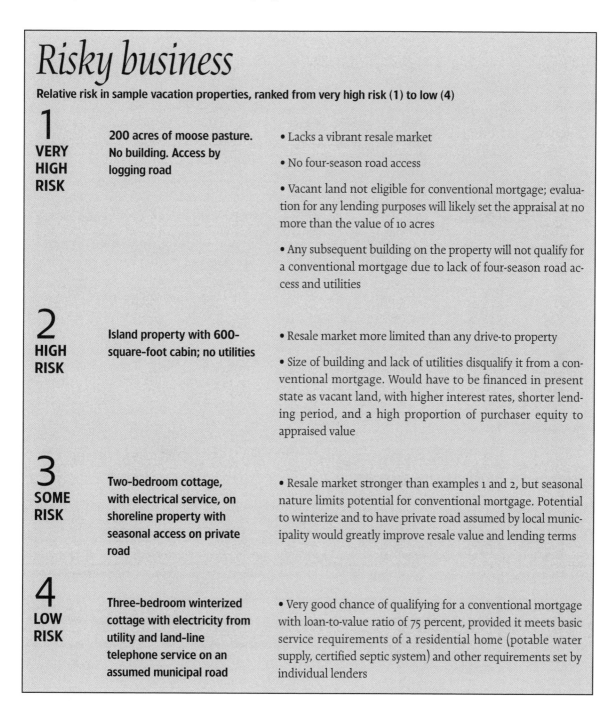

Risky business

Relative risk in sample vacation properties, ranked from very high risk (1) to low (4)

1 VERY HIGH RISK

200 acres of moose pasture. No building. Access by logging road

• Lacks a vibrant resale market

• No four-season road access

• Vacant land not eligible for conventional mortgage; evaluation for any lending purposes will likely set the appraisal at no more than the value of 10 acres

• Any subsequent building on the property will not qualify for a conventional mortgage due to lack of four-season road access and utilities

2 HIGH RISK

Island property with 600-square-foot cabin; no utilities

• Resale market more limited than any drive-to property

• Size of building and lack of utilities disqualify it from a conventional mortgage. Would have to be financed in present state as vacant land, with higher interest rates, shorter lending period, and a high proportion of purchaser equity to appraised value

3 SOME RISK

Two-bedroom cottage, with electrical service, on shoreline property with seasonal access on private road

• Resale market stronger than examples 1 and 2, but seasonal nature limits potential for conventional mortgage. Potential to winterize and to have private road assumed by local municipality would greatly improve resale value and lending terms

4 LOW RISK

Three-bedroom winterized cottage with electricity from utility and land-line telephone service on an assumed municipal road

• Very good chance of qualifying for a conventional mortgage with loan-to-value ratio of 75 percent, provided it meets basic service requirements of a residential home (potable water supply, certified septic system) and other requirements set by individual lenders

• **Income property.** Conventional mortgages generally aren't offered for pure rental properties.

• **Nothing standing.** Lots cannot qualify for a conventional mortgage, because a building is required. But they can serve as collateral for their own purchase loans.

• **Tear-downs.** This means different things to different people. A lot of cozy retreats that even a bank will consider as collateral of some kind are viewed as bulldozer fodder by some buyers. Nevertheless, if the building has serious inferiorities or simply cannot be lived in, forget about a conventional mortgage and look instead to finance the purchase on the same terms as an empty tract of land.

• **Potable water problems.** You can't secure a conventional mortgage without proof of a reliable source of potable water, be it a well, an intake from a lake (with the water then run through a purification system), or a municipal system. If the water source is polluted, or if your drinking water has to be brought in for whatever reason, a conventional mortgage is out of the question. And you can expect less-favorable terms when it comes to a collateralized mortgage.

• **No approved method of sewage disposal, be it a septic or municipal system.** If there's a holding tank, some lenders will still consider issuing a conventional mortgage, provided the loan-to-value ratio is sufficiently low (on the order of 50 percent).

• **Too cozy.** Even if you insist the property will serve as a primary residence, a conventional mortgage is unlikely to be available if the cottage is just a

CAUTION: If the bank won't touch it with a 10-foot pole, maybe you shouldn't either

We would be remiss if we didn't state one caveat: If a banker is too nervous to accept a particular property as collateral for a loan, then you owe it to yourself and your family to make sure you aren't placing your financial security at serious risk. It's technically possible to borrow every nickel necessary to acquire a vacation property. But in the process, if you've mortgaged your primary residence to the hilt *(see p.152)*, you might be overexposing yourself financially.

Vacation property values have been strong in recent years, but as with any real estate sector, there can be reversals – many of them localized, many of them temporary. However, if such a reversal coincides with an unexpected development in your own life, such as a job loss, you could find yourself in a difficult situation. Restructuring your finances would be difficult if a substantial piece of your main equity (your home) is pledged as security for a loan that funded a vacation property which has dropped in value or proves difficult to sell.

wee bit too cozy. Standards vary, but many jurisdictions have minimum size requirements. (Routinely, the hammer drops on buildings less than about 720–750 square feet with a basement, or less than 1,000 square feet without one.) Some lenders will also look for at least one bedroom. Even if the cottage is being used to secure a collateralized loan rather than a conventional mortgage, the bank is probably going to want to see a building no smaller than 600 square feet. Another potential difficulty is a property in which the value essentially lies in the land, not the building, although cottage lots can be used to secure loans.

• **Too rustic.** Conventional mortgages generally aren't available to properties without some kind of central heating system and electrical service of at least 60 amps.

• **Too remote.** Yep, the perfect quality in a cottage is just about the worst thing for a property on which you want to place a conventional mortgage. In a lender's terms, "remote" means sufficiently isolated that it lacks an identifiable real estate market, making an accurate appraisal to set the lending value difficult.

• **Too pristine.** Any building that falls within an area designated in some way as "environmentally sensitive" gives the conventional mortgage fraternity the willies.

• **Too historic.** If your eye happens to be caught by a designated historical building, no conventional mortgage for you, my discerning friend.

• **Too distinctive.** Banks really hate adventurous architecture. And not just houses shaped like giant shoes, or ones built from salvaged sheet metal 40 feet off the ground in a tree. While this is a pretty subjective area, real estate appraisers get the whim-whams (similar to the willies) when they encounter a structure that's just a little too "out there." You may have an architect for a brother-in-law who thinks the perfect thing for you to build on your newly purchased waterfront lot is a crinkled-titanium tribute to the genius of Frank Gehry, but the bank may beg to disagree if you're thinking of getting a conventional mortgage. They may go for it, but only at a low loan-to-value ratio. Similar complications may arise if you try to collateralize a loan with a distinctive design statement.

• **Right cottage, wrong location.** Any number of circumstances can lead a bank to decline to issue a conventional mortgage on a first-class structure. For instance, suppose you buy a 100-acre backlot property with a 4,500-square-foot retreat. It's close to a public boat launch – but happens to be across from a dairy farm. The bank will have trouble imagining that enough similarly minded potential purchasers – people who want a luxury retreat and can tolerate farm odors – exist to create a resale market, and is unlikely to issue a conventional mortgage unless there's a low loan-to-value ratio.

TIP:

Can you afford the monthly payment?

Want to quickly get a sense of what your monthly payments would be for a loan or mortgage of a certain amount? You'll find numerous interest rate calculators on the Internet, and most word-processing packages these days come equipped with a home-finance template. In the popular Microsoft Office suite, look under "Project Gallery," under the File menu. Then under the "New" tab, go to "Home Essentials" in "Groups." You'll find a "Home Finance" selection, and that opens a gallery of templates, including "Loan Calculator" and "Standard Loan." Play around with these – you can set the interest rate, principal borrowed, borrowing (amortization) period, and number of payments per year.

American taxpayers for whom interest on the loan is tax deductible can see exactly how much interest will be claimable at different periods of the loan.

Other forms of financing

After reading this chapter so far, you're probably thinking that banks are spoilsports, expecting every cottage property to conform to the conventional. Fear not: Just because your dream cottage has one or more of the factors described above doesn't mean a bank won't lend you money to buy it. There are ways to finance your cottage purchase that *don't* require a conventional mortgage or using the cottage as collateral.

So celebrate *la différence*, sharpen your pencil, and start thinking a little more unconventionally about financing. And don't get hung up on the idea that being unable to secure a conventional mortgage means you're being forced to resort to less-desirable options. In many ways, the options can be superior.

Use your home as collateral to secure cottage financing

If you already own a principal residence when you begin shopping for a vacation home, the equity you have in that residence is a powerful lever in securing financing for a vacation home. It is, in fact, the best source of funds you have. You're unlikely to secure a loan with better interest rates, even using the vacation property itself as collateral. And if the principal residence serves as the underlying security for the vacation property purchase, there's no need to make the purchase measure up to the lending criteria that apply to a purchase where the financed property serves as its own collateral.

Leveraging the equity in the homestead has been one of the great financing revolutions of recent consumer history. As real estate values steadily marched upward and mortgage balances steadily retreated with each payment, the average North American homeowner began building an impressive war chest of high-quality equity. Unlike a strong stock portfolio, a portion of which can be sold off to realize cash, you can't sell a chunk of your house to release the equity. You can, however, employ that equity as desirable collateral in order to borrow money.

Homeowner equity is tapped essentially in two ways: by refinancing a first mortgage, or by taking out what amounts to a second mortgage by pledging a portion of the equity as collateral for a loan, which can include a personal line of credit. In both cases, you gain considerable freedom.

Because your main residence's equity is serving as the security for your borrowing, not only are you able to borrow at favorable rates, but you can also spend the funds on whatever you want. The bank doesn't care what you're buying, because what you're buying isn't serving as security for the loan. The bank only cares that you can service the resulting debt with the required monthly payments. As a result, people hankering after a vacation property that falls well short of conventional mortgage guidelines – the island and seasonal-access properties, the small rustic cabins, the empty

Using other assets as collateral

Banks will accept things other than real estate to collateralize loans, including stocks, bonds, and other securities. The highest-quality securities for collateral purposes are ones with an absolute value: investment certificates, treasury bills, savings bonds, and other quality instruments with a set maturity and worth. (These can be used to collateralize loans at 100 percent of their value.) Less attractive are shares in public companies, which have virtually no nominal value and depend on the whims of the stock market. Your bank probably will accept them in some form of margin. Fine art and family heirlooms, however, are generally considered too volatile in value to serve as security.

lots, the crinkled-titanium tributes to Frank Gehry built in the midst of moose pasture – can buy whatever they want without getting a banker's or a real estate appraiser's approval of it.

Option #1: Refinancing

Let's say you own a home with an appraised value of $300,000, on which $50,000 remains to be paid off on your existing mortgage. That leaves you with $250,000 in equity. The bank might consider remortgaging your home up to 95 percent of its appraised value, or $285,000. Because $50,000 still remains to be paid, the total new borrowing available is $235,000. Provided you qualify to make the payments on a mortgage of this size, you can use these funds as you wish, because the debt has been secured by your home.

(Technically, you could borrow everything you need to purchase a vacation property under this scenario. If the cottage you are interested in is actually $245,000, a separate loan facility could be negotiated for the $10,000 shortfall. As always, this is provided you meet the main lender's debt-carrying requirements.)

Remortgaging is often considered more attractive than using the available equity to secure a second mortgage. That's because a second mortgage, having a lesser claim on the underlying security than the first, commands a higher interest rate.

However, if there is a significant difference between the interest rate on the first mortgage and the current market rates, a borrower might not want to interfere with the first mortgage. For example, if the first mortgage has an interest rate of four percent and current rates are six or seven percent, the homeowner might choose to leave the first mortgage alone and create a second mortgage for the cottage purchase. (*See next page.*)

In any event, refinancing would require a "blended" mortgage, in which the existing first mortgage and the equity to be added to it in a replacement mortgage require the interest rates applicable to the first-mortgage and to the new borrowing to be merged into a single applicable rate. Very simply put, an original mortgage rate of 5 percent and a current

TIP:

Terminology: A "home equity" loan here is not a "home equity" loan there

In Canada, second-mortgage products are often known as "home equity" loans. For tax purposes in the U.S. "home equity" loans are defined not by how they're secured, but by how they're *employed*. If some form of loan collateralized by the main home is used to acquire, build, or improve a designated second home, such as a cottage, the interest charges retain their "home acquisition" tax deductibility. Otherwise, the loan is considered to be for personal use and is categorized as a "home equity" loan, in which case the tax deductibility on the interest paid is limited to a maximum borrowing of $100,000 (if married and filing jointly; $50,000 if filing separately).

market rate of 7 percent could result in a final mortgage rate of 6 percent. The exact rate blend depends on factors such as the relative sizes of the new and old borrowings and their terms.

In the case of declining rates, a blended mortgage can work to your advantage by reducing borrowing costs on your primary residence while providing the funds to purchase the secondary one. But every refinancing situation is unique, and depends on many factors beyond interest rates, including possible restrictions or penalties on refinancing a current mortgage. And there will be tax implications for Americans because of the regulations affecting the deductibility of interest costs on mortgages and home equity loans. (*See "Mortgage Interest Deductibility for American Buyers," p. 157.*)

Option #2: A second mortgage

With a second mortgage, equity is used to collateralize either a loan of a spe-

Working with a line of credit

The line of credit's flexibility makes it an ideal tool for cottage purchases, even if it isn't the entire source of financing. One significant benefit is the way you can use it to customize your borrowing and repayments, making useful distinctions between the purchases or expenses you're funding.

Let's say you qualify for a $200,000 secured line of credit (LOC). You need $140,000 to fund the purchase of the cottage, leaving $60,000 unused. You should be able to have your bank subdivide the total available borrowing into as many separate facilities as you require, without cost, and with no difference in interest rates, as they're all secured by the same collateral: the equity in the main home.

Each line of credit facility exists as its own bank account. In this scenario, Account 1 is used to fund the cottage purchase, against which you draw the $140,000. While a conventional mortgage can have a term as long as 30 years, if you decide you want to structure the payments to have the cottage paid off in, say, 15 years, all you need is a do-it-yourself payment schedule. If the LOC's current interest rate is 5 percent, a quick loan calculation (done on a PC; *see Tip, p. 151*) tells you that you need to assign $1,107.11 per month to payments against the balance of Account 1 to do so.

You will probably also have several other expense categories for the cottage, which is where the different credit facilities created with the line of credit come in handy. Furnishings might require an account with a total available draw of $10,000. A boat and motor might require an account with a draw of $20,000. A new dock calls for an account with a draw of $5,000.

For U.S. taxpayers, there are good tax reasons for isolating the interest expenses on distinctive borrowings: Interest on LOC funds used to pay for things that don't qualify as an acquisition, construction, or improvement of the main or second home are treated as "home equity" debt (*see Tip, p. 153*), and face restrictions on maximum permitted tax deductibility of interest. The LOC you use to build a new dock, for example, may qualify under the "home acquisition" category, if it can be shown to be a "substantial" improvement to the property. But another LOC you use to buy furniture falls into the "home equity" borrowing category. And if you started out by buying undeveloped land, the interest costs on a dedicated LOC may be eligible for deduction as an investment expense.

Beyond these tax implications, you want to split up various purchase categories into their own LOC accounts because they're different kinds of assets, with different depreciation rates. Only the cottage is going to appreciate,

cific size or a line of credit on which you can draw. You will pay a slightly higher rate than on a first mortgage, but for valued customers the difference might be only half a percentage point. A second mortgage can, in fact, be a cheaper source of money than securing a loan for a cottage with the cottage itself.

(Of course, if you own your main home outright, such a loan would be a first mortgage; you would just use the borrowed funds to purchase the cottage.)

Using some form of second mortgage to finance a cottage purchase has a number of advantages over refinancing a first mortgage, despite the slightly higher interest rate. For one thing, if it takes the form of a line of credit, it's far more flexible. You only borrow what you need, and repayment terms can range from a certain percentage of the outstanding balance per month to simply servicing the interest charges. You can pay it down in

and because of the large borrowing attached to it, you naturally want to take longer to pay it off. But furnishings don't deserve to have money borrowed for years on end, nor should a boat or a dock. These should be paid down more aggressively, to avoid the classic pitfall of LOCs: undisciplined borrowing. People often run up the LOC with a series of purchases and make minimal monthly payments. Only when the LOC is fully drawn do they try to attack the outstanding balance, and as that balance drops, room for new borrowing opens up. The problem here is that they've created an initial lump of borrowing that is never really retired.

If you use an LOC indiscriminately, without identifying the specific assets within it, the facility can turn into a bottomless pit of borrowing, in which you can end up spending 12 years paying off a gas barbecue without really being aware of it.

In the above case, we might decide that furnishing purchases must be paid down in two years (or sooner, with some items), the dock and the boat in five years. Because some of these facilities aren't going to be drawn down with a single purchase, you should manage every significant purchase as best you can, by recording its purchase date,

Sample spreadsheet:
Using a line of credit to buy cottage furnishings

Purchase date	Item	Cost	Payment period	Payment (int. rate 5%)	Total interest
June 2005	sofa	$400	2 years	$17.55	$21.17
April 2006	kitchen lights	220	6 months	37.20	3.22
July 2007	bunk bed	800	2 years	35.10	42.33
Total current monthly payments:				**$89.85**	

assigning it a term in which to pay it off, and calculating a monthly payment. (*See sample spreadsheet.*)

With this approach, these items, totaling $1,420 in value, generate total interest payments of $66.72. But if they're paid down as part of a single facility over a 15-year period, they would generate interest charges of $601.27. You would still be paying interest on a sofa that you probably got rid of five years before the payments stopped. You can see why banks love lines of credit.

Unless a line of credit is managed in a disciplined fashion, the interest costs relative to the value of the purchased items can be ridiculous. Using a spreadsheet and separate facilities allows you to impose discipline on spending, and live to an appropriate budget when borrowing to pay for assets that have different lifespans.

TIP:

Move to the cottage, and you might be able to move the mortgage with you

If you invested in the cottage as a future retirement home and have now chosen to sell your main residence and relocate to the cottage, you could be eligible to transfer (or "port") the first mortgage to the cottage with you without penalty – provided the cottage meets the bank's main-residence standards and loan-to-value ratio requirements. If this is your plan, you should discuss the financial implications with your lender right up front, at the time of the cottage's purchase.

whole or in part whenever you like, without penalty, unlike a conventional mortgage. If cash flow becomes a temporary issue, you can lower your payments to the monthly minimum, without having to go cap in hand to the banker, as you would to change the terms of a conventional mortgage.

The downside of using your primary residence for collateral

One of the foremost reasons people avoid this financing route if they have other options available is that they prefer not to have their cottage finances tangled up with those of their main residence. Even if they end up with a higher interest rate, some people just sleep better knowing they still have a large, unencumbered lump of equity in their main home.

That aside, you might want to think twice about employing equity in your main home as collateral for a cottage loan if there's a chance you might move to a new home after buying the cottage. In a worst-case scenario, your lender might not allow you to transfer the first mortgage on your old home to your new home because of the complication of the cottage loan. You could end up paying a discharge fee on the old mortgage, having to requalify for the total lending amount, and paying a registration fee on a new mortgage.

To sleep better at night, before you use collateral in your home to fund a cottage purchase, you should map out with your lender what might happen if and when you sell your home.

Financing land

Can you borrow money to buy land or a cottage lot, using the land as collateral? Yes, but it won't be a conventional mortgage. Banks will consider collateralizing a loan with the land, but expect to incur an interest rate higher than for a conventional mortgage, a much shorter borrowing term, and a low loan-to-value ratio, although some banks will offer loan-to-value ratios as high as 75 percent, depending on the property.

It helps if you have immediate plans to build when approaching banks about the financing options. Some banks offer construction loan plans, in which you are given an approved maximum for a project, and the bank releases the required payments to the contractor either on receipt of an invoice or on a percentage-of-completion basis as work proceeds. (*See Chapter 8 for info on claiming an interest deduction in the U.S. for funds borrowed to buy undeveloped land.*)

Large acreages, however, can be tricky as collateral. You might buy 100 acres (about 40 hectares) of former farmland, but a bank may only be willing to consider the market value of 10 acres (4 hectares) of it as security. That's because you're unlikely to be able to sever the acreage into a number of building lots with their own resale potential.

Mortgage interest deductibility for American buyers

Mortgage interest payments are tax deductible by American taxpayers, and can be claimed for two residences. And the IRS's definition of a residence is pretty flexible: It's any sort of accommodation, anywhere in the world, with some kind of kitchen, toilet, and sleeping facilities. That includes mobile homes, house trailers, and boats – so a cottage is pretty easy to have qualify as a first or second residence.

You have to designate one home as your "main home," and the other as your "second home." The main home is the one you live in most of the time. You don't even have to occupy the second home during the tax year in order to claim it. However, if you rent out the property, you have to occupy it yourself for at least 14 days of the year, or 10 percent of the total time

---

Q & A:

Can we claim the deduction?

Q: Does my second home have to be in the U.S. to qualify for mortgage interest deductibility?

A: No. American taxpayers can claim as their first or second home any qualifying property, anywhere in the world. This naturally means that you can buy or build a cottage in Canada and claim it as one of your homes for tax purposes.

Q: My spouse and I file separate tax returns. Can we each claim both a first and a second home?

A: The IRS says every married couple gets a maximum of one first and one second home, whether they file separate or joint returns. Each spouse can only claim the interest deduction on one of those homes. If you file separately, it's permitted for one spouse to claim the interest deductions available for both properties, an important strategy if one spouse's income triggers limitations.

Q: My bank doesn't think the cottage I want to buy measures up for a conventional first mortgage. Can I collateralize a second mortgage with my main home in order to finance the purchase of my second home, and still get my full deduction for a "home acquisition" loan?

A: The tax code requires that interest deducted for acquisition purchases be secured by a qualifying property, and not by other assets. It does allow a loan properly secured by one qualifying property to fund the acquisition of another qualifying property. So, yes, you can use some kind of secured loan on the main home to fund the acquisition (or construction or improvement) of the second home.

---

it is rented out, whichever is longer, in order for it to still qualify as a second home.

Two basic kinds of debt are covered by mortgage interest deductibility: *home acquisition debt* and *home equity debt*. Home acquisition debt is any borrowing used to buy, build, or "substantially improve" a home, and is secured by the home itself. (By "substantially improve," the IRS says the renovations must add to its value, prolong its useful life, or adapt it to new uses.) Home equity debt consists of any other borrowings secured by the home's equity. This commonly involves a line of credit used for purposes other than making substantial improvements to the house – such as paying for a vacation, funding a child's college education, refinancing credit-card debt or a car loan, or just making ends meet between paydays.

For home acquisition debt, a qualifying taxpayer can claim interest payment on all loans on all qualifying properties up to a combined value of $1 million ($500,000 if filing separately from your spouse). With home equity debt, the maximum permitted total loan value for the claimed properties is $100,000 ($50,000 if filing separately). But both maximums are subject to how much "grandfathered" debt you have, and other conditions. And your home-acquisition borrowing is limited to the cost of your home plus the cost of any improvements permitted under this debt category. Anything beyond that is home equity debt.

The actual fascinating calculations can be explained to you by your accountant, or slogged through in IRS Publication 936, "Home Mortgage Interest Deduction."

Smart owners start saving right away

Congratulations! You've signed the papers, turned over the certified check, and are now the happy owners of the cottage of your dreams. It's time to relax, enjoy the lake – and start saving.

Not money. Paperwork. A complete collection of receipts for all cottage purchases, upgrades, improvements, and repairs – not to mention service records and owner's manuals for cottage equipment – will serve you in good stead when you ultimately pass the cottage down to your kids, sell it, or rent it. *(See Tip, p. 200, and "How to Build a Cottage Operating Manual," p. 208.)*

10. Sharing a cottage

I n considering the cost of a particular property, along with the limited time you have to use it, you may be struck with the inspired idea of getting friends or family to join with you, pooling your resources to buy a property none of you might be able to afford alone. You share not only the upfront costs, but also the ongoing expenses – as well as the work required to keep the place running.

Co-ownership is a viable option for acquiring a vacation property, but it does require like-minded individuals and some realistic legal forethought. And no legal document, of course, can avert or resolve all potential flashpoints of human behavior.

Prerequisites for success

Co-ownership with friends might seem a high-risk proposition. Friendships don't always last a lifetime, and these relationships lack the peculiarly resilient glue that allows blood relations to go through Hades together and back. Nevertheless, co-ownerships don't have to be seen as a "till-death-do-us-part" undertaking. They can be an effective way for people to get their feet in the door of cottage ownership. After a few years in a co-owned property, they might decide to cash in their equity and purchase a property of their own. The whole co-ownership might be terminated after a few years, as one co-owner assumes complete ownership and the others seek their own cottages.

Co-ownership is often a consequence of bequest, of parents handing down the family retreat to their children. We'll deal specifically with bequest issues in Chapter 14, including the strategies for minimizing financial and legal problems. For now, let's consider the prerequisites for successful co-ownership.

They boil down to one word: compatibility. People who share ownership and use of a property also need to have a shared vision for it. This includes both how the property is to be used, and what its future nature might be.

Needed: A compatible vision for how the property will be used

Co-ownerships can founder because of incompatible visions of what a vacation property is for. One owner might see it as a quiet, contemplative retreat, a place to admire sunsets, catch up on reading, and paddle a canoe. The other owner might see it as party central, a place for huge bonfires and multiple motorized watercraft. Not even a bulletproof legal agreement spelling out who gets to use the cottage when might save this owner partnership. Even if they don't ever inhabit the property at the same time, the "quiet" owner is going to end up catching flak from the unhappy neighbors who don't appreciate the other's antics.

Differences in vision can arise as children of co-owners grow up. One co-owner might feel it's okay for their 18 year old to have the place to himself and his friends for a weekend. The other might be adamantly opposed to leaving anyone's teenagers in charge.

One owner's vision might include occasionally renting the place out to improve the bottom line – while the other wants no part of an income-producing property. Both sides may even agree that the property is not going to be used formally as a rental unit, but then one owner realizes she can't make it to the cottage for a certain week and decides it's okay if she lets a friend or coworker use it in exchange for some cash that she wants to apply to her share of the property taxes. She doesn't think this is really "renting the place out," but the other owner is entitled to disagree when she learns a total stranger has been sleeping in her bed.

Needed: A compatible vision for change

As for "future nature," the owners need a compatible vision of the property's character. You might be happy with a rustic retreat, but your co-owners might be thinking "tear down" or "winterize" or "new boathouse with sleeping space for six guests."

An agreement can – in fact, must – cover how costs are going to be shared, but the agreement isn't going to be much help if the parties can't at the same time agree on what constitutes "necessary improvements." And co-owners must be prepared for the reality of changes in financial status. One party may fall on hard times; the other might develop the financial wherewithal to pursue renovations that his co-owners cannot afford.

Co-owners will face other changes in their lives, too – the arrival or departure of children, divorce, or a job change that takes one family far from the cottage. As a result, they have to agree (and spell out in a legal agreement) what the rights and obligations of co-owners are in such situations. (*See "Co-ownership Agreements: Dealing with the What-Ifs," p. 168.*)

Co-ownership structures

Co-ownership of a property can be organized in two basic ways:

1. joint tenancy or tenancy in common (*see Tip, at right*)

2. a legal entity such as a partnership, trust, or not-for-profit corporation.

Typically, a home is owned through joint tenancy or tenancy in common, with both spouses (or other owners) named in the title deed as well as in any mortgage. Such a simple arrangement can also be used successfully in multiple-owner cottages. All the investors can be named in the deed as co-owners, and they can all sign any mortgage attached to it (*though see "Financing the Purchase," next page*). The co-owners can then agree to the ground rules of usage and finances in a co-ownership agreement.

For many legal and financial reasons, it may make more sense to organize ownership within a framework such as a limited partnership, a trust,

TIP:
The type of tenancy matters

While joint tenancy and tenancy in common are much the same when it comes to the actual ownership of cottage property, they do differ when it comes to passing along title to a property should one of the co-owners die. In the case of joint tenancy, title to the property automatically passes to the surviving owners without becoming part of an estate. (This avoids the expense of probate, but means a joint tenant can't bequeath his share of the property.) With tenants in common, ownership passes to the deceased's estate, and is bequeathed subject to the terms of a will.

TIP: **They may be your friends or family, but think of them as your business partners**

However it's structured, treat a co-ownership like a business partnership. For starters, you should have a written agreement in place that sets out the terms of ownership, provides a method for ongoing decision-making, and addresses major questions, such as what happens in the case of divorce or nonpayment of fees. (*See "Co-ownership Agreements: Dealing with the What-Ifs," p. 168.*) You'll also need someone to take on a management role – to oversee the time-allocation process, deal with income and expenses, and chair the meetings. (And, yes, you'll want occasional meetings; *see Tip, p. 165.*) If the co-ownership is in the form of a limited partnership, trust, or non-profit corporation, the management structure may be dictated by the legal structure. Otherwise, the management job can rotate from year to year.

or a not-for-profit corporation – some legal entity in which the property is not owned in the name of the individual investors. This option has some disadvantages, mainly in the area of the expenses of registration and meeting accounting requirements and tax filings. But there are significant advantages as well:

• Foremost is a partnership's or corporation's limitations on individual liability and protection of the co-owned asset from actions of creditors of a co-owner. If one owner in a traditional joint tenancy/tenancy in common co-ownership arrangement is pursued by creditors, the vacation property could be seized by them to satisfy debts wholly unrelated to the property.

• There may be tax advantages to these ownership structures for the individual investors, although this depends entirely on the jurisdiction, the tax circumstances of each investor, and how much the cottage is used as an income property.

Issues in co-ownership

Financing the purchase

Mortgages can be complex in co-ownerships. As an example, there could be a single conventional mortgage to which all co-owners are cosignatories, and their obligations in paying it down are proportionate to their ownership interest. That doesn't necessarily mean everyone pays a share of the

CAUTION: Do you plan to rent the co-owned cottage?

On both sides of the border, rental activity – either by the group as a whole or by individuals of their own time blocks – can have taxation consequences.

In Canada, for instance, if one co-owner in a partnership decides to rent out his allotted blocks and operate his interest as a rental business, this changes the nature of the property and affects capital gains reportage.

U.S. tax law is not absolutely clear on how rental activity affects mortgage interest deductibility in the case of multiple owners. Unless the co-owners have banded together to purchase the cottage mainly as an income property, they are likely able to meet collectively the minimum annual personal-usage test that permits the deduction (at least 14 days, or 10 percent of the total days rented out, whichever is higher). But the issue can be complicated when an ownership arrangement permits individual owners to rent out their allotted blocks of time and keep the revenue for themselves and the property *overall* meets the personal-use test for interest deductibility, but an individual owner's usage does not.

Bottom line? Get professional tax advice if you're purchasing with partners and plan to rent out the property.

monthly bill in proportion to their stated interest. It's possible for four people to agree to acquire a $200,000 cottage, making them each responsible for $50,000 of its cost. One partner might pay $40,000 in cash; two others might put down $20,000 and $10,000 respectively, while the fourth owner might have no equity to contribute at all. This results in a $130,000 mortgage with a $70,000 down payment. At 5 percent interest over 20 years, that creates a monthly payment of $857.94. The payments would work out per partner as follows:

Partner 1 (*$40,000 down payment*): $65.99
Partner 2 (*$20,000 down payment; $30,000 financed*): $197.99
Partner 3 (*$10,000 down payment, $40,000 financed*): $263.98
Partner 4 (*zero down payment, $50,000 financed*): $329.98

Is this a good arrangement? Fundamentally, no. The partners who put in most of the equity have no more claim on the property under their agreement than the ones who contributed less initially. And spreading out the amortization period to make the purchase affordable for partners 3 and 4 likely means that partners 1 and 2 are paying more interest than they would have if they'd financed their debt obligations on their own, over a shorter period.

Another potential problem is the exposure of the property to seizure by debtors of the partners with less initial equity, should they run into financial problems elsewhere in their life.

The co-ownership would be much simpler if each partner arranged his or her own financing to acquire the money needed for the acquisition, and the partnership paid cash for the cottage. This way, the property is left clear of shared debts.

Who gets to use it when?

This is the main issue with multiple-owner properties, and percentage ownership is the simplest way of dividing the time. The trick then becomes figuring out who gets which blocks.

Not all blocks are created equal: In seasonal getaways, height-of-season weeks attached to holiday long weekends are always going to be the most appealing. Every partnership can come to its own solution, but here's a basic approach:

• Divide the vacation season into the most appropriate blocks of time. Depending on the number of partners, a block could be an entire month, single weeks, or even days and weekends.

• If the property is co-owned by family or close friends and space permits, the block distribution might begin with setting aside joint holiday times, in which owners share the property. The remaining blocks are then distributed for individual use. (It's possible, with a small number of co-owners who

TIP:

Be flexible when divvying up cottage time

A rigid co-ownership risks failure if it cannot accommodate the special circumstances of its participants. Some partners may have strict limitations on when they can take their vacations – a scheduled plant shutdown, for example, or school holidays. Others may have special circumstances in certain years that need to be worked around. A partnership that hopes to survive long-term and in good humor needs to be able to accommodate the "human factor."

know each other well, to divvy up the usage blocks without a highly formalized process.)

• Since some blocks are more desirable than others, making sure there is a fair distribution every year is crucial to the success of the co-ownership. If rights to blocks are held equally, a lottery could be used for determining the initial selection order, much like a draft-pick system of a sports league. With every year, the selection order can rotate. The problem here is that if a cottage has, say, six co-owners, the most desirable summer blocks can be gone by the time the fifth or sixth pick comes along, and if you are unfortunate enough to draw the sixth pick in the initial year, it will be six years before you move into the top spot. Consider instead using a system that creates more rapid rotation in the selection order from one year to the next. For example, instead of the winner of the initial lottery beginning the picking first, second, third, fourth, fifth, and last over the course of six years, have the pick positions shift by two. *(See the sample picking chart, below.)*

• If ownership is not held equally, then the selection process becomes more complicated. A partner with 40 percent of the equity is going to be entitled to 40 percent of the available time. Deciding how they get to select, without having them dominate the most desirable periods, requires careful planning. The simplest method is to create a set of "pick positions," and divvy up those positions according to the number of pick rights each person's equity entitles them to. In the case of a co-ownership being divided into equities of 40, 20, 20, 20, there would be five pick positions to rotate through, with the largest equity interest holding two of them.

• To make the distribution more equitable with numerous partners, you may wish to designate certain highly desired blocks as "hot zones," and no one can secure more than one hot-zone block until everyone has been able to make a selection in a hot zone. (This would occur over the course of two or more seasons, or within the same season if someone has more than one "pick position," as above.)

Choosing time slots: A sample picking chart

Initial Draw	Year 1	2	3	4	5	6
Partner 1	1	3	5	2	4	6
Partner 2	2	4	6	1	3	5
Partner 3	3	5	2	4	6	1
Partner 4	4	6	1	3	5	2
Partner 5	5	2	4	6	1	3
Partner 6	6	1	3	5	2	4

• If the number of partners doesn't divide equally into the number of available weeks, consider setting aside the extra block (or blocks) as a rental period for which the co-ownership shares the revenues, or permit a co-owner to "rent" the extra week and use the funds to reduce the collective expenses. Another possibility is to assign odd blocks in the calendar to property "down time," and use them to take care of maintenance.

• Set some ground rules about slot trading. Can it occur in the midst of the selection process? Are individual partners permitted to lock up consecutive blocks of time, particularly at the height of the season?

• If the co-ownership intends for the cottage to serve in part as an income property, some method of setting aside rental periods might be required. The choice depends on whether rental income is to be pooled, or if the rental right remains with individual owners for their blocks of time. If it is to be pooled, and rental income is critical to the co-ownership's bottom line, the distribution of blocks should begin with an agreement on which blocks (and how many) should be set aside for rental, before divvying up the available times among co-owners. If the rental right is an individual one, co-owners are free to rent out any of the blocks they secure, subject to general agreements on how much rental activity the partners agree to allow.

How will expenses be divided?

You need a clear understanding of what the shared costs are, and what expenses are to be individually shouldered. Every co-ownership needs to come to its own resolution of how to deal with this, including who pays the bills and ensures all the co-owners remit their share of the expenses promptly.

The simplest strategy is to divide shared costs such as property taxes, utilities, maintenance (including roads and docks), and capital costs (including major repairs and renovations) according to equity interest. However, payment according to actual individual usage is sometimes employed as well, if a feasible system can be arranged. If, say, one partner has the cottage for all of July, he can be responsible for the phone and electricity bills for that month. Some co-ownerships – particularly those involving large properties used by multiple owners at the same time – assess an annual fee per owner to cover fixed costs (such as taxes, utilities, and major capital expenses), plus a per diem charge for the time each person spends on the property, to cover other expenses such as maintenance.

One way to deal with expenses is to have the co-owners essentially "rent" their blocks of time from the group. You have to begin with a good sense of what the annual operating expenses for the property are, and use the total as the basis for setting usage rates for the blocks. The number of block entitlements still depends on the proportion of a co-owner's interest in the property. Each co-owner remits to the group the "rent" that his number of blocks demands. These payments are then used to handle the operating expenses. At the end of the year, any operating deficit has to be addressed in proportion to the individual's interest in the property. If there is a surplus, it can either be carried forward (depending on the legal structure) to address the next year's expenses (thus possibly reducing the next year's rent), or distributed back to the co-owners in the appropriate ownership proportions.

TIP:
Hold budget meetings
Each year, hold a meeting – the dead of winter is a great time – to take stock of the cottage's financial standing and to plan and budget for any building projects or maintenance chores that need to be addressed the coming summer. Always build some leeway into the budget for unexpected expenses.

TIP: What about boats?

A common solution at shared cottages is to designate one boat for use by all and sundry and share all the associated costs. (With water-access cottages, a shared runabout is a necessity if you don't want to pay for multiple slips at the local marina.) Beyond that, if one of the owners feels a competition bass boat is critical to cottage enjoyment – a sentiment not shared by the other partners – then he should purchase the boat separately and the others shouldn't expect to use it.

TIP:
Money in the bank

Most cottage co-ownerships set up a separate bank account to pay communal bills and expenses, keeping the account topped up to a predetermined amount each year, according to the anticipated level of annual expenses.

Tracking and remitting expenses is made more complicated by rental activity. Co-ownerships that do casual or "hobby" renting often allow their individual owners to make their own rental deals and keep the money. If the property is held in a corporation or a limited partnership, this may not be practical. But in the case of American taxpayers, rentals of homes totaling less than 15 days a year don't require the income to be reported, and so the tracking of expenses for tax purposes becomes less onerous.

Changes in ownership

Co-owners should take as much care to ensure they don't wind up with strangers as future partners as they do when choosing with whom to purchase at the start. Whatever the legal structure of the ownership, the governing co-ownership agreement requires clear parameters and processes for transfers of ownership within the group. (*For the circumstances co-owners need to consider, see "Co-ownership Agreements: Dealing with the What-Ifs," p. 168.*)

A lawyer well versed in co-ownership agreements can provide the most appropriate options for a given group of investors.

Where trouble lies

Starting out with a shared vision of how the property is to be used is key. But as time progresses, decisions on any number of matters must be made, ranging from whether to proceed with a renovation to whether to chip in with the neighbors to have the private road regraded. Unanimity is the ideal, but it's not always possible.

A co-ownership with two partners who can never agree is not long for this world, but others can soldier forward with majority agreements. For the practical reason that there are only so many available weeks of summer holidays to share, it's rare to have co-ownerships consisting of more than a half-dozen equal votes (unless the property is large enough, and the partners willing, to allow multiple owners to regularly use it at the same time). There's always the possibility that two out of six co-owners are consistently outvoted on matters important to them, but that is a hazard of multi-owner properties. If they're truly unhappy as a result, they can be bought out by the others, or their interest otherwise sold, according to the terms of the co-ownership agreement.

Over the long term, the mechanics of how decisions are made through voting processes are probably less important than the co-owners staying on the same page with respect to the property's nature and use. If one partner wants major renovations, a new ski boat, more rental activity – or conversely, if one partner doesn't want to proceed with renovations, thinks the old aluminum boat is fine, and is opposed to any rentals to outsiders – the ownership arrangement naturally will become strained.

Don't sweat the small stuff

Pettiness is one sure way to destroy a co-ownership. Gas for the communal boat may be a communal expense, but if you and the kids spend a full week fishing and water-skiing with it, the cost for that fuel should come out of your own pocket. It's not rocket science, it's common consideration. (And agree to always leave a full tank of gas for the next person. Nothing can get tempers flaring faster than to arrive and find the boat tank empty – nothing, that is, except finding the propane tank on the barbecue in the same state. *See Tip, p. 169.*)

Similarly, while the cost of construction materials is definitely a group expense, if you buy a $5 box of nails to fix the outhouse, does it really have to become a line item at the next budget meeting?

Play to the partners' strengths

Inequities in contributions of elbow grease when opening and closing the cottage, tending to maintenance, and taking on larger projects such as a re-roofing or dock construction can be a source of contention. Right off the

---

There's a difference between breakage and breakdown

It makes sense to share repair costs for things that break down from normal wear and tear. Repairs or replacements necessitated by the actions of an owner or his guests, on the other hand – the bent prop, say, from an encounter with a rock – should be the responsibility of that individual owner.

Common sense, you say? Yes, but therein lies the rub: Even if you put a provision to this effect in your co-ownership agreement (and you should), it won't prevent squabbles over whether a particular problem is the result of wear and tear – or operator error. (When, exactly, did that prop get dinged?)

This is where the goodwill of the co-owners comes into play: Maybe it wasn't entirely your fault – but you can still take the high road and offer to pay, knowing you're helping to keep the co-ownership on an even keel.

---

bat, at your yearly meeting, you should decide which projects will be hired out and budget accordingly.

For do-it-yourself tasks, it's important to play to the strengths of each partner and, above all, avoid placing a higher value on certain types of labor than others. If a couple of people in your group are dedicated hammer wielders with the skills necessary for major construction work, their contribution – though large and laborious – shouldn't necessarily be valued any more than the green thumb who dedicates time to landscaping and gardening, the plumbing whiz who takes command of pipes, or the foodie who runs the "chuckwagon" and keeps the troops fed and watered on work-bee weekends. Not all co-owners share the same skills, but if each owner makes a fair contribution to the group, to the best of his abilities, everyone benefits. Remember: You're all in this together.

Other common causes of discord

1. Differing housekeeping standards. A co-owner arrives to find the place left in a state he finds unacceptable by the co-owner who had the previous time block. Differing standards can sometimes be evened out by the co-ownership developing – as a group – a set of rules or a checklist for how the

TIP:

A clue to compatibility

Working through the what-ifs can be a useful guide to the compatibility of future co-owners: If you can't agree at the planning stage, then you may be in for some rough times once you're actually sharing.

Co-ownership agreements: Dealing with the what-ifs

Co-ownership agreements not only have to provide an orderly method for managing a multi-owner property, but they also have to expect the unexpected. A common co-ownership mistake is assuming that your friendship is so solid or your family ties so strong that you can rise above any worst-case scenarios. But even if you never have to consult the agreement, it's simply smart planning to have it.

Although you can draw up an agreement yourselves, a good lawyer will help you make sure you've addressed all the issues and cast the whole thing in watertight language. Here are some of the what-ifs you and your potential partners need to think about:

- If there's a divorce, where does the ex-spouse figure in the ownership? Has the ownership been structured to prevent a divorce from cleaving a share in two?

- Are limits placed on an owner's use of his equity in the property to collateralize other borrowings? (If not, you could end up with the bank as your partner if one of the owners defaults on a loan collateralized by his share of the cottage.)

property is to be left. But how will the co-ownership deal with a partner who refuses to follow the rules?

2. Offspring. Are teenaged children allowed to use the cottage without adult supervision? If the kids leave the place messy – or damage something – who is responsible? At what age are children considered adults and allowed unfettered access to the property?

3. Non-payment. Slow payment is an annoyance, but how will you deal with a partner who can't (or won't) pay his share of the basic bills? Will you allow him to rent out his time slot if it means saving the partnership? Does he have to be bought out?

4. Unauthorized purchases. How do you deal with a situation where one partner decides to buy, say, all new deck furniture because he or she felt the old ones were too crummy for words, then submits the bill to the group? Should the group refuse to pay and return the chairs? Or pay up and hold bitter grievances towards the unauthorized decorator?

5. New spouse with a different mindset. What happens if a new spouse is introduced to the co-ownership through divorce and holds views towards

TIP:

Little things mean a lot

Sometimes, even cottagers who can happily work around major legal, social, and financial entanglements in their quest for co-ownership can get worked into a frothy rage over seemingly small annoyances. The following are a few common flashpoints that can drive even the most level-headed partners nuts. Avoiding them can go a fair way towards keeping a co-ownership chugging smoothly along:

- Slovenly housekeeping
- Dirty laundry
- Empty boat gas tanks and broken propellers
- Food freeloaders who don't replace the staple items
- Propane or charcoal for the barbecue used up and not replaced
- Dead flashlight batteries
- No toilet paper!

- If one owner decides he wants to get out of the arrangement, what mechanisms are in place for dealing with his equity? Do the others have first right of refusal to buy this owner out? What if the others don't want or can't afford to buy him out? Can he sell to a third party? Can he force the sale of the property?

- Can one partner acquire more equity in the property than the others? Does majority ownership imply control over decisions about the property?

- Can a co-owner be forced out? On what grounds?

- If equity is changing hands, how will its value be determined? (For instance, you could agree to get two appraisals and if they don't agree, to average them.)

- How is inheritance addressed, particularly if the co-owners are not related?

- How do you deal with a non-performing partner? If a partner is unable or unwilling to pay, what recourse is available? (For instance, an agreement could state that a failure to pay within one year means the partner forfeits his share of the cottage and it is divided among the other partners; or that it triggers the sale of his share to the other partners.)

- Is there a provision for making changes to the agreement?

maintenance and upkeep that are radically different from those agreed to by the original partners – in other words, he doesn't want to contribute volunteer labor and would rather hire others to do the work. Do you force a capable do-it-yourselfer to pay for outside help? Do the original partners continue to make all their own improvements while the new partner doesn't lift a finger?

Not every dispute can be foreseen and protected against. As a result, a dispute resolution mechanism should be written into any co-ownership agreement, providing for arbitration where issues cannot be resolved.

Time–sharing and fractional ownership

So maybe you don't want to co-own a cottage with friends or family members, but because of limitations in your available vacation time – and perhaps your budget – you can't justify outright ownership of a property. Time-sharing and fractional ownership are two possible alternatives.

Time-sharing

With a time-share property, the user has no equity interest. A co-tenancy – perhaps 50 years – is provided on a lease basis to each user of the property.

TIP: Two books that will help keep a co-ownership running smoothly

When different owners are using the cottage at different times, information-sharing is essential – not just to prevent problems and misunderstandings, but also to create a shared cottage history. Two books can help you do this: a cottage logbook and a cottage operating manual.

The logbook records the details of each cottage stay – who was there, what the weather was like, interesting wildlife sightings, and what people did (work as well as play). Owners can use the logbook to bring each other up to date and alert the next visitor to developing problems and successful solutions. ("Aluminum boat hard to start – cleaned sparkplugs.")

An operating manual – which compiles all the information about how the cottage runs in one handy spot – is absolutely essential when you're sharing a cottage. See "The Owner's Best Friend: How to Build a Cottage Operating Manual *(p. 208)* for advice on what to include, but here is one tip especially for a shared property: Develop an end-of-stay checklist of what every owner should do before leaving the property, and put it at the front of your manual. This can go a long way towards ensuring the happiness of the person who arrives next.

The user will also pay a property management company a fee for overseeing all aspects of the operation. Most cottage time-shares operate along the same basic lines as the one below, which was launched recently in Ontario's cottage country and overseen by Midland, Ont. lawyer Fred Hacker:

• Every cottage unit, newly constructed for the purpose and fully furnished, has 10 co-tenants, each acquiring a 50-year leasehold interest, granting them five weeks of use per year. The cost was less than $50,000 per co-tenant.

• Each co-tenant receives a package of usage: one summer week, two "shoulder season" weeks (spring and fall), one "prime" winter week, and one "off-season" week.

Case study:

A solid friendship is no guarantee of a trouble-free co-ownership

Joyce and Liz were good friends, and so they were confident they could successfully go halfsies on a large piece of lakefront land with an old cabin. They drew up an agreement themselves, which stated (among other things) that if one of them wished to terminate the partnership, the other would have first option to buy her out for half the appraised value.

The first few summers went fairly smoothly, with Joyce and Liz alternating months but sharing occasional long weekends – despite a difference between them that soon became a sore point: Joyce was a fairly casual housekeeper, while Liz was decidedly more fastidious.

The blow-up came the summer Liz arrived to start her stay and opened the door on what she described as "a real mess" – which included used sheets on the bed. It seems Joyce, without Liz's knowledge, had rented out the cabin for part of her month and had neglected to check before Liz arrived that the renter had left it in order.

For Liz, that was the last straw. The two continued to share the place, but basically stopped talking and made sure their paths never crossed. After a year of this, Joyce decided to try to buy out Liz. Liz refused and, after getting her lawyer's advice that the agreement they had written themselves was vague and open to interpretation, she threatened to sell her half-stake to a stranger.

Eventually, Liz conceded, realizing that no one would want to share a cottage with an unwilling partner. But for a while, it looked as if *both* owners would be forced to sell.

How could this situation have been avoided? Joyce says she should have been more careful in her choice of partners and looked for a better match. But, as in any relationship, you'll never *really* know how quirks and idiosyncrasies will affect your partnership until you're in the thick of it. A better co-ownership agreement – one prepared with the advice and assistance of a lawyer so that its language didn't leave it open to dispute – would have helped. And most importantly, what was missing in this partnership was a willingness to work out difficulties to foster the relationship. As Joyce concluded, "When the goodwill is lost, it doesn't matter a whit what you've got in writing."

Time-share checklist

☐ How are the maintenance and service package fees set? What controls do the co-tenants have over them?

☐ What are the terms for re-selling or bequeathing the co-tenancy? How easy is it to exit the co-tenancy if you decide you're ready to own your own cottage outright?

☐ Can you rent out your allotted weeks, either on your own or through the management services company?

Fractional ownership checklist

☐ What are the annual fees and how are they set? What controls do the co-owners have over them?

☐ Is it possible to buy more than one share if you want to have more time or accommodate a larger number of people at the cottage?

☐ Check the local real estate market in the area. Because you are buying a share of a property – not just leasing a piece of a building – you need to determine whether your investment will appreciate in value or sink like a stone. Do the same homework you would if you were buying a traditional cottage.

☐ If you don't want to rent out any of your weeks, is it possible to opt out of the time-sharing program and its affiliated costs?

• Each cottage is occupied for 50 weeks of the year. Two weeks are set aside for significant annual maintenance.

• Like a self-contained resort, the cottages in the development share waterfront amenities.

• There is no need to do any work at the cottage. The co-tenants share in the ongoing costs of maintenance through a maintenance service package, which also provides supplies and housekeeping services between individual weeks of use.

• There is limited interaction among "co-owners." The responsibilities for maintenance, financial accounting, and organizing the usage times is left to a contracted third party.

Fractional ownership

A relative newcomer to the cottage scene, fractional ownership operates much the same as time-sharing in that each newly built, fully furnished cottage is divided into a number of shares (usually 10), thus making cottage acquisition much more affordable. The big difference is that while time-sharing buys you a leasehold interest in the building itself (not the land), with fractional ownership you are buying a piece of the cottage and the land it sits on. You actually own a piece of the development and are free to sell it on the open market or pass it down to future generations as you see fit.

• Fractional ownership scenarios vary widely, from around $60,000 for a one-tenth share of a smaller development to $200,000 for a one-quarter share of a larger property.

• All maintenance and upkeep is contracted out. Most developments also offer weekly cleaning and the use of a communal dock, clubhouse, and water toys.

• Ownership grants you legal membership to a "club" whose annual fees pay for maintenance, upkeep, cleaning, and all shared amenities such as clubhouses, docks, water toys, and swimming pool (if there is one).

• Many fractional ownership developments are affiliated with international time-share companies and you are automatically enrolled in their organization upon closing. (The fees are part of the purchase price.) This provides a mechanism where you can deposit unused weeks to be rented out for profit, with the management company taking care of the marketing.

11. Renting out your cottage

*E*ven if you've bought your place by the lake for your own pleasure, renting may still be an important component of your ownership strategy. (This book doesn't concern itself with cottages purchased purely or substantially as rental properties.) Here are a few situations in which renting can make sense:

• The sort of rates your property can command may tempt you to set aside enough weeks to cover most or all of the property tax bill, or help with loan payments. As property taxes have soared in some vacation areas, owners of places that have been in families for generations sometimes have no choice but to rent the cottage for part of the summer, just to cover the tax bill.

• You have friends or family members who want to use the place on their own, not as your guests, and it only seems fair to everyone that some contribution be made to cottage overheads.

• Whether because of travel, work, family pressures, or other demands on your time, you find yourself unable, even for a season or two, to get to the cottage as much as you'd like. Sometimes, for instance, there are a few difficult years, when a son or daughter in high school has a summer job and can't be left at home alone. The owners want to hang onto the cottage through this stretch, and choose to rent it out in the meantime.

• The cottage is shared by family members, and one member who can't use his or her allotted time chooses to rent it out for that period. (*See Chapter 10 for more on co-ownership.*)

• The owners plan to hand the cottage down to their children, but neither they nor the kids are really in a position at this point to use it. Generating some revenue from it in these idle years simply makes sense, rather than letting it sit empty, piling up expenses, or selling it outright.

• You may be coming to the conclusion that, for whatever reason, it's time to sell the cottage – but you can't quite bring yourself to do so yet, and choose instead to rent it out while making up your mind.

• The cottage is in the process of being sold, and is being rented while it's on the market.

Still, renting isn't for everyone. For most owners, a cottage is as private a space as their main home, and some will never be comfortable allowing even friends and relatives, never mind total strangers, to have the run of the place. For others, the demands on their time in dealing with renters and housekeeping aren't worth the income gained. And renting has hidden costs – such as general wear and tear – that shouldn't be overlooked.

TIP:
Renting gives your place a lived-in look
Income aside, security is another advantage to renting your cottage when you're not using it. An empty cottage is more likely to attract thieves and vandals than an occupied one.

Finding renters

Who will your renters be?
More than anything, how well you know the customers dictates how formal or informal the rental arrangement needs to be. Renting the place to your sister and her family for a week or two is a handshake deal. Renting to a total stranger is another matter altogether.

If you're only renting occasionally, you may prefer to avoid the "total stranger" route. Essentially, you're turning over your house to people you've never met. You don't know them, their kids, or their friends who might be dropping in. Your cottage contains things that are precious to you, not to mention just plain valuable. You also value your good relationship with your neighbors, and don't want it jeopardized by renters' antics. (Even when the renters are well behaved, it can be a source of stress to neighbors to have to meet a new cast of characters every week and pray they won't be holding late-night parties.)

If you are going into what we might call the casual renting business, one time-honored option is to limit the pool of renters to people you know personally, or at least to people who are recommended by someone you know well. Another is to turn the entire operation over to an accredited cottage rental agency. (*See p. 182.*)

The upside of dealing with friends is that the complications of renting diminish substantially. You can eliminate advertising, damage deposits, contracts – unless you're a real stickler – and a host of worries. Just remember the caveat regarding doing business with people you know. Renting your place to Fred in accounting can make for awkward boardroom meetings if Fred sets your deck on fire, blames your barbecue, and doesn't offer to pay for the damages. (Even a handshake deal should be accompanied by an understanding of who's responsible for damages.) And even in less-drastic situations, it can be difficult to tell friends afterwards that you're unhappy with the state of the property.

Getting the word out

If you have an attractive, road-access property within a reasonable driving distance of a major urban center and a limited number of weeks available for renting it, you may be able to fill all your slots with renters you know or who are recommended by someone you know just through word of mouth. (Even if your cottage is water access, finding renters may not be impossible, particularly if a nearby marina rents boats or offers water-taxi service.)

Talk to cottage owners who rent out on occasion, and you'll generally find they're able to be highly selective about the people they're willing to give free rein to their vacation retreats. The best rental arrangements involve people you know who want to come back every summer in the same time slot. You're comfortable with them, and they're comfortable with your property and have learned the routines of vacationing there.

If your immediate circle of friends doesn't yield enough rental prospects, here are some inexpensive marketing techniques that can help you get the word out:

• Your company may have a staff newsletter that accepts ads, and you can reach a lot of people in the right demographic at little or no expense.

• Talk to your lake's cottage association for leads, or put an ad in the association newsletter. Other cottagers on the lake are often looking for a neighboring property for friends or family to rent so they can have a holiday together. Tapping into the association's web of contacts can net renters who come with some pre-screening by fellow area cottage owners.

• Ask at the local marina where you do business. Other customers may have made inquiries on behalf of friends and family. Again, there's a certain level of pre-screening built in.

• Work the contacts available to you through professional associations, community groups, and sports teams: everything from your book club to the other parents on the sidelines at your kid's soccer games.

CAUTION:
Check your insurance policy

Insurance companies have been striving to reduce their exposure to payouts in recent years by excluding property coverage (including liability) when a cottage is rented out, even on a casual basis. Consequently, it is essential that you confirm with your insurer that you are still covered when a renter is on site. Take heart: Even if your current provider won't offer it, insurance that covers rental usage can be found. You may need to shop around, but the coverage does exist, and renting without it is unthinkable.

TIP:

Setting the price

A bit of research on-line or in print publications will help you determine the going rate for cottages like yours. As with buying a cottage, location is the key factor affecting price, but the number of bedrooms (large cottages are in big demand), amenities (such as a dishwasher), and extras (such as a hot tub and canoe) can up the ante. And of course you can ask more in prime vacation periods and around holidays (such as Christmas and New Year's).

If you're tempted to under-cut the competition, keep in mind that a giveaway price can attract the wrong sort of renters.

• Contact a local real estate agent, perhaps the one you used to buy the place. They're usually happy to help because they know that cottage renters often become cottage buyers.

If you're willing to go the "total stranger" route, the options for advertising your rental can expand to include newspapers, magazines, and vacation rental directories (and their on-line counterparts). Or you can leave the marketing to a professional rental service. (*See p. 182.*)

When are you going to rent?

Figuring out when you should make the cottage available means striking a balance between your own use and the desire for rental income. Here are some of the factors to consider:

• The more closely cottage availability is aligned with popular vacation periods, the more likely you are to command top dollar and attract significant interest. From the beginning of July, when public schools are out and summer is at its height, until late August is peak season in most northern vacation areas, with heightened activity in the weeks around holiday long weekends. If you're willing to surrender some time in this period, you'll be better positioned to attract renters.

• One week is generally considered a minimum rental period, but many cottagers won't accept a rental of less than two weeks. Shorter rentals mean more back-and-forth for housekeeping and other changeover chores (such as orientation tours), and more bookings to worry about in a single year. Rental services often offer properties only on the basis of a two-week or a one-month rental.

Case study:

Getting a good fit

Bob and Leslie's cottage is on a three-acre private island. The marina that's the departure point for the island is a four-hour drive from downtown Toronto, and the place itself is very rustic – no hot water and no electricity. Its water access, distance from a major center, and lack of amenities are all drawbacks to attracting renters – yet the couple has managed to rent the place to strangers very successfully. (They even go against prevailing wisdom and include a powerboat in the rental.)

Their trick is to screen potential renters very carefully. Bob visits them in their homes to talk to them about the cottage and show them detailed photos. For starters, this allows him to see how they live which, he says, gives him a good idea whether they're likely to take care of his place. During the visit, he's "brutally honest" when describing the cottage, thus eliminating unrealistic expectations and a potential bad fit between renters and cottage.

Bob and Leslie also clean the cottage themselves between rentals. They've found that the condition the renters find the place in when they arrive sets the standard: "The cleaner I leave it," Bob says, "the cleaner I get it back."

• Weekend-only rentals are even more onerous – plus they mean missing out on longer rentals that would incorporate those weekends. That said, there may be opportunities in spring and fall for weekend rentals, depending on the cottage region. Many cottages are located in spectacular fall-colour areas. At that time of year, people are looking for a quick weekend getaway, and your cottage may fit the bill.

• Interest in winter sports has grown, and with it the potential for "off-season" rentals. A property within a reasonable drive of a downhill ski area or close to cross-country skiing or snowmobile trails can attract weekend rentals, as well as week-long bookings during holiday periods. The income opportunities from these rentals must be weighed against the expense of keeping the property operational during winter months.

Increasing the odds of a trouble–free rental

Is your cottage renter-friendly?

Cottage renters aren't necessarily cut from the same cloth as cottage owners. They're not usually do-it-yourselfers who won't object to doing a bit of fiddling with the composting toilet, or whose first instinct when a bat swoops out of the fireplace is laughter rather than wild panic about rabies.

Renters are generally looking for a carefree experience on their one significant getaway of the year. If you're going to join the rental business, for better or for worse, you're going to have to make your property match the expectations of a typical renter.

The big four for keeping renters happy

1. Maintenance should be up to snuff. Renters usually don't have much experience with things like wells and septic systems, and they don't want to learn about them the hard way. If there's a problem with a pump or the septic is working sluggishly, they won't be happy. And appliances must be in good working order. The stove can't have one functioning burner. The refrigerator freezer can't be iced over. Renters aren't willing to put up with the aggravations you're happy to live with: It's their vacation. "Rustic charm" isn't going to save the situation.

2. Nothing upsets a renter more quickly than an infestation of mice or bats. If you're going to be renting out, deal with the problem first. In a wooded or rural setting it's difficult to guarantee that no small creatures will make their presence known, but that's a far cry from letting a herd of mice have the run of the place.

TIP:

Tell it like it is

The word "rustic" means different things to different people. Be *very* specific in your description of the cottage. And then ask potential renters *very* specific questions ("will your children be comfortable walking to the outhouse at night?") to make sure they understand what the cottage is like.

3. It's a no-brainer: The property should be clean and tidy, inside and out.

4. The property can't have hidden disappointments. If renters think they're getting a cottage with a sand beach, the bottom can't be slimy mud. If they think the photos promise a quiet retreat, there shouldn't be a road or a marina next door. You can't do much about these features, but being deliberately misleading is not going to make for happy renters.

Establishing the conditions of rental

When the renters are close friends or family, the arrangements are often done on a handshake basis: Owner and renter agree to a rental fee and the start and end dates, and leave it at that. When you don't know your renters (or if you – and/or your friends – feel more comfortable with a more structured arrangement), you'll want to have a written agreement.

A rental agreement for a private cottage should be just that – an agreement, and can be as short and sweet as a single page. You don't necessarily have to construct an elaborate contract that imagines every possible consequence, but if you are concerned, have a real estate lawyer draft a basic agreement for you. Here are some elements to consider:

• **Deposit:** This helps firm up the commitment if you're dealing with strangers. If you offer a rental without requiring a deposit, there's no penalty for failing to appear, and you're leaving yourself open to someone making multiple bookings and then choosing the one they like best. If they drop you late, you'll have no time to find someone to take that empty period.

• **Cancellation policy/refund of deposit:** There's no hard-and-fast rule on how much notice you deserve to receive if someone, for whatever reason, decides to cancel. Most people are planning well ahead for summer vacation and don't pull the plug on a whim. But you don't want to lose an entire week's booking without compensation if someone decides not to come at the 11th hour.

• **Security/damage deposit (refundable after inspection at the end of the rental period):** Some cottagers set the damage deposit at the amount of their insurance deductible. That way, they won't be out of pocket if a claim is necessary.

TIP:
Gather references

Ask potential renters for references (preferably from a cottage owner or landlord if they have previous rental experience). And be prepared to give your own happy renter references if they request them.

⚠

CAUTION: Playing with fire

It's entirely your call whether you feel comfortable having renters hold a bonfire – or even use the fireplace. Make any restrictions clear in an information sheet, and leave it in an obvious spot. And if your cottage isn't already equipped with smoke detectors and fire extinguishers, you certainly want to have them in place before the first renters arrive.

• **Waiver** of your responsibility for any injury, loss, or damage the renters sustain while occupying your property – although by itself, this isn't enough to protect you. (*See "Managing Risk When Renting," p. 181.*)

• **Restrictions:** These should include your own restrictions on cottage use – such as no pets, no smoking, and the maximum number of people allowed – as well as any boating restrictions on the lake or noise restrictions in the area.

• **Refunds:** You may wish to specify some recompense for days on which a substantial problem (loss of electricity, water, septic service) interferes with renters' full enjoyment of the property.

What to include – and not include – in the rental

• **Staples:** When you start to think about it, there are a million and one things a renter might need on an everyday basis, from toilet paper and paper towels to dish soap, insect repellent, and sunscreen. Some cottage owners include all the basics; others include none. Some even leave a few staple foodstuffs in the pantry and fridge – and ask renters to replenish what they use. Whatever you decide to do, make sure you're clear about what staples renters should bring along with them and what will be supplied.

• **Bedding and towels:** Sheets, blankets, pillowcases, bath and beach towels, washcloths, and tea towels are usually (though not always) considered extras to be supplied by the renter. The whole idea is to eliminate the need

TIP:
Give 'em space
Leave renters lots of empty drawers and cupboard space. And even if you choose to leave no other staples, you might want to stock an assortment of cleaning products – to give renters a gentle hint to leave the place the way they found it.

Basic cottage gear for renters

• **A tool kit that can handle simple repairs.** A table saw or welding torch isn't called for, but do provide a proper set of screwdrivers, sockets, wrenches, and pliers. For more serious problems, leave numbers for local tradespeople and prearrange with them to respond immediately to renter calls.

• **Spare parts for things that may require unscheduled servicing.** You're not expecting the renter to perform essential maintenance, but you should leave a ready supply of bits and pieces for things that can quickly be set to rights: everything from extra wicks for the kerosene lamps to an adequate supply of light bulbs and fuses to a replacement cartridge for the tap-mounted water filter. And don't forget matches, a flashlight, and candles, in case of a blackout. And a secret stash of extra toilet paper.

• **Fuel.** Whether it's kerosene, gasoline, or propane, make sure there's an adequate supply. If the barbecue runs on propane, have a spare full tank standing by.

• **First aid kit.** Your cottage naturally should have one anyway, even if you're not renting out. But make sure it's fully stocked at the beginning of every rental period, and don't forget the antihistamines for insect bites and stings.

• Ensure every boat you make available has its own **full set of required safety equipment**. Don't expect renters to remember to take the bailing device and heaving line from the pedal boat when they get in the canoe.

---

to do laundry between rental periods. Renters will need specific instructions on what they need to bring along (e.g., what size sheets). Sometimes they can be encouraged to keep things simple for themselves, especially with kids, by bringing sleeping bags rather than bedding.

• **Watercraft:** For liability reasons, powerboats are almost never included in a rental. If renters want a powerboat, suggest they rent one from a nearby marina. If they wish to bring a boat of their own and you're agreeable, be sure they're aware of any local restrictions on operator age, licensing requirements, wake rules, speed limits, and hours of operation.

Cottage sailboats likewise should be kept off limits unless the renters can convince you they are competent sailors.

If you plan to rent the property regularly, you might want to invest in some boats you feel comfortable providing to renters. Cottages represented by rental services typically come equipped with a selection of pedal boats, canoes, and rowboats. Store the $3,000 wood-epoxy canoe in the boathouse and provide a secondhand one (with its own expendable paddles). Consider getting a plastic "sit-on" kayak. A pedal boat is a low-cost crowd-pleaser. If the boats are dedicated to the exclusive use of renters, their cost can be fully depreciated as an expense against rental income. (*See p. 184.*)

• **Lifejackets:** Because boating regulations require a lifejacket or PFD that is both approved and of the appropriate size for the wearer, it is a good idea to ask renters to bring their own with them, if possible. But if you are providing boats as part of the rental, there's an implicit requirement to ensure that operators and passengers have access to the appropriate flotation devices. Have an assortment of inexpensive ones on hand anyway, if you're going to be renting out regularly. You'll sleep better knowing that an eight-year-old who went out in your canoe had a proper PFD available.

Giving renters the information they need

Contracts and damage deposits can be skipped if you know your renters well, but whoever the renters, don't be casual about arrangements. You need to provide support to ensure the experience is an enjoyable one for both sides. Renters no more need to be flummoxed by problems with mechanical systems than you need to be fielding phone calls day and night from a frustrated renter.

Put together a cottage manual

A binder of material covering the many aspects of living in and enjoying your cottage is a major asset for renters. (And should you decide to sell one day, it's a value-added item for a new owner.) In addition to providing instructions on systems and information for emergencies, it should be leavened with details about the lake and your property that you've gathered over the years. (*See "How to Build a Cottage Operating Manual," p. 208.*)

TIP:

Add a few nice touches

While they aren't make-or-break necessities, a few small, homey gestures can help make your renters feel welcome and enjoy their stay at your place. (Remember: You want the good ones back.) Organize your field guides to birds, beasts, bugs, plants, and celestial objects in one handy place. Provide some binoculars that you can afford to have dropped over the side of a canoe. Direct guests to the cupboard full of board games and playing cards. Point out the stacks of vintage *Cottage Life* and *National Geographic* magazines and crossword books that make great bathroom reading. Some owners even leave a bottle of wine or a half-dozen bottles of beer in the fridge to welcome their renters to the lake.

Provide an information package beforehand

Not everything should be left for discovery in the cottage manual. There are things people need to know well before they get to the cottage, beyond the driving directions. Compose an information package, of as many pages as necessary, that highlights what is included in the rental (a 12-foot aluminum boat and motor, the trampoline, and two kayaks) and what is not (groceries, linens, fishing equipment, and charcoal for the barbecue), so that renters are properly equipped for their holiday and there aren't misunderstandings.

It's also helpful to point out the best places to stop on the way to get groceries, beer and wine, and fresh produce.

Give them a personal tour

You should try to meet renters at the start of the rental period (or even on a convenient day before that period) to give them a proper tour. Not everything about a property can be explained in writing. Some things, such as starting the water pump, benefit from hands-on directions.

But remember to provide written instructions as well. People can be overwhelmed by the information being conveyed to them on a single walkaround. Just because they're nodding in agreement as you explain how to prime the pump or relight the propane refrigerator doesn't actually mean it's all sinking in.

Managing risk when renting

Renting does carry the possibility of being dragged into a lawsuit by renters, as a result of personal injury, damage to personal property, or third-party damage sustained while they were renting your cottage. The worst thing you can do to manage the legal risks associated with renting is to just slap a generic liability waiver onto the rental agreement, and think you've taken care of things.

Waivers in and of themselves aren't worth much more than the paper they're printed on when it comes to protecting you from legal action. If you're doing any kind of renting beyond letting your brother-in-law use the place for a week in exchange for some money to help pay the property taxes (and even then, this depends on your brother-in-law), you need to undertake a risk-management look at your rental activity:

1. Identify the aspects of your cottage that present some liability risk, and figure out how that risk can be minimized or eliminated. This basically comes down to applying a critical eye to the current condition of the property, its appliances, and various amenities. A risk review can lead you to fix deficiencies such as the barbecue that balks at lighting properly and the rickety steps on the sleeping cabin; to make a note to regularly pressure-wash the deck to get rid of the slippery scum; and to exclude entirely from the rental the highest-risk amenities, such as the use of your own power-boat or sailboat.

2. Speak with your insurer to understand how renting affects your liability coverage. The insurer's willingness to extend coverage to certain rental situations (say, inclusion of a boat), and the cost, will drive the steps you take.

3. Speak with your lawyer about what sort of liability waiver you need to include in the rental agreement. (Your insurer might already insist on one.) Generally, waivers include a "hold harmless" clause to shield the property owner. Although a waiver won't prevent a suit from being filed, risk-management professionals like them because they require the signatories at least to acknowledge the risks involved in what they are about to undertake, and they can discourage legal action, particularly frivolous suits. But no piece of paper is going to protect a cottage owner if the renter is injured or suffers personal property damage because of faulty wiring, an exploding barbecue, or loose boards in a dock.

4. If you own a cottage with others, and if any of the co-owners are renting, be sure their desire to raise some extra cash doesn't place your investment in any danger.

Using a professional rental service

Most cottage rental services operate on an agency basis for the owner. They are basically in the business of marketing the properties, screening the customers, handling the rental paperwork, and collecting the rent. However, you can also find services that *only* market the property, leaving you to handle the rest of the functions yourself.

A good service will provide guidance on what a fair rental rate is, and on what should be done with the property to make it a rental magnet. Maintenance and housekeeping usually remain the responsibility of the individual owner, although services that operate in recreational hot spots (such as condo-based ski areas) sometimes retain a maintenance supervisor, and housekeeping is sometimes made available separately.

Types of rental services

Cottage rental services come in two basic flavors: ones that are registered travel agencies, and one that are affiliated with the real estate industry. (Ones that aren't affiliated with either should be treated with caution.) The difference makes for some important distinctions in services.

Real estate-based services fundamentally are a side business to selling property, though the rental properties are not necessarily all for sale. (If the property is for sale, the renter may not always come first; a rental contract may require the renter to allow the cottage to be shown to prospective buyers during the rental period – and may allow the agency to cancel the booking if the cottage is sold prior to the start of the rental.)

Dedicated rental services, on the other hand, including those that are travel agencies, have obligations to both the property owner and the renter. As well, the travel-agency-based rental services are interested in building a stable of properties that are worth renting. A good travel-agency service inspects the property and makes recommendations on what improvements or changes should be made before deciding to accept a listing. (Not all properties make the cut: Cottage Country Travel Services, a registered travel-agency service in Ontario that has been in the rental business for more than 17 years, reports that it turns down 20 percent of properties that it is approached to list.)

Screening the renters

The biggest challenge rental services face is vetting the renters for the owners. Some services allow the potential renter to consider specific properties in their listings before getting to the nitty-gritty of defining who they are. Other services are designed so that the renter first goes through a screening. Only when their characteristics are known are the cottage listings opened up to them.

Screening allows the service to identify smokers and pet owners, for

Items to consider when hiring a rental services company

- Is it a real-estate-based or a travel-agency-based operation? Or does it have no professional affiliation at all?

- Can it provide references from cottage owners who have used its service for more than one rental season?

- Does it demand an upfront registration fee? (Not everyone does.)

- Is it discerning about the properties it lists, or does it just take them on, regardless of condition?

- How does it promote its listings? Is the marketing entirely Internet based, or does the service advertise elsewhere as well?

- What services, beyond marketing, does it provide?

- Does it seem interested in a long-term rental relationship with you? Do staff provide frank and helpful advice on how to make the property rental-friendly?

- How is the agency paid? On a flat-fee basis per rental, or on a commission?

- If you are also attempting to sell the cottage, are your sales efforts considered an intrusion on the rental efforts, or vice versa?

example, who never get a chance to consider a particular property if the owner doesn't want cigarettes or dogs or cats on the premises. Rental agencies typically want to know how many people are involved in the rental, and specifically how many "guests" might be joining renters during the holiday – not only to prevent cottage systems, such as the septic, from being over-taxed, but also to reduce the possibility of large parties that would drive the neighbors crazy.

Since the rental service is choosing the renters, liability does come into play. The rental service will not assume legal responsibility for damages caused by a renter – any more than a travel agency will accept responsibility for mischief a customer inflicts on a resort in the Caribbean. The simplest way to deal with the consequences of a badly behaved renter is to require a damage deposit and have the renters agree in the rental contract that they accept full responsibility for any and all damages to the property. And the property owners are responsible for ensuring that their property insurance covers rental occupancy.

How much does it cost?

Fee structures for the services of a rental agency, whether real-estate-based or travel-agency-based, vary widely. Real estate companies often charge only a percentage of the rent, plus taxes, to act as an agent of the owner, but their role beyond marketing the property can be minimal. Travel-agency-based firms, because they are interested in building a stable of properties for rent, might include a flat fee for carrying the property for 12 months, plus an additional fee for Internet marketing. There may also be an additional "administration fee" that varies according to the property and the management services offered. Some companies also charge the renter a fee.

Renting and the tax man

Reporting rental income

If you rent out your cottage, you're generally obligated to report the income on your individual income tax return – though in the U.S., not if you rent for 14 or fewer days a year. While a lot of renting goes on "under the table," failing to report rental income as required can come back to bite you. If you advertise your property for rent, particularly through a rental service, and then don't show any rental income on your return, you can pique the interest of tax officials. Auditors have been known to call on rental services, asking to look at the rental records for particular clients.

While declaring rental fees increases income, you are also entitled to claim deductions of a long list of expenses associated with renting, such as depreciation on many assets (including the buildings), insurance costs, property taxes, utilities, fees paid to property listing or management services, and much more. It's not unusual for renting out to be a tax-neutral exercise, with legitimate expenses offsetting the income generated.

Rental expenses and Canadian taxpayers

The Canada Revenue Agency's permitted deductions include maintenance, improvements, and general expenses related to the running of any small business, such as travel to and from the cottage if it's dedicated to rental duties (and not just collecting the cheque, which isn't permitted). Run to your nearest accountant for help.

The general rule for the amount of general expenses that can be claimed against rental income is that the proportion claimed of the total expense must bear a rational relationship to the amount of time the property was rented out in a given year, particularly where personal use comes into play. Taxpayers have to take care not to be too aggressive in the expenses they claim. Claiming an entire year's worth of electrical bills, septic services, and depreciation on furnishings and the cottage building, when the property was only rented out for three weeks (and especially if there was personal use during the year), is risking an unhappy audit. If you do invest in some assets that are for renters' exclusive use (such as a canoe or pedal boat that you never touch personally), you may be able to claim the entirety of their capital cost allowance and associated maintenance.

CRA does permit losses on rental income to be claimed against other sources of income, but tread extremely carefully. If your costs are consistently higher than your income, you're not considered to be running a proper business, and the costs will be disallowed altogether. Auditors are also on the lookout for practices of renting at less than fair market value: They can conclude that you are undercharging friends and relatives to rent the cottage so that you can create a loss that can be applied against your other income.

Renting and capital gains on Canadian property

Use of a vacation home as an income property, even for just one year, can have an effect on capital gains taxes far down the road. The CRA is fairly generous in how it permits a seasonal residence to be designated as a principal residence, which exempts it from capital gains taxes. (*See Tip, p. 226.*) It also advises that "a person receiving only incidental rental income from a seasonal residence is not considered to own the property mainly for the purpose of gaining or producing income." Once a property is being used mainly to generate rental income, it cannot qualify as a principal residence and loses the capital gains exemption for those years.

There's no hard-and-fast rule on what constitutes "incidental" rental income. CRA approaches the issue case by case, and it's a judgment call. Before becoming involved in renting out a family vacation retreat, see an accountant who can advise you on how revenues need to be handled (and what expenses are legitimate), and what impact your rental plans might have on any current or future designation as a principal residence.

Under current regulations, a principal residence can serve temporarily in whole or in part as a rental property for up to four years without losing the capital gains exemption for those years. You can't have another property serve as your principal residence in those years, and you can't claim any capital cost allowance (depreciation) from rental activity. Again, speak with your accountant, and consult the CRA – see guide T4036(E), Rental Income – for more information.

Eligible U.S. rental expenses

Eligible deductions to offset rental revenues include mortgage interest (and "points"), utilities, cleaning and maintenance, advertising, travel and local transportation, insurance, taxes, commissions, equipment rentals, and tax return fees. (Consult Publication 527 for the full list.) It's important to keep careful records of expenditures, and to differentiate between expenses that qualify as upkeep (which are directly deductible) and those that are considered improvements. The former aren't considered to add significant value to the property, while the latter are. A good example is the cost of a furnace repair. A house call to fix the burner is upkeep, and can be claimed in the relevant tax year. But if you install a whole new furnace, that's an improvement, and the expense must be shown over time through depreciation.

Although you can't claim depreciation on a main or second home you can claim it for the proportion of its use as a rental property. (Technically speaking, you end up with a property that for tax purposes is, say, 80 percent home and 20 percent rental property. It's the rental property portion that's depreciable.) If you bought vacant land and then built on it, the portion of the property's value represented by the original land purchase can't be depreciated. You can't claim depreciation on land, since it is considered to be a permanent asset that never wears out.

Rental income and U.S mortgage interest deductibility

With second homes such as a cottage, the IRS has specific restrictions on rental activity. Ordinarily, you don't even have to occupy the place in a tax year to have it qualify as a second home. But if you rent it out, you must occupy it for at least 14 days of that tax year, or 10 percent of the rental period, whichever is longer. If you don't, it's no longer considered a second home.

When the property still qualifies as a second home but you have reportable rental income (*see p. 184*), the IRS requires you to distinguish between personal use and rental use in terms of days of occupancy in order to calculate permitted deductions. This is a complex area of taxation – particularly if there are co-owners – and you need to consult a tax professional to understand how to handle permitted deductions, and to avoid losing second-home status.

12. Selling your cottage

At the beginning of the book, we explored the ins and outs of purchasing a vacation property. Now, 12 chapters later, the shoe is on the other foot: You're the one doing the selling.

Much of the practical info on selling a cottage is common to any real estate transaction, whether it's in the city or at the lake. In a hot vacation property market, cottages can sell as quickly as homes in urban markets. But a number of factors encourage a more leisurely selling pace, including a smaller, more specialized pool of potential buyers and a strong seasonal cycle. And certain aspects are unique to cottage country or require more careful attention than you'd normally give them in a city-side deal.

Who's going to handle it?

One of those aspects is deciding whether you're going to turn the sales job over to an agent or handle it yourself. For a variety of reasons (we'll get to them below), owners consider selling privately more frequently when the property being put up for sale is a cottage rather than a home. Before we get to the complications of the "for sale by owner" – or FSBO – approach, let's assume you're going to go the conventional route and work with a real estate agent.

Choosing an agent

Finding a good agent in cottage country can be a little easier than in an urban area. To begin, the pool of potential agents is usually much smaller for a given vacation area than it is for a city or suburban area. The agents who are successful have been building up their local business for years, and they have to know the minutiae of the particular market – not only pricing trends, but also the basics of the bylaws and zoning regulations that affect a cottage's renovation or replacement.

This doesn't mean everyone working in a given area is an expert. But as a seller, you're way ahead of the buyer in choosing an agent in cottage country because you've owned the property for a while and have been able to see which agents are most active and most successful. If you own a property in a strong market, you've probably already received mailings from agents announcing that they have just sold a particular property or have ready-and-willing buyers looking for a place on your lake.

As with any hiring, get references from others who have used the services of the person you're considering. And don't just choose an agent on the basis of who proposes the highest listing price. (*See Tip, at left.*)

Selling privately

When the cottage real estate market is hot, owners preparing to put their property on the market – even those who never dreamt of handling the sale of their city home themselves – inevitably ask themselves: Why can't I just unload this place myself?

Most of us will never spend more on a professional service than the fee paid to a real estate agent, which routinely runs into the four or five figures. You can't blame people for looking at that stack of cash and wondering

TIP:

The bigger they are, the harder they fall

If you pick an agent just because he suggested the highest listing price of all the candidate agents, you're probably headed for trouble. Unrealistic sales expectations fall the farthest and the hardest, and create the most problems in the effort to realize a sale.

TIP: **Before you start, ask yourself these three tough questions**

Whether you have an agent representing you or you're selling the cottage yourself, here are three questions all sellers should answer before officially putting their property up for sale. Having firm answers helps ensure that everyone – that includes both halves of a couple – is on the same strategic page.

1. What is the asking price going to be?

2. How long are we prepared to wait before reviewing the asking price?

3. What's our rock-bottom acceptance price?

what it was they just paid for, and if they couldn't have handled the whole deal themselves for substantially less.

Selling your cottage yourself can be a good idea, but it can also end up being an awful experience. You might sell the property at considerable savings in agency commission, and even get a price higher than what an agent might. On the other hand, you might not find a buyer, or might underprice the property, or make such a mess of the closing that the whole exercise ends up with squabbling lawyers.

Red-flag reasons for deciding to do it yourself

Here are some of the oft-heard reasons why owners believe they can handle their own property sale and the warning flags they raise:

My prime motivation for selling privately is that I want to save money on agency commissions.

We all like to save money, but we need to know *how* to save money. If you don't have the necessary skills to step into the sales agent's role – and as a result can't find a buyer or sell for far less than you should have – you won't be saving any money at all.

The market is so hot that properties are just selling themselves.

If the market is really hot, buyers may well beat a path to your door with minimal encouragement. But don't confuse a hot market with a *crowded*

Got a buyer in mind? Then selling it yourself makes sense

Even when you're not predisposed to sell privately, it's a solid strategy in situations where the buyers and sellers already know each other: sales that occur within a family or between friends, or involve someone who has rented the property and is well informed and motivated. In every case, the significant challenges of advertising and showing the property – where an agent can excel – are eliminated. Real estate lawyers and professional appraisers and surveyors can take care of the rest.

Just don't fall into the trap of allowing an existing relationship with the buyer to obviate the need for all professional help. The better you know someone, the more care everyone should take that no hard feelings result from a transaction.

If a mortgage is going to be attached to the property, a formal appraisal will be required in any event. But a professional inspection that independently assesses the state of the property can save you from misunderstandings later on, thus preserving a friendship or keeping peace in a family. As the seller, you may want to make the grand gesture of suggesting to your friendly buyer that he really ought to have the property inspected, if only to save yourself from an unhappy brother-in-law coming to you later to complain about the expense of a roof repair you genuinely had no idea would be required.

CAUTION: Beware the paper chase

If you're selling the property on your own, you can acquire the necessary paperwork inexpensively on-line. But possessing forms with blanks to fill in is very different from knowing how to fill in those blanks – and the firms offering these forms typically advise you to take them to your lawyer and pay him to go through them. We can't put it any better than one service offering free forms does: "These forms are provided AS IS. They may not be any good. Even if they are good in one jurisdiction, they may not work in another. And the facts of your situation may make these forms inappropriate for you. They are for informational purposes only, and you should consult an attorney before using them."

market. When property owners start thinking that the market is hot and begin listing their properties en masse, it can be difficult to get those eager buyers to pay special attention to your property. If you can't cut effectively through the noise of the humming market, you're going to find yourself with a tough sell.

I've been through the purchase and sale of a couple of houses. I probably know as much about the real estate market as the average agent. I can't see why I couldn't handle a cottage sale myself.

Having been through the purchase and sale of a few homes doesn't necessarily mean you know much about the nitty-gritty of getting real estate deals done. What is it, exactly, that you contributed to the process of those other sales, besides putting up with an open house or two? A lot of selling experience for homeowners boils down to enduring the selling experience. Even when owners make a solid contribution to the process, it's often by working effectively *with* the agent, not by supplanting the agent.

No one knows my property better than I do. Who better to do the selling?

You might know your property all too well. Cottages are usually more of an

TIP: Get your lawyer involved

If you're selling privately, it is in your best interest to start by contacting the lawyer you're going to use and devoting some financial resources to having him walk you through the basics of the selling and closing process. Get a clear understanding of your rights, obligations, and liabilities as the property's seller. (Many of the "vendor due diligence" issues should be addressed at this time; *see p. 200.*)

Whether you sell privately or through an agent, however, don't imagine marshaling the final deal without a lawyer who knows the cottage market. There are simply too many potential tripwires in a property deal to try to fly solo.

You should also let your accountant know what you're up to, as vacation property sales invariably trigger some kind of critical – and potentially expensive – tax issue, and a bit of planning can minimize the impact.

Downsides to selling privately

The emotional roller coaster: Experienced agents know strong leads that never produce an offer, or aggressive lowballs, are part of the business. When it's your property and you're dealing with potential buyers directly, it can be hard to deal with the disappointments. Going through a showing to end up with nothing, or an offer so low you feel insulted, is part of the game. You also have to distance yourself from the emotional attachment to the property. A buyer is just trying to get the best possible deal.

The time commitment: Showing a cottage can be hard work. You probably face a round-trip drive of several hours, which means a full day's commitment for just one curious buyer, who may be on the lake looking at several other properties through an agent at the same time. You don't know if you're solidly in contention or just an afterthought to the day's outing. You also don't know if the prospect will fall in love with the first cottage he sees and cancel his appointment. There will be aggravations, and you will have to smile through them.

The pricing dilemma: Arriving at a listing price is tricky enough. *(See p. 196.)* But that price is often just an opening gambit, and if you're not in the real estate biz, it's difficult for you to judge the market's momentum. If you're not getting offers as soon as you thought, how do you know when or whether to make a price adjustment? Agents will know how deals on other properties are turning out. They'll know what's moving, and what's being repriced. They'll also have toured other properties, and their knowledge of competing properties can be intimidating when they show up as a buyer agent and start trying to talk down your price, based on what five other properties have sold for. Unless you've seen those properties yourself, you don't know if they're comparable or if this buyer agent is just blowing smoke.

Agent solicitations: Agents are always looking for new listings, and nothing says "I want to sell" more than listing your property privately. Hungry agents will be on the phone to you, looking for a way to convince you to list with them and give up the FSBO route. Not only will you have to stick to your guns about doing it yourself, but you'll also have to do so without giving offense. The hungry agent may end up bringing you a buyer, or you may indeed end up deciding that you don't have the wherewithal to sell privately and end up going to an agent. So don't dress down every good agent in the area: You might need their help down the road.

emotional investment than a residential home. The memories they contain give them a value that total strangers can't be expected to recognize. And they often have a lot of do-it-yourselfer handiwork that the do-it-yourselfer thinks looks like a million bucks, but that the prospective buyer wants to get rid of at the first opportunity. If you're the do-it-yourselfer doing the negotiating, it's not easy to hear a potential buyer tell you your wall paneling, instead of being an asset, actually has to be removed in order to make the place tolerable.

Owners, even with agents working for them, can be insulted by offers they think are too low. It's the agent's job to agree with the client, or explain patiently why, in fact, the offer is a reasonable one, regardless of whether or not the retreat has been in your family since your granddad built the original cabin and you're willing to throw in the moose head you carved with a chainsaw. A good agent brings emotional distance to the selling process.

Six for the sale

Regardless of how you decide to sell your property – privately or through an agent – six basic steps of the selling process must be completed for you to be successful:

1. Price the property appropriately, according to the current market conditions, and be prepared to revise the price as circumstances require.
2. Attract prospective buyers.
3. Deal with their information needs.
4. Show the property.
5. Negotiate effectively and fairly.
6. Close the deal.

Without an agent, you need to be able to step outside your own skin and think independently about your property's reasonable worth – and in the process hear some things you probably don't want to.

Five places recently sold on my lake. I have a pretty solid idea of my property's value as a result.

How much do you actually know about those other sales? Do you know what the closing price was, as opposed to the asking price? The conditions attached? Were any contents included?

And how much do you actually know about those other properties? Have you walked around inside them, taken note of the electrical service, the condition of the dock and the boathouse, the age of the septic system? Or do you know these places only from a passing view from your boat?

Advantages an agent offers

The only way you are going to do the job of selling your own cottage acceptably well and for much less than an agent is by contributing free labor (your own) and mounting a sales effort that is more focused and more cost-effec-

TIP: When to put your cottage on the market

In more northern climes, the opportunities to show properties are limited by seasonal considerations. Even if there is winter road access, buyers are reluctant to purchase a cottage in the dead of winter, without seeing the place in its summer-getaway glory. Market interest naturally is strongest in spring through early summer, fades into fall, then becomes close to nonexistent in the dead of winter. If a property enters the market at the wrong time in the buyer-interest cycle (October, for example, in seasonal-use locations), you could have a long wait before the market wakes up again.

tive overall than the scattergun approach that agents use. But be warned: Agents can use a scattergun approach because they enjoy economies of scale unavailable to you. They don't have to worry about whether to emphasize print advertising over an on-line listing: They can do them both, and more, as part of the brokerage's general advertising program. And it doesn't matter that, with property A, it was a print ad that drew the buyer, whereas with property B, an on-line MLS listing was brought to the buyer's attention by the buyer's agent. They can do all of them, all the time, and let individual buyers find their way to the deal.

And agents have resources that go beyond traditional advertising. They are constantly cultivating potential buyers for their listings, some of which take years to finally pan out. (*See "The Real Estate Agent as Matchmaker," p. 69.*)

So compared to a good agent, you're at a distinct disadvantage on several crucial fronts when it comes to finding a buyer for your property. Agents can advertise more widely and less expensively, and they have a multitude of potential buyers waiting in the wings (where you may have cultivated few or none for your particular property). And they have a wealth of

---

Q & A:

Getting a "for sale by owner" property listed on MLS

Q: I'm selling my cottage privately, and I've heard that I can get it listed on MLS even though I'm not using an agent. How does this work?

A: Since professional realtors have rapidly moved to the Internet as their prime source for promoting listed properties, being outside the MLS system is an ever-increasing disadvantage to the private seller. However, some realtors (more so in the U.S. at this point than Canada) are now marketing a "flat-fee" MLS listing. This allows a private seller to get a listing on MLS through a broker for a set length of time at a set fee – without actually having the broker formally take on the property as a listing. You're still "selling it yourself," since the broker isn't representing you, and you won't have to pay him any commission.

Essentially, you are using the MLS only as an advertising vehicle, so be sure the cost and duration of the advertising are appropriate to the amount of time you think it will take to sell the property, and not eat up all the money you planned to spend on marketing. Also be absolutely clear how leads that result from the listing will be referred to you.

And don't be surprised when agents start contacting you: Being on MLS as a private seller is inevitably going to bring overtures from agents inviting you to list with them – including, quite possibly, from the agent who sold you the flat-fee service.

Commercial real estate web pages outside MLS will accept private ads, but be sure to research their effectiveness. As with print media, the Internet is only as effective as the buyer traffic it generates. Find out how many hits a site is generating, and ask for references from previous users.

TIP:

Be prepared to do some legwork to help your agent

Don't just sit back and wait for your agent to come up with the perfect buyer: Help beat the bushes and feed him leads, using your own personal and professional connections.

On the other hand, if your agent isn't being of any use at all in delivering potential buyers to your cottage doorstep, fire him and get another one. Good agents exist, and they get results.

experience that you don't: in negotiating a sale, which also includes telling the difference between a good lead and a tire kicker; and in the market's ups and downs and how a property is positioned, pricewise.

The one thing they don't have is the ability to lend your property their undivided attention. But then, neither do you, if you have to earn a living and raise a family. For an agent in cottage country, showing a listed property is far less onerous than it is for you, if you live several hours away. While agents can't focus all their attention on your property, they are in contact with potential buyers virtually every day, some of whom can be directed to your listing. And with the property on MLS, other agents can bring their own clients in your direction.

Playing to your own strengths

If you're selling privately, you have to be able to play to your own strengths. One of them may be that you're not in as much of a hurry to sell your property as an agent is. As noted in the chapters on buying, agents make a living through cumulative sales, not by waiting for months on end in hopes of getting a few thousand dollars more for a property. One reason some people who successfully sell a property on their own are happy with their experience is that they end up getting more for the property than an agent proposed listing it for. Anyone, professional or amateur, can underprice a

The Return on Equity Rule: Holding out for the right price costs you money

Vacation properties often have less urgency attached to their sale than do conventional residential ones. Residential homeowners are regularly in the process of buying one home as they sell another, and face closing-date (and monetary) pressures from the new home that put the heat on getting a satisfactory offer on the old one as soon as possible. Unless you're in the process of selling a cottage to buy another property, with a fixed closing date looming for the new place, you probably aren't feeling particularly rushed about closing a deal on your sale. And that can lead you to wait far longer than you should for the right offer.

If you and/or your spouse think you can wait ad infinitum for the right offer to come along, consider what we might call the Return on Equity Rule. From the moment you list a property for sale, you have a fixed asset you are attempting to turn into a liquid one (cash) that can be deployed elsewhere. Every day that goes by without that asset having been liquidated is leaving that cash in suspended animation. That asset is not working for you. While the property continues to appreciate if the market is in good shape, you don't know what the starting point of its appreciating value is. Therefore, you're not really "making money" on this idle fixed asset while waiting for someone to meet your sales price. And in the meantime, the property is racking up a host of expenses that will disappear the moment you stop owning it.

Let's say you put the property up for sale in the spring for $204,995. By midsummer, you still haven't seen an offer, but you don't want to sell for a dime less than $200,000, so you don't want to drop the price. However, if the

property, but private sellers sometimes feel that agents are in such a hurry to get a deal done that they aren't willing to hang in for the time it takes to get the right buyer at the top price. There's no way to prove if this is true, and private sellers have to be wary of their own predilection for demanding more for their property than the market is willing to pay. As well, hanging onto the property for longer in order to get your price carries its own costs. (*See "The Return on Equity Rule," below.*) But differing pricing philosophies can be a factor in private sellers' favor…if they can actually get their price.

Another strength private sellers can draw on is their connections, which can be invaluable in turning up potential buyers. You may have people who have rented from you in the past and might now be interested in buying. Through ads in a corporate employee newsletter or a fitness or sports club publication, you may be able to reach hundreds of people with the right purchasing demographics. Better yet, you probably have an entire cottage or local ratepayers' association with whom you can network. Every cottage on your lake potentially contains a bevy of leads. The folks three lots down may know a family member who would love to own a cottage on this lake. The people across the bay may have renters who would be prepared to invest. All this is unknown to you, until you ask. And if such leads are readily available, it might be possible to arrange a quick deal privately.

The volume and quality of leads that result from putting out such feelers

property isn't sold before fall, it will probably be next spring or summer before it attracts an offer – that is, if it even attracts an offer at the desired price. Another year will have passed, and in the meantime there will be another round of property taxes, maintenance, and boat storage fees (not to mention the costs of continuing to advertise and show the property, if you're selling it privately). If there's a mortgage or some other loan financing the property, thousands more in monthly interest payments are waiting to be avoided through an immediate sale.

Get out the calculator: What if you dropped the price now to $195,000 and hope to attract an offer around $190,000 before the summer is over? Figure out how much $190,000 in the hand now (less the agent's commission) will be worth next year. Even a modest five percent return on equity would turn $190,000 into $199,500. Plus, you might find yourself easily saving $5,000 in cash flow by not owning the property for another year. Suddenly, selling now begins to look like a real deal. In fact, you may be willing to lower your rock-bottom acceptance price even further.

Unless a vacation property is so unusual that time and patience are required for the right buyer to come along, the first rule of real estate is that a quicker sale is better than a slower one. Time is money, and time also erodes money. A hot market can provide an exception to the rule – if properties have been appreciating 10 or 15 percent per year, you may well be tempted to hold on into the next calendar year and hope to get a top-dollar offer. After all, what might be a bit overpriced this year could turn out to be a middling price next year. (If you're selling this property to buy another one immediately, however, it's fair to say that this price increase will simply be transferred to the new property.)

Doing the return-on-equity and cash-flow-retention calculations may encourage you to be much more aggressive about getting your property sold sooner rather than later.

can be very helpful in making a final decision on whether or not to list with an agent. You can, in essence, take an initial, informal stab at finding out how strong a response you can generate to your plan to sell privately before beginning an active selling process.

Getting the price right

Whether you're working with an agent or handling the sale yourself, setting the price may well be the most challenging aspect of selling a cottage. Real estate pros like to counsel that owners tend to overestimate the value of their property – in the same way that car owners tend to overestimate the trade-in value of their jalopies – though letting an agent set the price is no guarantee it will be more realistic. Where there is plenty of competition for new-listing business, an agent may suggest a list price higher than the property has any likelihood of realizing, knowing that playing to the owners' fiduciary delusions can increase the odds of winning the listing.

So how do you know what your place should fetch? The clues to use are the listed prices of similar properties, the prices similar properties actually sold for, and formal appraisals of your own property.

While the easiest to collect, the listed prices of similar properties are the least reliable. First, a listed price is only what someone is asking, and may have nothing to do with what the property will actually command. Second, you need a reasonable familiarity with a listed property to know whether yours is actually in the same league. A curbside – or dockside – inspection is hardly going to tell the full story of the condition and amenities, or complications such as easements.

A major challenge in deciding what your property is worth is that most cottages are unique. The lake is not suburbia, where the same house is available in endless replication along the street. Rather, every cottage is a custom

TIP:

How much is too much?

How do you know if your asking price is too high? It's not merely that your property isn't attracting offers, or only offers you consider beneath your dignity. (Agents say purchasers are inclined to lowball when a property is overpriced.) But it's also that other properties are selling, and yours isn't. And while yours isn't selling, another wave of properties is coming on the market, giving your listing fresh competition.

TIP: **Attracting buyers is easier if you're in a "branded" area**

The two most significant factors in the cottage resale market are – no surprise – location and price. (These are pretty well the same as the main factors for home sales in general.) Potential buyers are as susceptible to the allure of brand names as consumers of sneakers are, and certain locations are better known than others and have greater cachet; buyers are going to focus on them, at least initially. With some education and guidance – and, sometimes, faced with the reality of the prices those branded regions command – they will look farther afield and consider locations they've never heard of. If you're selling privately, being in a branded area is a big plus, because buyers will already be motivated to seek you out. Being in a non-branded area, without an agent touting your property and without a position on MLS, makes attracting a buyer that much harder.

Cold feet? Stay out of the water...

If getting the asking price wrong really makes you nervous, you shouldn't be trying to sell your cottage privately. The rest of the process can be nerve-wracking enough without also having to worry about the fundamental pricing issue. You'd be better off having an agent set the price, explain why to you carefully, and have a mutually agreed on game plan about when to revisit the asking price if no satisfactory offers are forthcoming.

effort, some professionally built, some built by owners. And lot #52 as a property can be entirely different than lot #51: Great variation in the value of the underlying land can be found on a single lake or bay.

The upside of this uniqueness is that it affords you some flexibility in price point and you can leave it to the market to ultimately decide what the "real" value is. The downside is that you can get the price seriously wrong. And the odds are that, left to your own devices, you will overprice. While properties are invariably listed for more than they fetch, going significantly over the top on the price will seriously complicate the selling process – among other things, attracting lowball offers or no offers at all.

Unlike you, agents are immersed in the vagaries of the market on a daily basis. Coming up with credible valuations – and being able to show you comparable properties over a broad geographic area – is where seller agents earn their keep. That doesn't mean you necessarily have to list with an agent. You can get an agent to help in the pricing, by acting as an appraiser for you. Many real estate appraisal services are side operations of realty firms, although it's also possible to hire an independent appraiser.

Appraisal + market forces = asking price

An appraisal isn't necessarily the same as an asking price. Appraisers assess market values for mortgage, insurance, and property-tax purposes, and theoretically, what an appraiser decides a property is worth is what it should actually sell for. The final price, however, needs to also reflect market forces: Is it a buyer's or a seller's market? How many similar properties are on the market? How aggressively does the owner – you – want to pursue a quick sale? How accurately should the listing price reflect the likely (or acceptable) final offer?

Getting the asking price right gets trickier as the number of comparable properties declines. Pricing strategy is also complicated by the seasonal nature of the cottage market. There is naturally tremendous interest in the spring, and scarcely any interest in the winter. If you decide to list in late fall and want the property to move quickly, your asking price may well have to reflect the reduced pool of potential buyers at that time of year.

The asking price will fall into one of the following two categories:

1. Firm asking. You genuinely believe that this is a fair market price, and that it's not unreasonable to expect an offer within a few thousand dollars.

You think you should be able to hold out for an offer close to the asking price, rather than gratefully take the first lowball offer that comes along. And if the market is hot, you could be rewarded with a bidding war that takes the price even higher.

2. Testing the waters. The fair market value of your property is $250,000, but you think that the market is strong enough that you should be able to ask $300,000 and see what happens.

Putting together an information package

A good information package can give you a leg up on other sellers. If you're using an agent, he or she will prepare the listing, but beyond that, it's to your advantage to provide as much information to potential buyers as possible.

The basic facts

If you go the FSBO route, you'll need to put together a listing to start. This isn't rocket science: People want to know the number of bedrooms, room dimensions, property dimensions, utilities, property taxes, and the like. Look at a standard MLS listing and use it as your information template. (Keep in mind that the listing has legal weight. Don't stretch or fudge dimensions.)

You want to make sure to position the property correctly in your description: Are you offering turnkey luxury? Comfy cozy? A fixer-upper? It's very difficult to anticipate how different people will react to the same property. Some buyers break out in hives at the sight of linoleum flooring. Others will think that a cottage you feel is ready for a complete interior overhaul is just fine the way it is.

If you're doing it yourself, the listing can take the form of your own web page, but you'll also need a print version. In the real estate business, "print" these days also means having it in a digital format, such as a PDF, that can be e-mailed easily to potential buyers.

Pictures are worth a thousand words

People want to see what the property looks like, inside and out. And they want to see it as it appears during the summer, with all the leaves on the trees and the ice gone from the lake. Views to and from the waterfront are also a priority. If there's an amateur videographer in the family, so much the better. A cottage video can be a terrific sales tool.

Photos that include people enjoying themselves may sound like a good idea but, in fact, peopleless photos – empty chairs lined up invitingly along the deck or water toys at the dock waiting to be used – can be even more appealing. They allow viewers to picture *themselves* in that setting, to imagine themselves as owners of the property. Which, of course, is exactly what you want. (Besides, distributing photos that show family members can raise personal security issues; be careful what you choose to show to total strangers.)

Pictures should highlight the property's strengths, of course. And cameras can discreetly omit as much as they show – for example, cropping photos so they don't reveal the close proximity of the neighboring cottage. But buff your property's appeal at your own peril. There's a difference between maximizing the positive and misrepresentation. If you fool people in order to get them to come look at the property, you can be certain there won't be any offers forthcoming.

The value-addeds

Think beyond your immediate property line when touting the appeal of your cottage. Does your lake have an active cottage association that holds regular family events? A local sailing club? Are there hiking trails near or accessible from the property? Do winter recreation opportunities exist (even if you don't partake of them yourself)? Does the lake connect to other lakes? If the cottage doesn't have a sandy beach, is there one nearby on Crown land or public parkland? Such value-added opportunities can help your cottage cut through the clutter of other cottages competing for buyers.

What about the services in the nearest town? Is there a fully stocked grocery store? A liquor store? A movie rental outlet with more than 15 titles in stock? Is Internet service available (even if you don't have or want it yourself)? Does the local marina have a great mechanic? Use the points in Chapter 3 (which is devoted to buyer research on cottage areas) and make a list of your lake's pluses and the nearby amenities that will attract a buyer.

No cottage deal is going to live or die on the basis of whether the full Adam Sandler oeuvre can be rented locally in director's-cut DVD format. But covering all the bases of your property's appeal can include remarking that a fully stocked hardware store is just a 10-minute drive from your laneway, and that there are three good plumbing contractors in the area. And don't be afraid to point out that you can buy the Sunday *New York Times* and fresh bagels in town. A buyer often will be comparing your property to competing properties on different lakes in entirely different vacation areas that are all about the same driving distance. Be prepared to sell the appeal of *your* lake as a vacation destination.

Provide documentation

By giving buyers as much information as possible about the cottage itself, you accomplish several things: You save them the time and trouble of tracking it down themselves; you make the purchase seem less risky by providing the complete lowdown; you distinguish your cottage even further from the

TIP:

Let photos do most of the talking

Make the verbal description of the property brief, using words to provide basic statistics and fill in what might not be obvious from the photos – things such as deep-water docking, a year-round road, and the Crown land or parkland bordering the property. And, yes, the quality of the fishing. More detailed descriptions can wait until prospective buyers ask questions on the things that are important to them.

competition; and in the process you may "push the right button," highlighting something of particular concern or interest to the potential buyer. All of these can give you an edge in the market.

Some jurisdictions require a seller to complete a vendor disclosure document, but even if it's not a legal requirement, you should seriously consider conducting "due diligence" on your own property and providing a report to prospective buyers. (*For a checklist of what to include, see the section that follows.*) Other paperwork you should have available for prospective purchasers includes:

—a list of the contents included in the sale
—the previous year's utility bills
—the previous year's property tax statements
—the cottage operating manual; *see p. 208.*

TIP:
Keep good records and you'll thank yourself later

It's important to retain detailed records of any capital improvements you make to the cottage throughout your ownership, be it installing new windows, adding a screened porch, putting in a new dock, or drilling a new well. Proof of upgrades is a wonderful sales tool, demonstrating to potential buyers that the place really is worth every cent of your asking price. But beyond that, whether you plan to sell the cottage or hand it down to your kids, the costs of these improvements can be added to the cottage's base cost to you, thus reducing the amount of capital gains taxes you might have to pay. *(See Chapter 14, p. 225, for more.)*

The two VDDs: Vendor disclosure documents and vendor due diligence

Assuring buyers that the property they're purchasing is free of worries makes good legal as well as strategic sense. Many states and provinces are now making vendor disclosure documents a mandatory part of real estate transactions, and even where they're not mandatory by law, some real estate boards are requiring them as a condition of listing the property. (These documents go by various names; in Ontario, for instance, they're called "Seller Property Information Statements.") Sellers are being asked to sign documents in which they provide basic "to the best of their knowledge" statements about the condition of and issues surrounding the property and acknowledge any known faults or deficiencies.

Vacation properties are increasing in value at the same time that serious issues in many cottage areas are compounding: from building code violations to failing septic systems, from encroachments to undocumented easements for private roads. Risks for purchasers have increased, and have become less tolerable as asking prices have climbed. Rather than view vendor disclosure documents as a burden, sellers who want to give their properties the strongest market potential should be embracing them. Instead of waiting for a purchaser to request certain information, vendors should be preparing it in advance, as part of the selling package.

This proactive approach is known as vendor due diligence, and it is a transplant from the world of corporate mergers and acquisitions. Corporate takeovers aren't much different from buying a cottage: The buyer is trying to settle on a fair price for a takeover target while striving to determine if

 **OREA** Ontario Real Estate Association

Seller Property Information Statement
Schedule for Water Supply, Waste Disposal, Access and Shoreline for use in the Province of Ontario

Form 222

This Schedule is attached to and forms part of the Seller Property Information Statement (Form 220) for:

PROPERTY:..

SELLER(S)..

WATER SUPPLY AND WASTE DISPOSAL:	YES	NO	UNKNOWN	NOT APPLICABLE
1. (a) What is your water source? ☐ Municipal ☐ Drilled ☐ Bored ☐ Dug ☐ Lake ☐ Community ☐ Shared ☐ Cistern ☐ Other..				
(b) If your water source is Community/Shared, is there a transferrable written agreement?				
(c) Are you aware of any problem re: quantity of water?				
(d) Are you aware of any problems re: quality of water?				
(e) Do you have any water treatment devices?...				
(f) Is your water system operable year round? Heated lines? ☐ Yes ☐ No				
(g) Date and result of most recent water test...................................				
(h) Are any documents available for the well? If yes, specify				
(i) Does the property have any abandoned well(s)?				
2. (a) What kind of sewage disposal system services the property? ☐ Municipal ☐ Septic tank with tile bed ☐ Holding tank ☐ Other............................				
(b) Are you aware of any problems with the sewage system? Date septic/holding tank last pumped.................... Age of system............................				
(c) What documentation for the sewage system is available? ☐ Use Permit ☐ Location Sketch ☐ Maintenance Records ☐ Inspection Certificate ☐ Other				
3. Are the well(s), water line(s) and waste disposal system(s) within the boundaries of the subject property?				

ACCESS AND SHORELINE:	YES	NO	UNKNOWN	NOT APPLICABLE
1. (a) Is property access by municipal road? If yes; ☐ Open all year ☐ Seasonally open				
(b) Is the property serviced by a private road? Cost $..................................... per year.				
2. If your access is across private property, access is: ☐ Right of way ☐ Deeded ☐ Other .... Cost $................................... per year				
3. (a) If water access only, access is: ☐ Deeded ☐ Leased ☐ Other..........................				
(b) Water access cost of: Parking $..................... Dock $..................... per year				
4. (a) Is the original Shore Road Allowance owned?				
(b) Are there any pending applications for shoreline improvement?				
(c) Are there any disputes concerning the shoreline or improvements on the shoreline?				
(d) Are there any structures or docks on the original Shore Road Allowance?				
(e) Is the original Road Allowance included in the lot size?				
5. Does the boundary of the property extend beyond the water line? If yes, explain				

ADDITIONAL COMMENTS:..

....
....
....

Form 222 R01/2006

Property disclosure statements such as this one – part of one used by the Ontario Real Estate Association – ask vendors to provide basic "to the best of their knowledge" information on cottage systems and property issues such as access.

there are any skeletons in the potential acquisition's closet. With vendor due diligence, instead of leaving it to the buyer to do the work, the vendor first performs due diligence.

Before listing a cottage property, you should consider conducting your own vendor due diligence. While the effect is difficult to quantify, when well executed, it promises to pay for itself in stronger buyer interest that can produce a top-dollar offer in a shorter period of selling time.

A vendor due diligence checklist

- **Verify title and the rights associated with the property.** If access to neighboring properties is required – for example, an easement for access to a private road, or to cross another property to reach the water – find the documentation. If you acquired your shoreline road allowance, dig out your proof of purchase.

- **Produce an acceptable, up-to-date survey of the property and its buildings.** Even though you're not legally required to have one, if an up-to-date survey doesn't exist, hire a surveyor and have one done. Now is the time to know if your cottage is encroaching on an easement, a road allowance, or a neighboring property, or if your property has inadvertently "sprawled" onto adjoining public or private land.

- **Have the chimney and fireplace cleaned and inspected and certified as in proper working order.** If there is a woodburning appliance, confirm that it is certified to Canadian or U.S. standards, and whether its installation met the local building code. You may not be able to warrant this, but if you can, it will be a load off the mind of the buyer.

- **Have the septic tank pumped, and produce service records.** And confirm that the system conforms to current regulations and passes local inspection.

- **If the cottage has a private water source (a well, the lake), have all the records you can muster on hand.** If you have a well, find the well record (the document created by the driller with info about well depth, casing, flow rate, etc.). If the pump was recently replaced or serviced, have the receipts and documentation on hand.

  If the cottage can serve as a main home, the buyers may try to secure a conventional mortgage, which will require them to provide proof of a potable water source. They will probably have to produce a test of their own, but a basic test by the local health board or a private lab is worth securing. Just be sure that you're only warranting that the water was contaminant-free on the test date. It should still be up to the buyer to verify that the water source is potable at closing.

- **If you have undertaken any renovations or repairs that required a building permit, provide the evidence.** As discussed in Chapter 7, the problem of "overbuilding," when a cottage is expanded beyond the capacity of the permitted septic system, is a growing concern among buyers. Show buyers that the local planning office approved of the work performed, especially if it increased the living area.

  In addition, do a little research into local building restrictions, to help buyers know whether their own reno plans are feasible.

- **If you're selling any boats with the property,** either separately or as part of a "with contents" offer, consider having a mechanic perform a basic tune-up on the engines, and have the service records available.

So what does well-executed vendor due diligence entail? The owner approaches his own property as a highly discerning buyer, probing it for every possible weak spot. *(See the checklist on the facing page.)* The due diligence may turn up problems that require remedy or repair. Taking care of them before the property goes on the market means that skeletons are eliminated and the property can be presented as a lower-risk investment.

Boosting market appeal

Adding value to the property

Some improvements are certain to add value to a cottage property, while others aren't – or at least have costs that are far less recoverable.

The reason for performing improvements can be misunderstood. It's not necessarily a case of spending $10 in improvements to realize $12 in purchase price. Well-considered, well-executed improvements increase buyer interest, and make a quick sale more likely – and that is a considerable payback in itself, regardless of the final sales price.

It's important to stress "well-executed." Cottage country is a do-it-yourselfer paradise, and with projects that have a high dollar-return value, such as a deck *(see "Tips from the Frontline," next page)*, it's possible to come out ahead if you provide all the labor. But there won't be any cost recovery if the deck isn't built to the local building code (or is ugly as sin) and buyers have concerns about it. Do it once and do it well.

In many ways, cottages are no different than homes in the sorts of improvements that enhance value or saleability – and in the ones that don't. Interior changes that are very taste-specific – such as wallpaper – generally don't provide a value boost. Repainting an interior always brightens things up but, as with a home, you should stick to white if all you're trying to do is freshen the place up for resale. Strong colors only make buyers think of what it's going to cost to repaint the place the way they want.

As you follow the general rules for home improvements, keep in mind that for most cottage buyers, an unpretentious, low-maintenance getaway is still the purchasing priority. In considering upgrades and renovations, focus on satisfying your own desires, and don't "improve" the cottage beyond your needs, or the essential resale market's needs. Unless there has been a major shift "up market" in the area since you bought the cottage, the person you're going to end up selling it to is probably going to be a lot like you.

Purchaser expectations for seasonal cottages still cover a wide range: Some buyers want a rustic "cottagey" place; others, one that replicates all the comforts of their suburban home. You shouldn't feel obligated to transform your cabin into a facsimile of city living in order to find a buyer. If you start spending money trying to turn the 40-year-old cabin into the modern city residence, you can find yourself suspended between two markets, with

CAUTION:
You've got to tell what you know

Don't think that the absence of a vendor disclosure document means you can "overlook" a problem with your property and it's up to the buyer to find it. If you knew about it and didn't disclose it, the buyer can hold you responsible after the sale. *(See "Seller Disclosure: Telling It Like It Is," p. 125.)*

TIP:
Forget the designer kitchen and focus on the septic tank

The improvements that reap the biggest return in cottage country are those that fall under the purview of vendor due diligence. Any measures that provide more certainty for the buyer of problem-free ownership are a boon to resale. Installing new flooring will be a totally unrecoverable cost if there are serious shortcomings with the septic system that stand in the way of any kind of sale.

Tips from the frontline: Where to focus your renovation efforts

Shirley Davy is an experienced cottage-country broker in central Ontario (and a cottager herself), whose office handles deals in one of the strongest vacation property areas in North America. We asked her what she and the other brokers and agents in her office would recommend to would-be sellers looking to focus their renovation efforts. Here's their hit list of what pays off:

- **Decks.** They provide the biggest payoff of any addition. Cottages are purchased to bring people closer to the great outdoors, and structures that do so are a big plus.

- **Screened-in porches.** Particularly appreciated by those who already know about pests such as blackflies and mosquitoes, they're a far less expensive add-on than a four-season sunroom. And for many buyers, the simplicity and atmosphere of the porch actually make it preferable.

- **Steps.** If the grade from the cottage down to the water is steep, a set of steps rather than a goat trail is a selling bonus.

- **Sleeping space.** An extra bedroom or a bunkie is usually well-received – making the cottage all the better for accommodating family and friends.

- **Septic system.** A newer system is definitely a purchasing plus, since buyers don't want to find themselves worrying about sewage problems and the need for an expensive replacement.

- **Fully winterized.** The retiree segment – including buyers who want to be able to retire to the cottage some day, rather than right away – is producing a shift in demand towards properties that have been fully winterized. It's still a submarket but, nevertheless, these buyers are looking for features such as proper insulation and heated water lines or a well.

- **Easy maintenance.** As sophisticated as vacation properties have become, buyers are still mainly looking for simplicity and minimal demand on their time – which is what vacationing is all about.

- **An exterior that fits in.** Don't paint or re-side the exterior in a bright color. "People like a cottage to fit into the woods," Davy says. Choose a color that allows the cottage to merge with its surroundings: In a wooded setting, green or brown is more saleable than fire-engine red or banana yellow.

a property that isn't simple enough for the rustic market, and not finished enough for the virtual-suburban buyer. Don't feel you have to install granite countertops and rosewood kitchen cabinets when the market is perfectly happy with clean, neat, assemble-it-yourself stuff from IKEA.

The land is ultimately more important to the long-term value than the structure, and it's entirely possible to put too much cottage on a particular property. You may have a challenge recovering the costs of an elaborate building if it's sited on an indifferent lot. If a lot has low appeal – poor swimming, too much boat traffic, too close to a marina or a major road – you're probably better off selling the old two-bedroom bunkie in serviceable condition and starting over with more ambitious renovation plans elsewhere, than you are sinking a lot of money into a major renovation on the existing lot and then trying to recover the costs in the resale market.

Getting the cottage ready for showing

One point realtors stress when they're showing a property for sale is that the devil is in the details – details that can send a potential buyer running in the other direction. Whether you call it "fluffing," "dynamizing," or "tarting the place up a bit," a bit of prep work is in order before you open your door (and dock) to potential purchasers.

Clear out the clutter: Clutter is the number one detractor when you are showing your cottage to strangers. Unfortunately, they might not share your affinity for garden gnomes, collectible teaspoons, or the plastic beach toys strewn throughout the place. Buyers tend to focus on the clutter instead of on the cottage itself – something you definitely do *not* want.

Unlike the average house, cottages also tend to accumulate furniture, which can make small rooms seem positively claustrophobic. Haul away those extra foldout couches and chairs you use when guests visit before you show the place to potential buyers.

Depersonalize: When you show the cottage, you want potential purchasers to imagine themselves enjoying the place with their family. Things like your wedding photos, family snaps, and a refrigerator door full of pet pictures tend to break this reverie. Impersonal neutrality is best: Let the cottage, the lake, and the view from the deck do the selling for you.

Empty the job jar: Any real estate pro will tell you that small things that need fixing – like the wonky hinge on the kitchen cupboard, or the cracked

TIP: **What's included?**

Cottages – more so than homes – are sometimes put on the market with their contents as part-and-parcel of the deal. From the owner's point of view – especially if you're not buying another cottage – selling the place "as is" is easier than emptying it out. Which, of course, means it's not always a plus from the buyer's point of view. *(For more on the strategy of an all-inclusive deal, see "The 'With Contents' Purchase," p. 66.)*

Including a basic boat, such as a canoe or a runabout with a small outboard, however, can sometimes be a way to seal a deal without having to make a significant price reduction – particularly with first-time cottage buyers, who like a turnkey purchase. This is a far better use of the asset than selling it separately in the want ads.

If it's a more valuable boat, such as a sterndrive ski boat, be prepared to have a discerning buyer look this gift horse in the mouth before accepting it in lieu of a major price reduction. Maintenance records may help convince him it's a worthy quid pro quo, but you may have to agree to at least split the cost of a marine survey as a condition.

TIP:

Be clear what you're selling – and what you're not

If you're selling the cottage with contents, try not to confuse the buyer by displaying stuff that isn't part of the deal. Of course, you can't be expected to remove everything, and no one expects you to throw in your car because it's sitting in the driveway. But you should make it clear whether items such as deck furniture and water toys are included or excluded to avoid misunderstandings at closing.

Easing the pain of taxes

In Canada, one way to reduce the reportable capital gains is by claiming the cost of renovations or improvements that enhance the value of the property or extend its useful life. *(See "Using the Cost of Cottage Improvements to Offset Capital Gains," p. 225.)*

pane of glass in the spare bedroom window – can convey to a buyer a sense of larger neglect. If you leave them unaddressed at selling time, you could be encouraging tip-of-the-iceberg fears in prospective purchasers.

Freshen things up with a coat of paint: There's an old saying in the real estate biz: "$100 in the bucket is worth $3,000 on the walls." Doing some painting yourself can pay huge dividends when you show the cottage to strangers. (But heed the notes about color choice on pp. 203 and 204.)

Increase the curb – or gravel driveway – appeal: First impressions count, so spend some time on the exterior of the place, especially in those areas potential purchasers will see when they step out of the car or boat. Replace that broken board in the dock. Sweep the pine needles off the deck. Cut the grass, clip the bushes, and tidy up any gardens. Maybe even put out some potted shrubs and flowers to maximize your property's "first glance" appeal.

And if you have stuff on the property that should have gone to the dump months (or years!) ago, now's the time.

Selling and taxation

Whether you're Canadian or American, selling a cottage will very likely trigger a tax bill for the net capital gains realized since you acquired the property (back to the point at which capital gains taxes were introduced), unless you are able to shelter the property from those gains in whole or in part by having it qualify as your "main home" (Americans) or "principal residence" (Canadians). Some advance planning can save you a bundle.

Taxes in Canada

Regulations for Canadian taxpayers on what constitutes a "principal residence" are fairly generous *(see Tip, p. 226)*, making it easy for a cottage to qualify for the exemption. You only have to designate your principal residence at the time you sell it (and if the property has been your principal residence since the day you acquired it, you never have to make the designation or declare the sale to CRA at all). If you're selling the cottage and it has appreciated more than your main home, it may be in your best interest to designate the cottage as your principal residence for a year or more of the ownership period when you file your return – assuming, of course, it can qualify. Since 1982 you have been permitted *only one principal residence per family*. (The definition of family has been shifting since then, but it now includes you, your spouse – who can be a same-sex or common-law partner – and your children, provided they are not 18 or older with a spouse of their own. Consult the CRA for the exact years when the definitions applied.)

Another reason to designate the cottage as your principal residence for at least part of the ownership period is if you intend to remain in your "real" main home and not sell it. While transferring the capital gains tax exemption to the cottage will remove protection from your "real" home for that period, if you and your spouse remain in your home for the rest of your lives, the capital gains tax obligation on it will be left to your estate to deal with. (*See Chapter 14 for more on capital gains tax strategies.*)

Taxes in the U.S.

American taxpayers have a huge incentive to make a cottage qualify as their main home at the time of sale. Since 1997, taxpayers have enjoyed an exemption of $250,000 for single filers and $500,000 for married couples on net capital gains on the main home. The second home has no exemption at all. And if the second home is considered a "personal use" property, which is most likely the case (unless you are using it as a formal rental property), you cannot reduce the capital gains hit by applying any sort of depreciation, or claim a loss if its value drops below purchase price. However, you only have to establish that a property served as the main home for two of the past five years in order to get the exemption – which then applies to all capital gains for the history of ownership.

The IRS considers your main home to be the place where you reside most of the time, whether you own it or not, and that could be an apartment where you live for nine months of the year. If the IRS isn't sure about the "main home" designation, it will look to clues such as the mailing address on your voter registration, the location of your place of work, the church you attend, and other social-scene indicators that tell them you're not actually at the cottage property most of the time. In any event, you must designate your main (and if applicable, second) home every tax year if you're claiming appropriate deductions such as mortgage interest.

Nevertheless, since the cottage only has to serve as your main home for two of the past five years to qualify for the exemption, you've got some wiggle room. The year leading up to the sale is considered critical in convincing the IRS of its status, but you don't have to be actually living in the main home at the time of sale to secure the exemption, and it could be used mainly for rental purposes during portions of the five-year lead-up period. You can also use the capital gains exemption for the main home repeatedly, as long as at least two years pass between sales of qualifying homes. (And even if two years haven't passed, you may qualify for a partial designation or for an exemption based on military service, health issues, or change in workplace.) This means that, in our five-year qualifying period, another home could be the main home during the first two years. This home could be sold, with the capital gains sheltered by the main home designation. You could move into the cottage in year three and designate it as the main home, rent it out in year four as you travel the world, move back in for year five and use it as your main home, then sell it and get the main home exemption all over again (to the maximum exemption available).

The owner's best friend: How to build a cottage operating manual

Every cottage should have one: an owner's manual for the entire property. A complete, up-to-date manual is a real bonus to potential purchasers – and therefore it's a great tool when it comes time to sell your property. Until then, it's terrific for jogging your own memory, and an indispensable resource if different family members use the cottage at different times or you rent out the place or lend it to friends. (Not only can it make their stay more enjoyable, but it can also save you from their well-intentioned – but misguided – efforts.)

Compile your operating manual in a three-ring binder: That way, you can add (and delete) pages as cottage systems and procedures change. Divide the info into sections to make it easily accessible. Have sections covering day-to-day operating instructions and ones devoted to "once a year" processes – opening and closing procedures, for instance. (Since renters don't need to know how to start the water system in spring or pull out the floating dock in fall, these sections can be removed from the binder when the cottage is rented out.)

Mechanical systems

The big three – water, waste, and electrical – require their own sections in the manual. They should cover how things run normally, the symptoms when they aren't running normally, and what to do when they aren't. (Include owner's manuals for all equipment in your operating manual.)

Photos work wonders in making operating instructions clear. Use a digital or film camera to snap a few pictures and compose step-by-step illustrated guides – to getting the water pump going, for instance, or performing the required once-a-week maintenance on the composting toilet or water purifier.

TIP: If you rent your place, give tradespeople and neighbors a heads-up

Get in touch with the service people you list in your operating manual and let them know that you're including them as a source of help. You can arrange for them to contact you first before proceeding with any repairs, but in a rental situation it's better to have the service calls happen automatically, rather than have a plumber's response unnecessarily delayed while he tries to get in touch with you. For both the renter's sake and your own, let a trusted tradesperson deal with the problem pronto and bill you directly.

Likewise, if you're on good terms with your neighbors, you can list them in the manual as a contact for renters in the event they need help with something. But you should also make such neighbors aware of when you're renting, and tell them to call *you* if they see any problems.

And since breakdowns can occur that are beyond the fix-it skills of even a handy cottager – let alone a renter – provide contact information for local tradespeople who can provide service on an emergency basis. (*See Tip, facing page.*)

Other cottage know-how

Where does garbage go?

Your manual should explicitly explain what's to be done with the garbage: Does it get stored in a shed until pick-up day, left in the bin by the road, or taken to the local dump? If it goes to the dump, include directions and operating hours. (The manual is a good place to store your dump pass or permit, if one is required.) How are recyclables handled? Does the cottage have a compost bin? If so, what are its dos and don'ts?

Especially if you rent or lend your cottage, you can't be too clear about garbage processes. City folks not used to marauding wildlife might not have the same appreciation for orderly trash disposal that you do. (To help motivate renters, it can be handy to overstate the presence of garbage-seeking black bears in your locale.)

Boats and other watercraft

Where is the key for the runabout kept? How about the canoe paddles? What's the trick for starting the old 9.9 hp? What's the mix in its fuel tank? Go through your watercraft one by one, think about their quirks and equipment, and include all relevant information. Don't forget maintenance records and repair manuals.

Go through the rest of the cottage in the same manner and write down operating procedures and troubleshooting tips. Of course you'll explain where the kindling is kept, but it would be a mistake to assume that everyone knows to open the fireplace damper before lighting a fire.

Emergency information

Don't just include "9-1-1" or the local variation. Provide the name and location of the nearest hospital and a map that shows how to get there by road and/or water. If there's a walk-in clinic, include hours and contact info. And remember to include the vet – name, phone number, and directions.

Fire service may be provided by the municipality or on a volunteer basis by the local lake association. However it works, explain it, including (if applicable) a map showing the location of the nearest fire pump.

Local amenities

In many cottage communities, there's not a whole lot of mystery to where you get groceries or beer. But every vacation area has its quirks, and a manual is a great place to outline them. You don't have to provide a written guide to the entire business district, but do share your favorite haunts: the best farm stand for fresh corn, the burger joint with the great shakes, the antique shop, the store

More handy inclusions:

- [ ] contact numbers (other than 9-1-1) for police and ambulance

- [ ] location of the first aid kit and fire extinguishers

- [ ] names, location, and phone numbers of helpful neighbors

- [ ] if there's no phone at the cottage, location of the closest neighbor with a phone

- [ ] cottage lot and concession numbers, or whatever numeric system your municipality uses to direct emergency services to your property

- [ ] sketches showing the location of wells, septic tanks, and leaching beds

- [ ] records of major repairs

- [ ] records of regular service and maintenance (for instance, septic tank pumpouts)

- [ ] receipts and warranties for equipment, as well as the instruction books

- [ ] location of closest suppliers of propane, firewood, charcoal, boat gas, etc.

- [ ] system limitations (what should and shouldn't be put into the septic system; how many consecutive showers can be had before the water goes cold)

Cottage Manual *continued*

with the best selection of magazines and newspapers. Include a warning of any oddball business hours. People can become so accustomed to 24-7 services in the city that they might not realize the local grocery store isn't going to be open on Sunday evening.

Insider tips on your property and the lake

If you have kids, enlist their help with this part of the manual. Have them describe all the attractions: where they like to swim (and the safe places to jump in), the spot they see the snapping turtle, the location of the beaver lodge. The list is endless, and it's a fun and practical exercise for them that can impart useful information to guests of their own age. Be so bold as to reveal the location of your favorite fishing hole, and the kinds of fish to be caught.

Local attractions

Beyond the business-district diversions mentioned above, there are bound to be rainy-day distractions within a short drive of the property: a local movie theater, a wildlife center, a museum. Keep restless kids in mind. You may have no interest in the local go-kart track, but they might. If you rent, you might even pick up some brochures and put them in the binder. Just remember to get fresh copies every year.

Official and unofficial lake rules

Provide new owners, as well as guests and renters, with guidance on both official regulations (a speed limit on the lake, for instance) and local etiquette. Different cottage areas have different cultures, and the ground rules may not be obvious to newcomers. Don't assume they'll know that soaping up in the lake is an environmental no-no, or that a bonfire sing-along that goes on after midnight is verboten. Put it all in the manual so that they – and you – don't incur the wrath of the neighbors.

Natural hazards

Cottage country often comes equipped with wildlife wild cards. Few creatures present a real threat to life and limb, but without being alarmist, your manual should explain what's out there and what's required to avoid problems.

If raccoons and bears regularly ransack unsecured garbage bins and greasy barbecues, stress the importance of proper disposal and cleaning procedures. If there's a persistent patch of poison ivy beside the shed, point it out. If mice are a problem, include a reminder about keeping food properly stored. If the rocky point is home to massasauga rattlers, explain that free-running children and pets should stay away. Excellent information brochures are available through provincial ministries and state departments. Include them in your binder.

TIP:

X marks the spot

In your manual, include a map of the lake with points of interest and practicalities marked on it. Show marinas, stores, and the route to the hospital. Point out your favorite picnic spot, the marsh that makes a good paddling destination, and the sand beach where the kids like to swim.

13. Relocating to vacation country

*I*magine not having to make the commute back and forth. Imagine being able to spend every day by the lake. The cottage that serves as a sanctuary from the nine-to-five routine can beckon as a permanent sanctuary when working life is finally behind you.

Alternatively, maybe you're thinking of relocating to the cottage *before* you retire. Thanks to the Internet, telephone and video conferencing, and the flexible work arrangements offered by some companies, more and more people are considering themselves "work from the cottage" candidates.

Bottom-line basics

At whatever age you make the transition, you need a few things in your favor for it to be successful:

• The community that's closest to your cottage must be at a distance *you* consider acceptable for regular, year-round access.

• It must be able to provide practical support for residential living year-round – stores that stock whatever *you* consider essential (from groceries to hardware to books to magazines), tradespeople, repair and personal services, schools (if kids are involved in the transition), library, restaurants, and entertainment. If that support isn't available in the closest cottage community, it must be found at a distance you find acceptable.

• Health services that meet your needs must be available at a distance that satisfies your comfort level.

• The relocation ideally will provide a desirable lifestyle change, but it cannot demand changes you are unwilling or unable to make.

• Relocation can result in changes in social patterns, and even enhance them. But it cannot disrupt social patterns you view as irreplaceable.

If you're buying a property now for retirement later

We stressed it in Chapter 2, and we'll stress it here again: If you are buying a property for eventual, rather than immediate (or close to immediate), retirement, buy what makes you happy now – not what you think will make you happy far down the road.

The character of an area can change dramatically in just a few years. If you're not planning to retire for another decade or two, choosing a property now, based on how you judge its suitability for retirement living, may cause you to reject potential properties that could turn out, down the road, to have everything you're looking for in a retirement retreat.

The lake itself can swing from mostly seasonal to mostly permanent residents, a change accompanied by improved road access and organized year-round social activities. Even where the character of the lake remains constant, local communities can change tremendously in less than a decade: better medical facilities, more social services, larger and more varied retail outlets.

On the other hand, some things *don't* change. A cottage high on a hill with 200 steps to the lake is unlikely to become more retirement-friendly as the years pass (though you can make some changes to compensate; *see "Retirement Retrofits,", p. 218.*)

But also keep in mind that you can't be sure you'll actually *want* to retire to the property when the time comes. Priorities and interests change, and retirement living in vacation country often proves to be something people dream about rather than actually do.

Vacation communities that are largely seasonal can be lonely places in the dead of winter. You may realize when it comes time to retire that you enjoy the cottage for those halcyon days between May and October, and that for the rest of the year you'd rather be in the sunny south, or home in the city, with your friends and relatives and the social life you've developed there. The cottage chores you enjoyed a couple of decades ago may just be too much hard work now. Or medical issues may have emerged in your life that require the attention of specialists who are nowhere to be found in cottage country.

Bottom line? Don't buy as a 40 year old what you think you might want as a 60 year old.

A starter kit of questions if you're thinking of year-round cottage living

☐ How many local residents are seasonal? Will you be comfortable living in relative isolation if most neighbors are using their properties as summer-only retreats?

☐ Is the property on a school-bus route? If so, you can rely on the road being plowed. If the road is private and jointly maintained by fellow cottagers, is winter plowing covered by your regular contribution to a road association or do you have to pay extra for winter services? Using the road regularly year-round may also affect general maintenance costs: If other users aren't interested in keeping the road open year-round, they may also expect you to pay a disproportionate share for spring grading and graveling.

☐ Are area businesses strictly seasonal? If the closest store is at the local marina and it's only open during boating season, how far will you have to drive to buy milk and bread?

☐ What's the "cabin fever" quotient? How close are diversions such as restaurants, movie theaters, and shops?

☐ Is the cottage itself big enough for year-round occupancy? What might seem cozy for an occasional winter weekend might feel claustrophobic on a full-time basis. You'll be spending a lot less time outdoors, so porches, decks, and docks – which expand living space in summer – don't count in winter. (*For other considerations about the cottage itself, see "Assessing the Cottage: Is It Ready for Year-Round Living?," p. 218.*)

Assessing local services

When we spend most of our life in a major urban center, we tend to take the availability of certain services for granted. It's only when you move to a more remote area that you realize it might not be easy to find a particular service after all. This can range from the relatively trivial – where the heck is the nearest Ford dealer? – to the serious.

People routinely relocate to small centers without giving thought to the possibility that they might have a problem finding a new physician or dentist, and be relegated to waiting at a walk-in clinic or a hospital emergency

TIP: **Three things to help smooth the transition**

• Before you become a year-rounder, investigate the social network opportunities in the community. There may be arts groups, fitness clubs, regular recreational and sports groups (bridge clubs, book clubs, walking groups, curling leagues), or volunteer organizations in which you can become involved.

• Consider easing into retirement at the cottage by trying the spring–fall part of the calendar first. Don't burn your bridges in terms of winter accommodation in case year-round cottage living isn't right for you.

• Have a proper guest bedroom at the cottage, and not just a pullout couch. It will make friends and family more inclined to visit and stay, rather than dropping by for a few hours.

CAUTION:

Are you the type that needs a get-out-of-jail-free card?

Some people feel more trapped than they anticipate when they move to the cottage full-time, especially once the activity of summer is over. Even if they didn't take regular advantage of everything that was available to them in the city, they knew they *could* if they wanted to – which gave them a sense of freedom that they now miss.

For them, urban life is like having a get-out-of-jail-free card: Even if they never use it, they need to know it's there.

room for basic service. Those with medical conditions that require ongoing care and monitoring are more aware of the need to ensure that a specialist and facilities are close at hand. But health is unpredictable, and you have to consider that complications could arise in a few months or years that might be difficult if not impossible to treat in a small community.

Lifestyle "transference"

By "transference," we mean the ability to relocate key parts of your current lifestyle to the retirement area. Some things – the hustle and bustle of the city – you want to leave behind. Other things you hope to take with you, and it's sometimes difficult to know what those things are until you no longer have them.

Perhaps the best way to approach this is to think of how you now spend a typical week or two at various times of year. (Go through an old calendar or appointment book to jog your memory.) Some components are easier to identify than others: the theater performances, the curling bonspiel. Others are less obvious. It's only after you move that you might start wondering how you're going to get your favorite daily newspaper, or who's going to cut your hair.

If you've had a cottage in a particular area for years, it won't be hard for you to put your finger on how transference is going to work out in terms of both obvious and less obvious things. But if you're choosing a cottage area with an eye to retirement, you need to think through the impacts of the lifestyle change. Some aspects of your old life will be left behind. Other aspects will undergo an adjustment. You will miss browsing the neighbor-

---

Case study:
Retooling the retirement dream

Dave and Donna had long planned to retire to the remote cottage they'd built themselves on an isolated lake eight hours from their home. Both teachers, they had always spent two consecutive months there with their son and daughter each summer, longing for the day when they wouldn't have to leave come Labor Day.

When the kids reached their teenage years, Dave and Donna got a foreshadowing of what could happen to their dream: Jobs, travel, and friends became compelling reasons for the kids to want to spend summer at home, rather than at the lake. Donna and Dave still moved north – but found they were going home themselves occasionally, rather than staying for two straight months. How else would they see the kids?

When they retired, the fantasy unraveled further. Older now, Dave discovered that keeping the bush beaten back, once part of the cottage adventure, was more pain than pleasure. Donna worried about being left a widow with no way to get to the cottage since Dave did all the long highway driving.

hood bookstore, and you know that there isn't a comparable one in the cottage area, but you can manage to visit the old store when you're back in the city once a month and bulk-buy on a single browsing.

Overall, you expect to gain a better quality of life with a relocation to cottage country. The gains tend to be intangibles: the life by the lake; the view; the clean air; a healthier, more active lifestyle. You need to be sensitive at the same time to what you might be giving up in relinquishing your old home. Your social network can take a body blow. Friends and family might express delight at the idea of coming to the lake for a visit, but when the time comes, they might not be able to visit as often as either of you thought.

Making a cottage retirement work

Many people find retirement a difficult adjustment – even without a location change. We all know people who lived to work, and when they stopped working, didn't know what to do with themselves. Suddenly they have "nothing to do."

For some, the move to the cottage circumvents the problem, since it comes with its own workload and offers a chance to set new goals. For others, the relocation compounds the difficulties caused by the loss of a lifelong working routine.

In our workaholic world, successful retirements are most often

Their lifestyle had changed too, their high-pressure work days replaced by the more leisurely pace of retirement. For years, the cottage had been an escape, a reprieve from their stress-filled lives, but now they didn't need an escape anymore. The distance to their place had always discouraged drop-in guests – and they had liked it that way, because they treasured their solitude. Now it began to seem lonely. They decided to sell the cottage.

But their story has a happy ending: They bought another place, on a larger lake, much closer to home. Here, they are part of a community of cottagers; plus, the new place is close enough to "civilization" that friends – and family – come to visit regularly. They don't live at the new cottage full-time either (they held onto their home), but they can come and go when the urge strikes – especially since Donna is comfortable driving the short haul herself. Instead of a bush road, the route to their door is now via well-maintained country roads – which offer the pleasurable side effect of allowing them to take up biking again. Dave paints watercolors instead of beating back the bush; Donna plays the organ in the community church. And they see their kids more now than they had in the previous 10 years.

TIP:

It will take a while to settle in

Successful cottage retirees report that they went through an adjustment period before they reached the point where they said, "We'd *never* go back to city life." For those accustomed to active, social summers, it takes a while to get used to – and enjoy – the slower pace of the off-season. And when the weather turns cold and neither of you has a job to head off to each morning, it can take a while simply to adjust to being together with your partner all day in a small space. "For the first year we were really at each other," one cottager admits, "then we got overinvolved in local activities." Eventually, they reached a balance, settling into the rhythm of retirement, each other, and a pace of life that changed with the seasons.

achieved by people who establish a fulfilling life (and identity) outside the workplace – *before* they put the workplace behind them. Then when they do, there's no better place than cottage country to continue that fulfilling life.

Year-round versus seasonal occupancy

"Retiring to the cottage" can mean very different things to different people. For some, it's a year-round commitment as the cottage becomes the main home. For others, the cottage is still strictly a seasonal abode, albeit one occupied full-time from May through October, after which they head to a warmer climate. Even "year-rounders" are known to take a midwinter break and head south for a month or two.

If you're considering year-round occupancy, try to get a good sense of what the area is like in winter before committing to the plan. In northern areas, it's not simply a matter of being able to cope with snow. (Though that's certainly a consideration: Cottage winter neophytes report being surprised by the severity of the weather and the sheer volume and frequency of snow.) Seasonal communities become different places in the off-season.

Take, for example, the couple who decided to move full-time to a waterfront community that was spectacular in the summer. But come Thanksgiving, virtually all the neighbors left. They were alone, with a 20-minute drive

For Americans: Make sure you're covered

 Americans planning to retire to a Canadian property need to confirm whether their medical insurance or pension plan offers coverage if they're living in Canada all, or most, of the year. If it doesn't, don't count on securing public health care in Canada.

Eligibility has nothing to do with where you pay either your income or property taxes. The most basic way for a non-Canadian to qualify for a provincial medical insurance program is by securing permanent residence status. However, your chances of becoming a permanent resident in Canada diminish as you grow older.

Canada no longer recognizes retirees as a separate eligibility category. A close relative or family member age 18 or older who is a Canadian citizen or permanent resident can sponsor you in your application to become a permanent resident yourself, but otherwise, you most likely have to qualify under the "skilled worker" or "business immigrant" categories – and under the Canadian points qualification system, your eligibility as a skilled worker diminishes with every passing year. The younger you are, the higher you score. The older you are, the harder it is to achieve the required number of points.

(in good weather) to the nearest town. The isolation was unnerving, and the next year, they relocated much closer to town, sacrificing life on the waterfront for a more established community.

Fretting over fitting in

Some retirees worry – with good reason – whether they'll be accepted locally. Even when you're living there permanently, it can take a long time to integrate into a rural community. To the locals, you're still a cottager.

Be realistic about how quickly you can expect to be embraced in a small community where you didn't grow up with long-term residents, attending high school together, going to each other's weddings, coaching each other's kids in hockey or Little League. But if you're looking for a way to jump-start the ice-breaking, don't insist on returning to the big city for goods and services because things are "better" or "cheaper" there.

Spend your money locally: Get your car from a local dealer; risk having your hair cut in town; patronize the local hardware store instead of always driving to a big-box outlet (even if a lot of the locals do). Nothing makes you fit in faster than taking a car to the local mechanic or lube shop. Nothing makes you stand out like a sore thumb more than never setting foot in the local grocery (or, worse, standing in line at the checkout and loudly complaining to each other about how expensive everything is "up here").

A ratepayers' association will help you meet people quickly, but don't limit your social circle to the people on your shoreline road. Get involved in a local service group or charity fundraising. Volunteer at the library. Join the local curling club. To be part of a community, you have to be active in it.

Unfortunately, "fitting in" becomes much more difficult if an area has

The "retirement effect" on local communities

When you retire to a cottage community, you'll likely be part of a larger process of change, as the municipality shifts from a largely seasonal to a more year-round population. In general, municipalities welcome the influx of year-rounders. They increase spending in the local economy, giving local businesses and trades a more stable year-round cash flow, spur new investment in the retail and service sectors, and improve the tax base. On the other hand, retirees can put strains on local infrastructure, particularly health care; but the solution is usually to get services improved and paid for, not to blame retirees for creating problems.

The downsides for "the people who were there first" are environmental and political. If once-seasonal waterfront properties are expanded and made into year-round homes, septic systems can be strained, to the detriment of water quality. The solution may be a municipal waste-water system that the existing residents never wished for − and now have to pay for. And an influx of year-rounders on the waterfront, who may be paying a disproportionate share of the property tax bill, can quickly change the political landscape as they demand a greater voice in local government. But change overall is usually gradual and, if properly managed, beneficial to both sides.

become polarized politically, which tends to be along property lines. The waterfront property owners try to secure a voice on local council, and the townspeople and backlot owners try to make sure they're not drowned out in the process. Relative property tax burdens and public access to the waterfront can raise the political temperature. Attending a local council meeting is a good way to start fitting in, but you might end up hearing others carp about people who sound a lot like yourself. At least you'll know where you stand, and where bridges need to be built.

Assessing the cottage: Is it ready for year-round living?

If you've never stayed at your cottage in the winter, or if most of your winter visits have been short-term, you'll want to think about the state of the cottage itself before embarking on your first full year-rounder by the lake. A substantial gap lies between fond memories of spending Christmas at the cottage and the reality of living there for the entire winter.

Retirement retrofits

Even if you're planning only a three-season retirement at the cottage and will retreat elsewhere in winter, you may find the place becomes a bit challenging as you get older. The steps down to the dock seem steeper, and the meandering walk from the parking area to the cottage door seems longer – and the groceries heavier. (Plus, you're doing it more often when you're living at the lake full-time.) And diving into the water (not to mention hauling yourself out afterwards) isn't quite as much fun as it used to be.

Take heart: This doesn't mean you have to trade the place in for a bungalow in a suburban seniors' development. A few retrofits can make any cottage a little more age-friendly:

• Long, steep flights of steps become more difficult with age. Break them up with landings to provide places to rest. And build (or buy) benches for the landings.

• Add sturdy, easy-to-grab railings – not just on steps, but also along whatever paths you walk on regularly.

• Make sure paths and steps are well lit to help avoid missteps: Add motion-sensor lights, or close-to-the-ground guide lights and mark "dangers." (For instance, if a tree root extends across the path and you can't route around it, paint it white so it's obvious.)

• Change the rise-to-run ratio on stairs so they're easier for aging knees to negotiate: Make the tread depth wider and the height between steps a little lower, adding an additional step or two if necessary. Paint the risers a contrasting color, so aging eyes don't misread the stair heights in dim light.

• Eliminate steps by extending your driveway so it brings you as close as possible to the cottage door. This reduces the distance you have to carry stuff and makes getting to the car more comfortable in bad weather.

If you have a newly built dwelling that's fully insulated, complete with a garage and a driveway to your door, you'll probably be facing fewer challenges than a cottager with an older place that has been slowly renovated and improved over the years – without much thought given to eventual year-round living. You may decide you still want to retire to the cottage, but that it's easier to start over with another cottage: one that is more a fully serviced waterfront home, and one that is also closer to the shops, services – and medical facilities – of town.

Access

• Is your cottage road plowed by the municipality or is it a private road, where maintenance is undertaken by local residents?

• If maintenance is privately contracted, how quickly is the road cleared after a snowstorm? Is winter plowing covered by your regular contribution to a road association or do you have to pay extra for winter services?

• Do you have a long driveway? Are you able to clear it yourself? If not, you'll need to secure the services of a local contractor for prompt, regular driveway plowing.

• If space permits, install an entrance ramp to replace the stairs into the cottage.

• If your cottage is high above the lake and the steps are simply getting to be too much, look for ways to decrease the number of times you have to make the trip from cottage to dock: One cottager put a mini-kitchen (with a fridge and microwave) in a shed near the dock to eliminate "snack runs." Another added a larger deck to the cottage itself to create more outdoor gathering space that didn't require a climb.

• Can you use a different route to get from cottage to dock? Is it possible, say, to put in a longer path with shallow switchbacks and several short sets of steps?

• If all else fails, investigate a lift. They're not cheap – but if this is the only serious drawback to a cottage you love, it may be the answer.

• A set of wide, shallow stairs that leads right into the water is much easier to manage than a dock ladder when creaky bodies go swimming. Add a handrail, too.

• If you have a two-storey cottage, add a bedroom and bath on the main floor and commandeer it for yourselves. Let the kids climb to the second floor.

• The crawl space under the cottage that was once merely inconvenient can make maintenance and repair a truly painful experience as you get older. Think about relocating the pump and other equipment or otherwise improving the access.

• Consider the same interior retrofits for your cottage as one would make to an urban home, such as grab rails in the bathroom and electrical outlets at a more comfortable height.

• Does your driveway go all the way to your front door? What might be a pleasant stroll to a parking area in summer can be an onerous struggle if you have to do it regularly in winter, especially with an armload of groceries. To avoid the labor of clearing a path each time it snows, many cottagers opt to extend their driveway right to their door – where it can be cleared with a snow blower or a contracted plow truck.

• Open-air parking means clearing and scraping your vehicle each time you want to go for a drive and, when the weather gets really cold, plugging in a block heater. For convenient winter access, many year-rounders choose to add a garage or carport before retiring to the lake.

Water and septic

• Unless you have the luxury of a municipal supply, having a reliable source of water in winter means having either a well or a heated or self-draining line running from the lake. Wells are basically immune to the cold, but if you'll be relying on a heated or self-draining intake line from the lake, it might be a good idea to have it inspected by a contractor before putting it to the test of a full winter.

• To prevent freezing, a properly installed waste line running to the septic tank should be buried deep enough to insulate it from the winter weather and pitched in such a way that liquids never sit in the pipe. Cottages built on elevated piers or pilings that have been subsequently converted to winter use sometimes end up having a waste line that is either completely exposed to the elements or partially buried under shallow soil. This isn't a problem in warm months, but can cause sewage to freeze and block the pipe when used year-round. If you have never used your septic system in the winter, check it carefully. Problems with fully or partly exposed drain pipes can usually be solved by either reburying the pipe (if possible), adding insulation to the exterior of the pipe, or wrapping the pipe with heating cables specifically designed for plumbing applications.

Heating

• Because power outages can occur frequently in the winter months, you need to assess how many of your cottage systems rely on electricity. If the entire cottage runs on electricity – including heaters, water pumps, heated intake lines, and cooking appliances – you should definitely think about having a backup generator installed to prevent freezing in the dark. (Even forced-air gas or oil furnaces require electricity to run their blower motors.) The number of systems you run with electricity will determine the size and cost of the generator.

• Mixed systems offer a higher degree of redundancy against power outages by combining electricity, propane, natural gas or oil, and wood to keep things comfy when the power fails. By being able to fall back on wood heat (via a woodstove or fireplace insert) and propane gas for cooking, short outages can actually be romantic. Longer-term comfort can be achieved with a small (less-expensive) generator used to run the water pump, a heated intake line if necessary, and a light or two.

• If your cottage uses propane or heating oil and you have poor access because of a steep driveway or some other obstacle, check with your fuel supplier. Many difficult locations simply can't be accessed by fuel delivery vehicles in the winter, a problem remedied by installing larger or additional tanks to meet an entire winter's demand.

• If you'll be heating with wood, make sure you lay in an adequate supply of dry firewood well in advance. Consider building a woodshed that's close or connected to the cottage.

Structure

• If you're planning to live at the cottage year-round, it goes without saying that the place is properly insulated. But if your cottage started life as a summer-only retreat and was made winter-ready by a succession of renovations and upgrades, you might want to make a quick inspection tour before you make the big move.

– Are there any old-style single-pane windows? If so, replace them with thermal windows.
– Are existing thermal panes in good condition? Are they sealed properly around the exterior?
– If the plumbing resides in an insulated crawl space under the cottage, is the insulation in good condition and airtight? Check for critter damage.

• Cottages originally designed for bright and breezy summer living may lack an airlock entryway, great for keeping heat where it belongs – inside the cottage. They also prove handy for keeping snow and mud outside. Airlock entries can be added to the inside of the building, space permitting, but are more easily created by enclosing a section of covered porch or adding a small "bump-out" to the building.

Special considerations for the working set

If you consider yourself a "work at the cottage" candidate, here are a few additional points to consider before you make the big transition:

• Living two or more hours away from your worksite becomes feasible if most days are spent working remotely at home, or if job duties require you to be on the road far from the office anyway. Determine how often you actually need to be at the worksite or, if you're self-employed, in a particular city for face-to-face meetings with clients. And think about how flexible those times are. Can you time them to avoid rush-hour-in, rush-hour-back traffic patterns? If you can't make a critical meeting because snow squalls trap you at the cottage, will it damage your career or a client relationship? Invest in a four-wheel drive vehicle and be prepared to stay overnight in the city at a hotel from time to time.

• Scope out the communications infrastructure in your part of vacation country. What are the options? How reliable are they? (*See "What Sort of Communications Systems Are Available at the Cottage?," p. 95.*)

• What are the opportunities for spousal employment? The relocation will be easier if your spouse is looking for an opportunity to try something new, or circumstances allow one of you to take a break from full-time work.

• Living year-round in what is still substantially a summer vacation community can mean a complete lack of kids the same age as yours within walking distance of home during the school year. Be prepared to do a lot of driving, and host a lot of sleepovers.

• Attending school – particularly high school – can mean long bus rides for the kids, and fewer choices of specialized programs. There's simply not the student population to support the range of specialization available in many urban areas. This can be a serious problem if your kids are destined for college or university and a sufficient variety of "academic stream" courses isn't on offer. Services for children with special needs can also be difficult to secure. On the upside, many kids excel in smaller schools, great summer jobs can be had in vacation areas, and recreational opportunities abound.

• And if you're used to interacting with co-workers in an office all day, working by yourself at the cottage can have you talking to the squirrels in no time.

14. Handing down the cottage

Most real estate isn't handed down from one generation to the next. Homes that are part of an estate are usually sold, and the proceeds distributed among the beneficiaries according to the directions of the will. Cottages are different: Many adults who harbor fond memories of childhood summers there have gone on to deliver the experience to their own children, and would like to imagine their grandchildren enjoying the same rites of passage. A cottage is often a rare touchstone among the transitions of modern life and, as such, it carries a level of emotion and possessiveness unlike that generated by a family home.

Many examples exist of cottages that have passed down through multiple generations of a family. But even those families have come to recognize that the hurdles – practical, legal, and financial – have become higher with each passing year.

Bequeathing a cottage can indeed be done successfully, but thanks to certain tax law amendments and the soaring value of cottage real estate, it has become more complicated than it once was. In this chapter, we'll first explore ways to reduce the tax burden as much as possible, then look at practical ways to hand down the cottage successfully to one's offspring.

Taxation issues lie at the root of many cottage bequest problems these days. They can be extremely complicated, and exploring them in their entirety for the North American cottage market would require two complete books, one for the tax regimen of each nation. That said, some effective general strategies for dealing with these issues do exist. Armed with a general understanding of possible solutions, you can then seek professional help, consulting an estate-planning lawyer, a tax accountant, and maybe even a financial planner.

Planning ahead for the tax bite

The greatest hurdle to handing down a cottage successfully is poor estate planning. Title can be conveyed to one or more beneficiaries in a will, but the capital gains taxes payable on the property when it changes hands can be so high that the only way for the estate to settle the tax bill is to sell the cottage to raise the money – hardly the desired outcome of the bequest.

Avoiding punitive tax bills that can defeat bequest intentions requires planning, and that planning often needs to occur years in advance. Owners of Canadian and American vacation property alike face taxes on capital gains on its "disposal" through sale, gift (in Canada), or bequest. Sound estate planning strives to minimize the capital gains payable by either the estate or the present owners during their lifetime.

Capital gains taxes can be minimized in two basic ways:

1. By deeming the cottage a principal residence (in Canada) or a main home (in the U.S.), which shelters it from taxes on capital gains.

TIP: Communication is key

Before you meet with a lawyer or a tax accountant, who typically charge hundreds of dollars per hour for their services, it's important that family members are all on the same page. First off, what are the parents' wishes? Can they truly afford to bequeath the cottage, or could the funds from its sale be better used for medical or retirement costs down the road? (Not surprisingly, many parents put the happiness of their kids ahead of their own well-being.) Are *all* the children interested in keeping and sharing the property or would some prefer a cash settlement to use as they please? *(See p. 228.)* Is sharing one cottage property a desirable outcome? Is it even possible, given inequities in the heirs' finances? Will all the children even be able to use the cottage on a regular basis if family members are scattered across the globe? Is it possible (or desirable) to sever the property into separate lots for each sibling? Parents and children need to take the time to determine what outcomes work for each family member before seeking advice from a tax or estate professional.

Gifting a Canadian cottage: The piper must still be paid

Whether you leave the cottage to your kids in your will, give it to them as a gift in your lifetime, or sell it to them for a nominal fee, the outcome for tax purposes is the same: The property is considered to have been sold *at fair market value*, and you (or your estate) are liable for the tax on the capital gains from the sale. *(For gifting a U.S. cottage, see p. 236.)*

2. By documenting expenses that enhance the capital value of the property (and, in the U.S., other expenses related to acquisition and ownership), which can be used to offset capital gains, whether or not the property ever qualifies as a main home or principal residence.

A few specialized strategies can also be employed to minimize taxes, such as transferring the cottage to a trust or non-profit organization, or by making a charitable bequest. (We'll explore these strategies later in the chapter.)

Using the cost of cottage improvements to offset capital gains

Canadian and American tax law approach capital gains on a cottage property from a similar angle. Both require the owner to arrive at a value for the property at the time it was acquired, whether it was purchased, inherited, or (in Canada) received as a gift. *(See p. 236 for the special circumstances of determining value when "gifting" property for U.S. taxpayers.)* Both systems then allow the base cost of acquiring the property to be increased by adding on the expense of capital improvements that increase the value or extend the life of a property. These can be used to offset any reported capital gains.

In arriving at what we might call this "what you put into it" value, you must take care to differentiate between *repairs* and *improvements*. The IRS and CRA have similar approaches to this distinction, and an accountant can help you with the borderline expenditures. Generally, capital improvements include things such as an addition or a new dock, windows, well, or roof. But while reshingling the entire roof *is* a capital improvement, the IRS, for example, advises that having the corner of a roof repaired is *not*. Similarly, replacing a cracked window pane is a repair, while installing a new energy-efficient window is an improvement.

Unfortunately, neither U.S. nor Canadian tax authorities allow you to "charge" your own labor as an offsetting expense for capital improvements you do yourself. Only the amount paid to others is allowable (though the cost of materials – keep those receipts – can be included).

Much can be done to minimize capital gains over the years by keeping careful track of expenditures. This is a prime reason for planning well in advance on bequest issues. Ten or 20 years from now, you might not know what you did with the bill for the contractor's charges for the new bathroom or the new deck. Even if you're not going to include the cottage in

The three priorities of bequest planning

While tax and estate laws differ greatly in Canada and the U.S., and the circumstances of individual cottage owners vary widely, the priorities of bequest planning are still fundamentally the same:

1. Avoid or reduce capital gains taxes.

2. Avoid the expense and complication of probate.

3. Ensure an orderly transfer of title that meets the wishes of the present owner and provides the most favorable possible result for the beneficiary(ies) – legally, financially, and practically.

your estate, you're going to want to keep track of these expenses in order to minimize your capital gains obligations if you decide to sell the property.

Using residence/home status to reduce – or entirely avoid – capital gains

For both Americans and Canadians, moving the "main home" (in the U.S.) or "principal residence" (in Canada) designation to a vacation property can have significant tax advantages, reducing or altogether eliminating capital gains obligations on it.

American taxpayers face restrictions in how the main and second home designations can be changed. (They are explained in the section on selling your cottage; *see p. 207.*) Canadians have more flexibility with the principal-residence designation, and are allowed to assign it to one qualifying property in one tax year, and change it to any other qualifying property the next year. *(See Tip, below.)* Capital gains can then be excluded for the years during which the principal-residence designation applied.

The idea for Canadian taxpayers who own both a home and a cottage is to designate the property that has gained the most in value each year as their principal residence. (You are allowed to claim only *one* principal residence per tax year.) Shifting the designation in this manner can make a significant difference in the accrued capital gains.

Canadian taxpayers don't need to identify a principal residence until that residence is sold or ownership is otherwise transferred. This means the designation can be applied in hindsight, by reviewing the history of the changes in value of the house and the cottage, and moving it between them for particular years to minimize the capital gains impact. This can be done

Even Americans must pay tax on Canadian capital gains

American taxpayers do have to pay the Canada Revenue Agency tax on capital gains from the disposition of Canadian properties. However, you then secure an exemption so you are not double-taxed when filing your U.S. personal tax returns.

TIP: Designating the cottage your "principal residence" doesn't mean you have to live there all or even most of the time

Although the Canada Revenue Agency allows you to claim only one principal residence in any tax year, its definition of "principal residence" is exceedingly generous. You don't have to live at the cottage a certain number of days per year, or use the cottage address on your tax return, or receive your postal deliveries there in order to designate the cottage as your principal residence. The term the CRA uses is "ordinarily inhabited" – which boils down to the property qualifying as a principal residence if you, your spouse, or one of your kids under the age of 18 sleeps there occasionally.

Better still, you don't have to make the decision about whether your home or your cottage is your principal residence until the time you sell or hand down one of the properties. And you can change the designation from year to year – making the cottage your principal residence some years and the house your principal residence in other years – depending on which showed the greatest increase in capital gains each year.

either as part of settling an estate or when selling a property. Here's how it can work:

Let's say an estate includes a main home in the city and a retreat in cottage country. There may have been a period – let's say 1991 to 1994 – when the market value of the cottage soared from $140,000 to $210,000, while the main home's value remained relatively flat, only increasing from $230,000 to $255,000. By changing the principal residence designation to the cottage for those years, the estate avoids taxable capital gains on the cottage of $70,000 while incurring a gain of $25,000 on the home in the city – putting the beneficiaries ahead by $45,000. The same strategy can be used when selling a cottage. And remember that the taxable gains are only recognized when you dispose of the property. (*To estimate the capital gains tax on your own cottage, see "Number Crunching for Canadians," p. 230. For a case study on how the principal residence designation can work to your advantage, see p. 232.*)

Practicalities of bequest

Tax and estate-planning professionals are accustomed to spelling out the strategies necessary for achieving a bequest with minimum financial impact. But you will find an increasing number who are also sensitive to the "human factor" that underlies legal and financial matters, and who are prepared to counsel clients on what might be called the practicality of bequest. As heartfelt as the desire might be to keep a cottage within a family, some

TIP:

A good-news reminder for Americans with cottages north of the border

If you are an American who owns cottage property in Canada, although you are subject to capital gains taxes when the property is sold or otherwise "disposed" of (including by gifting or bequest), your actual estate is not subject to Canadian estate laws.

CAUTION: **But there's a limit to the Canada Revenue Agency's largesse**

The basic rule is that land up to a half hectare (about one and a quarter acres) with a principal residence on it qualifies for the capital gains tax exemption. Any land beyond that amount is generally subject to capital gains tax on disposition.

"Generally" is the key word here. There are exceptions – which are important in the case of cottages, since they sometimes include more than a half hectare of land. The determining factor is whether the additional land is "necessary for the use and enjoyment of the house as a residence."

A foolproof test is whether the additional land can be severed; if so, it's deemed superfluous to the use and enjoyment of the house and loses the capital gains tax protection of the principal residence. Other indicators that would allow the additional land to qualify fully for the tax exemption include: The land is necessary for access to and from a public road; the size and character of the residence, along with how it is sited on the property, make the additional land indispensable to its use and enjoyment; and a minimum lot size larger than a half hectare is specified in a subdivision plan. As well, if your ability to sever the land is the result of a zoning change that post-dates acquisition of the property, you may also be able to maintain your tax exemption on the entire property.

Did you use these loopholes?

In Canada, two other tax loopholes – long since closed by the government – for several years created other opportunities to reduce capital gains tax. Offspring who are assisting with a bequest process need to keep their eyes peeled to see if their parents took advantage of them – or, in the case of one of the loopholes, if it can still be used to reduce capital gains during the years it was in effect.

 First, there may have been a large "forgiving" of the capital gains in the mid to late 1990s. On February 22, 1994, the basic $100,000 lifetime personal exemption on capital gains was eliminated. (The exemption for a principal residence continued, however.)

At the time it was eliminated, Canadians were given the opportunity to secure the exemption on up to $100,000 worth of capital gains, without having to dispose of the underlying property. The tax people considered the property to have been "sold" and immediately "bought" back at that time. People who opted for this measure had until 1997 to finalize the basket of assets they wished to include in the maximum $100,000 forgiving for the 1994 tax year.

For many cottage owners, it made sense to take advantage of the exemption and eliminate up to $100,000 in accumulated capital gains in one stroke. For others, particularly seniors, it didn't make sense, as the increase in reported income would mean they faced clawbacks in Old Age Security. Others used the exemption for their stock portfolios, or simply didn't look far enough down the road to realize the effect using this exemption could have. (*See "Number Crunching for Canadians," p. 230, and the case study, p. 232.*)

Second, for a full decade after capital gains taxes were introduced in Canada on January 1, 1972, couples could have *two* principal residences, provided the property titles were registered separately and not jointly. In this way, a couple could enjoy *two* principal residence exemptions from capital gains tax. One spouse could claim the main home as the principal residence, and the other could claim the cottage. The second principal residence exemption was eliminated on December 31, 1981, but if the cottage owners took advantage of the "double principal residence" designation before that date by registering separate titles to the properties, the cottage is still exempt from any capital gains accrued during those years.

Children who are planning a cottage ownership succession with their parents need to confirm if the 1994 capital gains election and/or the double principal residence option were taken advantage of, and to what degree. (The capital gains election would have required the parents to have filed form T664 with their 1994 return; be sure they didn't later change the assets they were including, which could have occurred as late as 1997. The double principal residence option depends on how the property titles were registered from 1972 through 1981.)

bequest situations are simply unworkable, or at least invite a high degree of unhappiness a few years into the next generation's ownership if not approached strategically.

Treating heirs equally doesn't mean treating them the same

Equitable treatment doesn't require every asset to be divvied equally between all heirs. If you have two children, one can be given a painting worth $50,000, the other a plot of land worth the same amount. They don't have to be given half of each asset. Most people would agree that, short of entering into a time-sharing arrangement on the painting, it's impractical to expect valuable assets like that to be shared by siblings. And you can see where this sort of literal-minded asset-dividing might lead: The painting shared by two offspring in the second generation would have to be shared by their own offspring in the third generation. A handsome painting that hung in Grandma and Grandpa's dining room ends up being shuttled between the homes of eight different grandchildren on a tight time-share schedule.

This, naturally, is an absurd way to treat a painting. One of two strategies would be infinitely more practical. The painting could be sold by the estate of the last-to-die grandparent, and the proceeds distributed between the two children. Or the painting could be left to one child, and another asset of similar value (or some other share of the estate equal to the painting's value) left to the other child. The decision might be easier to make if one child is particularly fond of the painting.

Sometimes, a cottage is a painting. As much as the present owners would like their offspring to share in its enjoyment after they've gone, the practical considerations overrule good intentions. While the challenges to the offspring are not insurmountable, several circumstances should lead parents to consider leaving the cottage to one offspring (or two of four, for example) and providing the other offspring with comparable assets, or disposing of the cottage as part of the general contents of the estate and distributing the proceeds. This sort of solution may be necessary if:

• There are too many offspring to reasonably expect them to share in use of the cottage.

• An estrangement between offspring makes it unlikely that sharing the property would work out.

• One offspring adores the cottage; the other has no interest in it.

• One offspring lives so far away she can't use it as much as her sibling(s).

And while it might make far more sense, for any one of the above reasons, to leave the cottage to one offspring, the estate may not be large enough to provide an asset of equal value to the other one. In this case, having the cottage liquidated in order to share its value equally could be distressing to the one offspring who would dearly like to have it. Alternatively, the offspring who wants the cottage can agree to buy out the interest of her sibling after the bequest occurs.

Thinking about situations such as these can be unpleasant, but they are eventualities that should still be considered, discussed, and planned for beforehand by all concerned.

Leaving a cottage to one of several offspring

• If the estate decides to share assets equally, some care should be paid to ensure that those assets are similar in their potential for appreciation. Real estate, as a rule, appreciates in value, sometimes dramatically. But boats,

TIP:

Use a mortgage to compensate siblings

If not all the inheriting children are interested in the cottage and the estate doesn't have other assets of equal value, a simple option to keep everyone happy is that the child who receives the cottage be required to take out a mortgage on it. Those funds are then used to compensate the other siblings for their share of the estate.

Number-crunching for Canadians: How to estimate the capital gains tax

 This calculation will give you an estimate of the capital gains tax owing if you disposed of your cottage now, *without the tax advantage of designating it your principal residence for any of your years of ownership:*

Step 1. Determine the cost base of your cottage. If you acquired the cottage *after* 1971, the cost base is its value on the date you acquired it. If you acquired the cottage *before* 1971, the cost base is its value on Dec. 31, 1971. (This is because 1972 was the first year the Canadian government began taxing capital gains. Any increase in the value of the cottage before then doesn't count towards calculating your taxable capital gains.)

Step 2. Determine the adjusted cost base (ACB) of your cottage. This is the cost base from Step 1 *plus* the total of all the capital improvements you made to the property since you acquired it.* (*See "Using the Cost of Cottage Improvements to Offset Capital Gains," p. 225.*)

*If you made use of the $100,000 lifetime capital gains tax exemption before it was taken away by the government in 1994, you do not need to pay tax on whatever capital gains you recognized at that time. Therefore, start with the cost base from the tax return in which you filed the T664 election (which may have been as late as 1997) and add any subsequent capital improvements to that. (*See "Did You Use These Loopholes?," p. 228.*)

Step 3. Determine the current fair market value (FMV) of your cottage. (For now, since this is just an estimate, you can check recent sales in the area, or ask a realtor for an opinion.)

Step 4. To determine the total capital gain, subtract the adjusted cost base (Step 2) from the fair market value (Step 3).

Step 5. To determine the *taxable* capital gain, divide the total capital gain (Step 4) in half. (The Canadian government currently taxes 50% of capital gains.)

trailers, recreational vehicles, and the like generally depreciate. In just a few years, a $200,000 cottage might be worth $250,000, while a $200,000 boat might be worth only $120,000.

There is no easy way around this, but it should be considered when placing fair values on assets that are distributed among heirs. Wills that distribute individual assets among heirs must be kept up to date to avoid bitter disputes over asset values. In the case of two offspring, where one adores the cottage and the other doesn't or lives too far away to use it regularly, it may still be more practical for the cottage to be left to both heirs, and for one to agree to purchase the other's interest at fair market value.

• If one sibling is particularly interested in the cottage, another option would be to leave it equally to all the children but include a proviso that it is to be sold and the proceeds divided – but that the interested sibling shall be given the right of first refusal to buy it at fair market value.

Step 6. To determine the amount of tax payable, multiply the taxable capital gain (Step 5) by your marginal personal tax rate. (For a rough estimate, use a rounded-up worst-case scenario of 50%. Your marginal rate may be much lower.)

This is the amount of capital gains tax you would owe if you disposed of the property today and did *not* take advantage of the principal residence exemption.

The principal residence exemption

Your cottage is exempt from capital gains tax for any years you designate it your principal residence. The following calculation will give you a rough estimate of how much the tax can be reduced if you take advantage of this exemption:

Step 7. Determine your "exemption fraction" using the following formula:

$$\frac{\text{\# years after 1971 cottage designated as principal residence} + 1}{\text{\# years after 1971 you owned the property}} = \text{exemption fraction}$$

(The government built the "plus 1" into the formula to cover the tax situation where one residence is sold and another acquired in the same year, so that you can designate both as your principal residence that year.)

Step 8. To determine the amount of the total capital gain that is tax exempt, multiply the total capital gain (from Step 4, above) by the exemption fraction (Step 7) or its equivalent percentage.

Step 9. To get your new taxable capital gain, subtract the tax-free amount (Step 8) from the total taxable gain (Step 4), then divide the result in half (as in Step 5).

Step 10. To determine the amount of tax payable, proceed with Step 6 as above.

Alternatively, the CRA permits you to calculate separately the capital gains for specific years in which the cottage was and wasn't designated the principal residence. If this calculation yields a lower tax obligation than the one that results from using the simple method (above), you're allowed to choose it instead for your return. (See the case study, p. 232.)

• Some means of addressing taxable capital gains must be arrived at if a cottage is not being left to all heirs. Those not receiving the cottage are hardly going to be pleased with taxable capital gains of $100,000 attached to the cottage diminishing their own inheritance. Some preplanning can avoid the problem. One option is to use the proceeds from a life insurance policy to pay the tax bill, with the premiums paid by the heirs who will inherit the cottage. *(See p. 238.)*

• Inheritance plans need to be discussed well in advance by cottage owners. There may be good taxation and financial reasons to transfer ownership in whole or in part to one or more offspring while the parents are still alive. *(See p. 234.)* But this strategy could backfire if an offspring subsequently divorces, and part of the cottage ends up in the possession of the ex-spouse. Generally speaking, property received as a gift or an inheritance, as well as property owned by a spouse before marriage, can be isolated from "communal" marital property and protected from division in the event of divorce. But family law in North America is full of twists and turns, and legal advice should be secured if the intent of an asset transfer before death (or any sort of bequest) is to leave the property entirely in the ownership of the offspring. While an offspring might be able to assert sole ownership to a prop-

---

Case study:

Using the principal-residence designation to reduce the tax bill: The simple method vs. the specific-years method

Canadians Cathy and Phil purchased a cottage in Ontario in 1995 for $145,000. In 2005, they sold it. Prices had skyrocketed on the lake, and they got $335,000. As a result, they were staring down the barrel of a capital gain of $190,000. With half of it taxable, and a maximum marginal tax rate of 46 percent in Ontario, Cathy and Phil were confronting a tax bill of $43,700.

They couldn't use the cost of improvements to offset the capital gains (*see p. 225*) because, frankly, they hadn't done much to the place beyond basic maintenance. And what few items might have qualified as improvements, they couldn't find bills to support.

But Cathy and Phil had an option. By shifting their principal-residence exemption from their city home to the cottage for as many years as they liked, they would gain relief from tax on capital gains on the cottage during those years. While their home wouldn't be sheltered from capital gains tax for the years they designated the cottage their principal residence, they had no immediate intentions of selling their home, so the tax bill would most likely be a concern of their estate.

Still, they decided to hedge their bets and split the principal residence designation between their home and their cottage. To begin, they shifted the principal residence designation to the cottage for five of the 11 tax years of cottage ownership from 1995 to 2005. Using the CRA's simple method to determine their "exemption fraction" (*see p. 231*), they would thus eliminate 6/11 of the capital gains, or $103,636. That reduced their reportable capital gain on the cottage sale from $190,000 to $86,364 ($190,000 − $103,636 = $86,364), and their tax from $43,700 to $19,864.

But their accountant thought they could do better if they didn't just use the simple method. Cathy and Phil had told him that cottage prices had gone crazy on their lake in the new millennium, and he suspected that most of the gain was in the six years from 2000 to 2005. He advised spending a little money for a professional appraisal, to determine the cottage value in 1999, before the boom.

The appraiser came back with a 1999 market value of $195,000 for the cottage. By designating the cottage their principal residence *specifically* for the years 2000–2005, and not using the exemption fraction, they would only pay tax on capital gains from 1995 through 1999. Therefore, the reportable capital gain was only $50,000 ($195,000 minus the purchase price of $145,000), with the $140,000 gain in the past six years completely sheltered. By calculating the capital gain this way, the 2005 tax bill for capital gains on the cottage sale dropped to $11,500.

This method may not work to everyone's advantage; consult a tax professional if you're thinking of going this route.

---

erty through a gift or bequest, if the $60,000 cabin was turned into a $250,000 retreat through a cash infusion from his or her spouse, all bets are off as to who might end up with the property should divorce occur.

• Parents who do their estate planning in advance must be prepared for the attitudes to cottage inheritance to change as children age. An agreement when a brother and sister are in their 30s that the cottage should be left to the sister may no longer be so popular when they're in their 40s. Circumstances in their own lives will change, and the cottage that the brother once thought he wasn't interested in can suddenly look appealing. If early estate planning is overly rigid, trouble down the road can be brewing.

Avoiding family friction once the offspring take over

How the cottage is going to be used by the next generation must be carefully thought through before succession occurs. Professionals who deal with cottage succession cite a long list of potential areas of conflict among siblings once Mom and Dad are gone, including who gets to use the place when, what the division of labor will be, how the costs are shared, and to what extent the cottage will be maintained and renovated. (Typically, a more-affluent sibling wants to redevelop the cottage into something more substantial while others want to maintain the status quo.)

To some extent, these are the same flashpoints that exist with cottage co-ownership generally, and the mechanisms for addressing them are much the same whether or not it's siblings doing the sharing. So if you skipped Chapter 10, "Sharing a Cottage," the first time around, now is the time to go back and read it.

Here are some other family-specific areas parents should think about when bequeathing a cottage:

• Will the property prove to be too great a financial burden for any or all of the kids who inherit it? If it has operating costs that could overwhelm the beneficiaries, then the bequest should, if possible, include a trust device containing a reservoir of funds to be drawn on for property taxes, maintenance and repairs, and other costs. (See "Testamentary Trusts," p. 239.)

If the beneficiaries cannot afford to own and operate the cottage, and the estate cannot provide a way for the costs to be addressed, it is probably better for all concerned if the property is sold and the proceeds distributed.

• It may not occur to the parents that one or more of their kids might not actually want to inherit the cottage. If two or more offspring become the owners of the family cottage and one or more of them wants no part of that ownership, the ownership will quickly disintegrate.

Parents may have greater sentimental attachment to the property than their children do. The kids may enjoy visiting their parents at the cottage one week out of every summer with the grandkids in tow, but when Mom and Dad are gone, the appeal of making the annual pilgrimage vanishes.

TIP:
Work out the details before the kids take over

Have the kids prepare a co-ownership agreement while you, the parents, are alive and able to assist – and mediate. *(See Chapter 10, p.168, for the issues that a co-ownership agreement should cover.)* Having such an agreement in place can help ensure workable solutions to problems that arise after your death.

• Alternatively, the offspring may want a cottage, but not necessarily the one that's in the family – especially if it means having to share it with other siblings. They may far prefer to have the property liquidated as part of the estate, the proceeds distributed among the beneficiaries, and then be able to use their share towards their own cottage.

As cottage owners age, they sometimes cling to a property they're not really able to use, and bear all its expenses, because they think they're supposed to "leave it to the kids." The kids may not want it, and the parents would have been better off selling it and using the proceeds for other activities, such as travel or a different kind of vacation property. And even if the kids do want it, they have to respect the ongoing demands it represents for their parents, and consider ways to relieve that burden if they want to benefit from it.

"Pre-bequest" changes in ownership

For a number of reasons, it may make more sense to begin the transfer of ownership of your cottage to the next generation while you're still alive. Taxes are one possible reason, but another is limiting the burden of ownership on you now.

Gifting the cottage to your offspring

"Gifting" is a way to transfer ownership of a property to an offspring (or some other beneficiary) during the owner's lifetime while minimizing the tax impact.

In Canada: A gift of all or part of a property is deemed by CRA to be a disposition, even if money doesn't change hands, and any capital gain must be

TIP: Talk is cheap – and essential

"The best advice that can be given to parents considering handing down the cottage," says Fred Hacker, an Ontario lawyer who specializes in cottage succession planning, "is to speak fully and frankly with the children individually and collectively, and to assist them to work out the issues that will arise with shared cottage ownership."

A frank discussion may reveal attitudes towards that cottage that surprise you. You may discover your offspring feel differently about it than you thought. If may turn out that none of your three kids really wants the cottage, or one does and two don't (or vice versa). You can then plan your estate accordingly, with an eye towards avoiding disputes after your death.

Kids, meanwhile, should encourage their parents to speak frankly with them about their own desires. They may discover the parents are – as always – putting their children first, while they're really hankering to sell the cottage and use the money for something else in their golden years.

Number-crunching for Americans: Being wise to capital gains reduction

For Americans who are well versed in home ownership, keeping track of property acquisitions and sales in their IRS returns is no great mystery. The only issue is whether the capital gains exemption applied to the disposition of a main home can be used for the cottage. (See Chapter 12, p. 207, for details of how the "main home" designation works.)

The generous nature of the main home exemption means property owners can get a little rusty on itemizing costs that reduce capital gains. After all, why go to the bother of preserving receipts for eligible expenditures when a $500,000 exemption for married couples is more than likely to wipe out any final gain, and then some? But if you acquire a cottage that might never qualify for "main-home" status, you may end up wishing you did a better job of documenting expenditures that would have reduced your capital gains obligation – either for your estate, or for you, when you sell the property.

Get hold of IRS publication 523 (Selling Your Home). Review the categories of settlement fees and closing costs that work in your favor in increasing the "adjusted basis," and be sure that you can document them for future use. Start squirreling away any and all receipts for labor and materials that qualify as improvements to the capital value. Study the list of permitted improvements carefully, as it includes landscaping, decks, walkways, and retaining walls. And with cottages often being in transitional communities, moving from seasonal to year-round residential, there may well be surcharges from the municipality to pay for road and other local improvements that you can add to the adjusted basis. A meeting with an accountant can help you understand what costs are eligible, and how to keep track of them.

Itemizing these expenses all might seem an enormous waste of time and energy if you intend to retire to the cottage some day and have the capital gains erased by the main-home exemption, should you then sell it (or leave it to your estate to worry about). But plans have a way of changing. Treat the cottage as if it will never enjoy main-home status. Because it just might not.

accounted for. Therefore, if parents give a child equity in a cottage, unless it has been totally sheltered as their principal residence, they will face a bill for capital gains tax based on fair market value at the time of the gift-giving. In addition to a significant tax bill (with no proceeds from gifting to pay for it), their resulting grossed-up income will also cause a clawback of Old Age Security. As a result, gifting real estate is a less-popular way of passing down ownership of a property in Canada.

But gifting can be worth exploring in a few circumstances with the following results:

• Assuming the cottage will continue to increase in value, gifting allows a smaller capital gains hit to be taken now, rather than a substantially larger one much later, when the cottage is included in an estate.

• Breaking down the change of ownership into a series of gifts can reduce the overall tax impact of one single large bequest.

• By shifting ownership while the parents are still alive, the expense of probate can be avoided.

• An offspring could put his or her own principal-residence exemption to work to shelter the cottage from future capital gains obligations, rather than waiting to do so after receiving it in a bequest, when the capital gains bill to be paid by the estate likely will be much higher.

• If the parents can no longer afford to hold onto the cottage, gifting it – with the offspring agreeing to pay the capital gains taxes – may be a way to avoid having it sold out of the family altogether.

• The new categories of living (*inter vivos*) trust also offer Canadians an effective way to hand down the cottage to offspring while the parents are still alive without triggering a capital gains tax bill. Actual title is held by the trust, and tax doesn't become payable until the property is conveyed to the heirs. (*See "Living Trusts," p. 239.*)

In the U.S.: Incrementally "gifting" a property has distinct advantages. Generally speaking, an individual can make a gift (including property) worth up to $12,000 (2006 limit) to another individual without either donor or recipient reporting the gift on their tax return, or triggering any federal gift tax. There's no limit on the number of individuals who can be gifted by a single person in a single tax year. If parents have two children to whom they want to leave the cottage, they could collectively hand over to them a total of $48,000 worth of interest in the property (using the 2006 threshold) this way every year.

While using the gifting strategy to avoid estate taxes down the road is unlikely to be an issue for most cottage owners (since estate taxes do not kick in until the estate exceeds $2 million for the 2006–2008 tax years, rising to $3.5 million in 2009), the strategy does allow them to avoid the capital gains bill their estate would otherwise face in bequeathing a property that isn't their main home.

When you're making a gift of property, the IRS essentially allows you to hand over the whole capital gains rigamarole to the giftee. The recipient is considered to have received the gift not at fair market value, but at the gift giver's adjusted basis (closing cost plus subsequent capital improvements), and does not have to report any aspect of the gift as income at that time. Capital gain is calculated only when the giftee disposes of the property. (Keep in mind, however, that if the cottage in question is in Canada, the CRA is going to want its capital gains tax on any change of ownership, and the gifting strategy falls apart.)

Let's say an American couple decides to gift their cottage (which is in the U.S.) incrementally to their daughter. The cottage does not qualify as their main home. It was purchased years ago for $60,000, and including closing costs from the time of purchase and subsequent capital improvements,

TIP:

Better safe than sorry: If you pass it on in your lifetime, be sure to protect yourself

Peter Lillico, a Peterborough, Ontario, lawyer with plenty of experience in cottage bequest issues, recommends that parents who transfer title to a family cottage in their lifetime consider securing a "life interest" (also sometimes called a life tenancy). This is a legal right to continue using the cottage while it is in their offspring's possession. In addition to guaranteeing access, it can prevent children from selling or mortgaging the cottage without their consent.

TIP: **Sell it to the kids for the amount of tax**

If you are ready to give up control of the cottage and one or more heirs has the means to purchase it, you might consider selling the cottage for an agreed-upon price right now. You will receive income from the sale and your estate won't have to pay any additional capital gains tax or probate fees at the time of your death. You can sell for any amount you choose but, of course, you will still have to pay capital gains tax on the fair market value of the cottage. If you don't need the extra income you'd get by actually selling it to your children at fair market value, one workable option is to sell it to them for the amount of capital gains tax you will have to pay based on fair market value.

it has an adjusted basis of $89,000. The fair market value at the time the gifting process began might be $190,000, but the daughter, taking incremental ownership with each annual gift, would receive it with a value equal to the adjusted basis calculated by her parents. Provided there were no further capital improvements (or any other changes to the adjusted basis), the $89,000 could be gifted over the course of eight tax years (at 2006 gifting limits) without any reportage requirements or capital gains taxes to be paid.

The downside? Should the daughter not plan to continue to own the cottage, when she sells it at fair market value, she could be on the hook for a substantial whack of capital gains, since the gain is calculated using the adjusted basis passed along from her parents, which might have been well below fair market value at the time she took ownership.

On the other hand, if the parents instead waited until they died to hand over the cottage, their estate would be liable for the tax payable on all the unsheltered capital gains, based on fair market value. If this was a substantial amount, there might not be enough money in the estate to settle the capital gains tax without having to liquidate the cottage. Having instead handed the cottage over incrementally as a gift while the parents were still alive would have avoided the tax hit and probate costs.

A purchase rather than a gift

An accountant can otherwise outline strategies for the children to compensate their parents for the cottage, up to and including an outright purchase of an interest in it. This strategy may be necessary if the parents are finding ownership financially difficult, and the only way to keep the cottage in the family is for the children to purchase some equity interest, either through a direct cash infusion or a mortgage.

Another possibility is to use the property's rental potential in association with a partial transfer of ownership to offset costs. Have an accountant or a real estate lawyer who is well versed in cottage properties and estate planning review all the options with you.

Using life insurance to pay capital gains tax

One of the most commonly cited strategies for dealing with estate-related taxation is the use of life insurance. It seems relatively straightforward and very clever. The current owner of the property secures a term policy on his or her life, with a death benefit of, let's say, $100,000. When he or she dies, the death benefit is paid to the estate and, in most jurisdictions, that benefit is tax-free. The benefit is then used to pay the tax obligations of the estate. If the cottage has a $95,000 capital gains tax obligation, the insurance benefit takes care of it all. Alternatively, if the cottage represents the bulk of the estate and only one sibling is interested in the property, life insurance could provide a way to pay a lump sum to the other siblings in lieu of inheriting the cottage. Life insurance can also be used within a testamentary trust to fund operating expenses. *(See facing page.)*

What's the catch? For starters, someone has to pay the insurance premiums. The usual pitch is that the kids pay the premiums, since they're ultimately going to benefit from an estate that isn't drained by a significant capital gains obligation. But since there's really no such thing as free money, the strategy has to be entered into with careful planning, as the actual value of the insurance benefit has to be measured against the cost of purchasing it. In some cases, another kind of investment, even one whose proceeds are taxable, will deliver a much better return than an insurance policy.

While an insurance-savvy accountant should crunch the numbers for you, some critical points you'll need to consider include:

• **The anticipated death benefit requirement.** You don't want to buy significantly more insurance coverage than is required – or less. But the requirement is very difficult to calculate with certainty, since the ultimate capital gains obligation is a moving target, as it depends on how long the owner lives, the fluctuations of the real estate market, and future changes in the designation of the property with respect to capital gains exemption.

• **The real return on the policy.** If it's guesstimated that $100,000 is a reasonable requirement for the estate, the premiums have to deliver an acceptable return on the investment. How much will the monthly premium be? How old is the insured person? What risks are associated with his health or lifestyle? Once a premium is determined for a particular amount of coverage, the return can be estimated, based on life expectancy.

Specialized strategies

In addition to the more traditional methods of handing down the family cottage outlined above, other, specialized options can work well in certain situations. The legal structures available for estate planning and organizing ownership for the beneficiaries include limited and general partnerships, limited liability companies, and corporations. Choosing one – if one even makes sense in your circumstances – requires consultation with legal and tax professionals. Get advice sooner rather than later. It's beyond the scope of this book to advise on the suitability of the many legal structures. But here are some of the more common approaches to specialized planning:

Non-profit organization

Transfering ownership of the cottage into a non-profit organization is a solution that works best for large, close-knit multi-generational cottage compounds. Under this arrangement, family members are no longer owners, but dues-paying members of a private club. (Membership can be limited to blood descendants of one set of parents or opened up to include all relatives or even family friends.) While the initial transfer will incur capital gains taxes, future generations of the family can enjoy the cottage in perpetuity without triggering another round of capital gains or probate fees. Should the board of directors of the non-profit, who can be family members, decide to sell the property and collapse the organization, taxes on capital gains would once again apply.

Some trouble spots with non-profits include an ever-growing membership that could simply get too huge after a number of generations. (In a non-profit, offspring become lifetime members at a specified age.) Non-profit organizations must also take special care not to support or subsidize any members who have trouble paying their dues or they could lose their status in the eyes of tax authorities. Also, beyond the set-up costs, a non-profit will be more expensive from an accounting standpoint on an ongoing basis.

Testamentary trusts

Essentially, a testamentary trust consists of a sum of money or a life insurance policy left in a trust specified in a parent's will, to be used exclusively for cottage purposes. The trust can also take the form of an endowment. An income-producing asset (such as a securities portfolio) can fund expenses through its profits, without eroding the underlying asset.

Testamentary trusts are particularly useful when a cottage is left to two or more children who have different incomes and financial resources. While maintaining the cottage may be easy for siblings with a solid financial base, others may not have the wherewithal to pay for ongoing operating costs or substantial capital investments such as a new septic system or major roof repair. A testamentary trust compensates for the financial inequities of various offspring.

Living trusts

Inter vivos or "living" trusts differ from testamentary trusts in that they exist while the cottage owner is still alive. Because a trust is a distinct legal entity,

Continued on page 242

Summarizing the options

The pros and cons of various bequest strategies

Strategy: Simple bequest

How it works: Cottage ownership is conveyed to beneficiaries on owner's death as stated in a will.

Most suited for: Simple succession situations, especially where minimal or no capital gains taxes will be incurred.

Pros: Wills are inexpensive to create. • Parents retain ownership and control of property during their lifetime. • Capital gains taxes can be left to the estate to worry about.

Cons: Property becomes part of estate and incurs probate costs and delays in transfer of title during probate period. • Unless otherwise provided for, the estate could face a hefty capital gains tax bill, possibly forcing the sale of the cottage to cover it.

Comments, caveats: Parents and heirs should take steps to shelter the cottage as much as possible from capital gains. If the property's gains are not sufficiently sheltered, a mechanism such as a term insurance policy should be considered to cover the estate's capital gains tax bill.

Strategy: Gift cottage to your children now

How it works: You transfer ownership of the cottage as a gift, either all at once or incrementally.

Most suited for: Those ready to give up partial or total ownership of their cottage • For Canadian taxpayers, properties that enjoy some principal-residence protection to minimize the capital gains bill triggered by the ownership change.

Pros: Probate costs avoided. • Children can assume ownership costs and responsibilities, relieving burden on parents. • Additional capital gains after the ownership change are deferred to recipients, who do not have to pay any tax until they dispose of the property themselves. • *U.S taxpayers:* Incremental gifting below annual IRS threshold can transfer ownership without requiring capital gains to be reported. In case of large estates, gifting can avoid estate taxes.

Cons: *Canadian taxpayers:* Gifting triggers an immediate taxable gain, based on fair market value. • *U.S. tax-payers:* If property is in Canada, capital gains tax must still be paid to CRA.

Comments, caveats: Parents should secure a "life interest" in the cottage, to be able to continue to have a legal right to use it and protect it from being sold or mortgaged unilaterally. • *Canadian taxpayers:* Children can relieve capital gains tax burden by agreeing to pay the tax for their parents. Incrementally gifting it can also spread out the tax bill over several years, and reduce the gross-up in the parents' income in individual years.

Strategy: Sell cottage to your children now

How it works: Your child or children pay an agreed-upon price to purchase some or all of the cottage.

Most suited for: Those who otherwise want or would be forced by financial circumstances to sell the cottage on the open market. • Those who wish to transfer ownership to children while still alive, but need help with the capital gains tax bill, or require funds for other purposes.

Pros: Parents receive income from sale. • Children can secure cottage that might otherwise have to be sold out of family. • Probate costs avoided.

Cons: Regardless of price agreed to, any capital gains to be paid are calculated on the basis of fair market value.

Comments, caveats: See "Comments, caveats" for gifting, above. • *U.S. taxpayers:* Parents can consider selling the cottage incrementally to offspring, to break up the annual capital gains tax burden.

Strategy: Make your children joint tenants

How it works: By making you and your offspring joint tenants, each of you shares an "equal and undivided" ownership of the cottage. The property is legally considered to have a single owner.

Most suited for: Those who wish to share ownership of the cottage with their children now, through gifting or sale (see above), and have them inherit all of it in the future.

Pros: At the time of your death, your portion of ownership will pass directly to your surviving joint tenant(s) without probate fees.

Cons: See gifting and selling above for general cons in the process that leads to joint tenancy. • May be difficult to establish in some jurisdictions, where the property was not acquired by all tenants simultaneously. • Survivorship rights of joint tenants override any bequest stipulations in a will. • Creditors of one joint tenant could force the sale of the entire property. • Where the joint tenant is not a spouse, capital gains are still taxable on portion that passes to surviving tenant(s).

Comments, caveats: It's a good idea to talk to your children about their future interest in the cottage and work out a co-ownership agreement. Be aware of limitations on your own rights, and the obligations of joint tenancy. A joint tenant could go to court and force a change ("severance") to tenancy in common (see below), in which case you would lose control over part of the property during your lifetime.

Strategy: Make your children tenants in common

How it works: You transfer a specific percentage of the cottage to offspring through sale or gifting

Most suited for: Those who wish to share ownership of the cottage with their children but retain a share that, upon their death, will become part of their estate. Also used for incremental sale or gifting.

Pros: Because your share of the cottage becomes a part of your estate rather than passing directly to your children, it may allow for a more equitable distribution of inheritance.

Cons: See gifting, selling, and simple bequest, above. • Unlike joint tenancy, because your share is part of the estate, you cannot avoid probate.

Comments, caveats: Many lawyers recommend tenancy in common over joint tenancy so your percentage of the cottage becomes part of your estate and is given to whomever is designated in the will.

Strategy: Transfer cottage to an inter vivos (living) trust

How it works: Property is transferred to a trust. Parent(s) no longer own cottage, but have control of it and benefit from it. Upon death of parent(s), trust conveys ownership to designated heir(s).

Most suited for: Those who wish to leave the cottage to children without the costs of probate for their estate, but do not wish to relinquish control.

Pros: No probate. • No capital gains tax payable at time of trust creation. Tax becomes payable when conveyed to heirs by trust. • Parents continue to enjoy use of cottage. • Trust provides legally unassailable provisions for inheritance, and a framework for protecting trustee's use and enjoyment in event of incapacitation.

Cons: In Canada, *inter vivos* trusts are only available to persons 65 or older. • Trust is generally more expensive to create and maintain than a simple bequest. • Trust provides shelter from reportable capital gains for a maximum of 21 years only. • Capital gains taxes payable on assets conveyed by a trust can be high. • Approval of third parties (such as a mortgage holder) for initial transfer of cottage to trust required.

Comments, caveats: Ideal for ensuring that the bequest wishes of the spouse who predeceases the other are not not subsequently changed.

Strategy: Establish the cottage as a non-profit organization

How it works: The cottage is transferred into a non-profit organization. Family members are no longer owners but dues-paying members of a cottage that operates like a club

Most suited for: Those with a large cottage property suitable to being shared by an extended family.

Pros: Enables successive generations of family to use the cottage without incurring capital gains tax or probate fees.

Cons: Initial transfer likely to trigger a taxable capital gain, which in the case of a large property could be massive. • Demographics can force sale of such compounds: too many members and too little space. • Expense of ongoing accounting fees.

Comments, caveats: Non-profits have to be careful not to subsidize members who are unable to pay their dues, as that puts them in danger of losing their special tax status.

once property is transferred to a living trust, you no longer own it, but as trustee you have control over and enjoyment of the asset during your lifetime. *Inter vivos* trusts are an estate-planning option for both U.S. and Canadian taxpayers.

Different tax schemes in Canada and the U.S. create different motivations for opting for some kind of living trust. (*For capital gains tax implications, see Tip, facing page.*) And trusts are so complex that you need to explore the options thoroughly with an expert in this field before considering creating one. But the main reasons for a living trust are:

• **Avoidance of probate:** Because the property placed in the trust is not part of a bequest through a will, it is not subject to the time-consuming and potentially expensive process of probate. Depending on the estate, probate costs might consume three to five percent of the total value of an estate, and the property can be tied up for months (at the least). While a trust is generally more expensive to create than a will, the savings to the estate in probate costs can be worth it. And some estate planners like the fact that

Protecting against loss of the property through mental incompetence

It's not a happy subject, but diminished mental competency of the elderly can have unfortunate consequences for the best-laid succession plans. Whether because of a stroke, an accident, or diminishment through age, Alzheimer's, or some other cause, a person can lose the capacity to manage his own affairs. In the absence of any other arrangement in Ontario, for instance, the provincial government, and not the immediate family, takes over the financial affairs – including the property – of a mentally incompetent person. If capital is necessary to produce income to support the incompetent person, the Public Trustee could assess the cottage as a large and unproductive asset, and sell it.

Mental incompetency is addressed differently by the laws in various jurisdictions. In New Brunswick, the preference of the courts in a circumstance of incompetency is to appoint a guardian from the immediate family. Ontario lawyer Peter Lillico strongly advises families to avoid the possibility of a parent losing control of a property to the state by having a lawyer prepare a power of attorney for property. "This document will ensure that if there is an incompetency, it will be your own chosen and trusted people who will control your affairs, to the exclusion of the government and the courts." At the same time, Lillico warns, this document immediately transfers control over your property, unless you include specific wording that it only takes effect when you are judged to be incompetent by a doctor.

Additionally, be aware that a simple power of attorney may cease to be in effect if the person assigning that power becomes mentally incompetent, unless there are specific provisions for that possibility. American property owners should investigate securing a "durable power of attorney," sometimes called a "financial power of attorney." It's a simple document, and it can extend as little or as much power to your "attorney in fact" as you wish in the event of mental incompetency or any other sort of incapacitation.

the inheritance stays out of the public eye when it doesn't have to go through probate.

• **Orderly planning in the event of incapacitation:** A living trust can provide power of attorney on how the trust is to be administered in case the trustee is no longer capable of doing so, due to accident or illness. (*See "Protecting Against Loss of the Property through Mental Incompetence," facing page.*)

• **Control of who ends up owning the cottage:** While the tax implications differ, both Canada and the U.S. have roughly similar trusts that provide a mechanism for ensuring an unchallengeable inheritance. In Canada, it's called a "joint spousal trust," while in the U.S. it's known as a "living trust with marital life estate," or more commonly as an "AB trust."

If property is jointly held outside a trust by a couple or willed from one to the other, in the event that the surviving spouse remarries, the new spouse (and any children he or she might have from a previous marriage) can end up with a claim to part of the cottage's ownership. For that matter, the surviving spouse could choose to bequeath the cottage in a way the deceased spouse would never have approved. One child might be favored over another, or an orphaned niece of the first spouse might be cut out of the will drawn up by the second spouse. A joint spousal or AB trust ensures that the ultimate beneficiary of the cottage is only whomever is named as such in the original trust document.

After the first spouse dies, the surviving spouse, as trustee, enjoys the

TIP: Putting the cottage in a trust no longer means triggering capital gains tax

Traditionally, *inter vivos* or "living" trusts were not used much by Canadian cottage owners because they required any capital gains incurred by the property to be recognized at the moment the cottage was transferred into the trust, which meant the trustee could face a hefty tax bill on capital gains in creating the trust.

Recently, two new categories of *inter vivos* trusts in Canada have changed that. Alter ego and joint spousal trusts permit a cottage property to be placed in trust without triggering the capital gains bill. Alter ego trusts are limited to trusts with a single trustee who benefits solely from it while alive, while joint spousal trusts, as the name implies, are designed for couples and limit benefits to them. In both cases, the trustees must be age 65 or older. The cottage is sheltered from any capital gains payable on disposition until the property passes to the ultimate beneficiaries of the trust.

Just bear in mind that the CRA won't allow an appreciating asset to be sheltered indefinitely from capital gains taxes in a trust. The cut-off is 21 years, at which point the CRA judges there to have been a deemed "disposal" of the property (even if no ownership change has occurred), and capital gains are assessed, based on fair market value. If you set up the trust at age 65 and you're still around and flipping pancakes for breakfast at the lake at age 86, you'll be facing a capital gains reckoning.

use and benefit of the property in the trust. After both spouses have died, the property goes to whomever was named as the ultimate beneficiary at the time the trust was created. After the first spouse dies, there's nothing the second spouse can do to change the ultimate beneficiary. While wills can be written that specify particular beneficiaries, they can always be challenged in court; a trust structure is essentially unassailable.

Charitable bequests and public donations

Some cottage owners do not have any descendants to whom they wish to leave a cottage, but they would still like to see the property be of benefit to a charity or the public at large. Real property can be left to any number of beneficiaries – charities, charitable land trusts, and various levels of government – with tax advantages to the estate. Such bequests can also be made in the owner's lifetime, with tax relief provided both in terms of credits and, in some cases, reductions in the reportable capital gains on the property's value. In Canada, for example, a donation of ecologically sensitive land results in a reduction of the capital gains "inclusion rate" (the amount you declare for tax purposes) from 50 to 25 percent. You may also be able to donate certain rights to your land, such as easements and covenants, and receive a tax credit.

If your cottage property contains a significant amount of land, give serious thought to a partial bequest to a land trust or a level of government for park purposes. Just be aware that land donated to municipalities for parks can't be relied on to remain parkland in perpetuity. Municipalities generally have the right to dispose of public lands, and you would be well advised to attach a bulletproof covenant to the transfer of title if you don't want to see a lovely waterfront lot flipped into a private cottage property by your local government. Conservation land trusts are generally a safer bet for preserving natural spaces.

In addition to preserving a treasured greenspace from future development, this may be to your and your estate's advantage if it avoids significant tax obligations on capital gains on the real estate. Canadian tax law, for example, limits the total land area of a principal residence to half a hectare under the capital gains exemption. The excess land could be disposed of through a donation, thus keeping it in a natural state while providing the owner with relief from capital gains obligations.

15. For more information

Magazines and periodicals

• **Cottage Life:** This award-winning, Ontario-based magazine is essential reading for anyone who owns or wants to own a cottage. Published six times a year, it features solid how-to advice on all aspects of cottaging. (The comprehensive article index on its website will give you an excellent idea of the kinds of practical information it contains.) **www.cottagelife.com**; 1-877-874-5253.

• A wide array of **regional lifestyle magazines** is published in North America. They are a useful source of information about particular areas you may be considering in your cottage search; plus, they often contain ads of waterfront properties for sale. (If you want to rent out your cottage, they're a good bet both for placing ads and for finding rental agencies.) Below are a few of the magazines that are devoted to popular vacation-property areas and/or offer coverage on topics of particular interest to waterfront cottage owners or cottage owner wannabes. For other areas, check the member list of the International Regional Magazine Association: **www.regionalmagazines.org**.

— **Adirondack Life:** Focuses on people, places, issues, and events in the Adirondack region of upstate New York; **www.adirondacklife.com**

— **Cabin Life:** Minnesota-based publication focusing on lakefront and rural properties; **www.cabinlife.com**

— **Cottage:** Focuses on country living in Western Canada; **www.cottage magazine.com**

— **Cottage Living:** U.S. lifestyle magazine, covering building, decorating, gardening, entertaining, and traveling; **www.cottageliving.com**

— **Lake Superior:** Directed at people who "live and play" in and around the greatest of the Great Lakes; **www.lakesuperior.com**

— **Midwest Living:** Focuses on lifestyle and property in Midwest Great Lakes states. **www.midwestliving.com**

— **Vermont Life:.** A quarterly celebrating life in the Green Mountain state; **www.vtlife.com**

— **Yankee:** 10 issues/year. Magazine of "New England living." **www.yankee magazine.com**

Books

• **Cottage Water Systems: An Out-of-the-City Guide to Pumps, Plumbing, Water Purification, and Privies** by Max Burns; Cottage Life Books, 1993; updated edition 2002: For cottage owners, both new and old, who are looking for information on any and all aspects of water and waste at the cottage, including getting water in winter and winterizing systems when the cottage isn't being used year-round; includes troubleshooting charts.

• **The Dock Manual: Designing, Building, Maintaining** by Max Burns; Storey Books, 1999: This is the place to turn for detailed info on docks – from planning and building a new dock to repairing an existing one.

• **Finding & Buying Your Place in the Country** by Les Scher and Carol Scher; Dearborn Trade Publishing (a Kaplan Professional Company), 2000: Issued in multiple editions since 1992, this is a comprehensive guide to building a rural retreat. Of some relevance to lakeside buyers, but content is strongest on ranches and farms.

• **How To Reduce the Tax You Pay: Professional Planning for You and Your Business** by Deloitte & Touche; Key Porter Books, 2005: A solid overview of issues for Canadian taxpayers, including estate planning and property ownership.

• **Inspecting a House: A Guide for Buyers, Owners, and Renovators**, 3rd edition, by Carson Dunlop & Associates Ltd.; Dearborn Trade Publishing (a Kaplan Professional Company), 2004: Although not specific to the cottage market, this covers the nitty-gritty of home inspection. (Note: Dearborn Trade Publishing has an extensive line related to real estate, including home financing.)

• **Renting for Profit: Making a Successful Business Out of Renting Your Cottage** by Heather Bayer; Cottage Knowledge Books, 2004: This book is aimed at those who have decided to rent out their cottage and want the fine details of making a successful business of it; includes a CD.

• **The Cottage Rules: An Owner's Guide to the Rights & Responsibilities of Sharing Recreational Property** by Nikki Koski; International Self-Counsel Press, 2005:

Covers the joint ownership of one specific type of property: a large place shared by numerous family members; includes a CD.

IRS and CRA publications

The following are the main tax documents that address the subjects in this book. They can be downloaded from the respective government websites. (As stressed throughout the book, however, consult a lawyer and/or accountant who knows his way around the tax code and can advise you on your specific circumstances.)

In Canada:

Canada Revenue Agency **www.cra-arc.gc.ca**

P 113(E): Gifts and Income Tax

IT-120R6: Principal Residence

T4011(E): Preparing Returns for Deceased Persons

T4036(E): Rental Income

T4037(E): Capital Gains

T2091(E): Designation of a Property as a Principal Residence by an Individual (Other Than a Personal Trust)

In the U.S.:

Internal Revenue Service **www.irs.gov**

501: Exemptions, Standard Deduction, and Filing Information

523: Selling Your Home

527: Residential Rental Property (Including Rental of Vacation Homes)

544: Sales and Other Dispositions of Assets

550: Investment Income and Expenses (Including Capital Gains and Losses)

551: Basis of Assets

559: Survivors, Executors and Administrators

561: Determining the Value of Donated Property

936: Home Mortgage Interest Deduction

946: How to Depreciate Property

950: Introduction to Estate and Gift Taxes

On-line resources (by subject area)

• **Lake science, water quality, fish habitat, and lake health:** To understand more about limnology (the study of freshwater lakes), including lake morphology and water quality, The North American Lake Management Society (**www.nalms.org**) is an excellent general resource. LakeStewardship.org (**www. lakestewardship.org**) provides extensive links to resources.

Regardless of where you want to cottage, the Wisconsin Department of Natural Resources provides a valuable overview of issues and an excellent primer on limnology through its Self-Help Lake Monitoring program. Go to: **www.dnr.state. wi.us/org/water/fhp/lakes/selfhelp/index.htm**

The Shore Primer, published by ***Cottage Life*** magazine for Fisheries and Oceans Canada, is a short guide to how to have a healthy waterfront; a companion publication, ***The Dock Primer***, explains how to construct a practical, shoreline-friendly dock. Both can be downloaded from *Cottage Life*'s website: **www.cottagelife.com**; follow the link to "Free Guides."

Individual provinces and states provide water-quality and fish-habitat information through their "natural resources" department or ministry. Obviously, you'll need the one that covers the part of the country you're interested in, so crank up your search engine and take a look. Among the ones that stand out for the quality of their information are Minnesota's Department of Natural Resources site (**www.dnr.state.mn.us**), which has an on-line "Lake Finder" tool that provides a wealth of data, including topographic and contour depth maps, and information on fish populations, water levels, and water quality; and the Ontario Ministry of Natural Resources little-known Land Information Ontario site (**www.lio.mnr. gov.on.ca/liohome.cfm**), which offers a searchable geospatial data tool. This Ontario Land Information Directory allows you to create custom maps that display a wide range of topographic and wildlife data, including the locations of 15 different fish species in lakes, rivers, and streams.

• **Waterfront property and public spaces:** In the U.S., the Coastal States Organization (**www.coastalstates.org**), which represents the interests of governors from 35 states, provides useful resources.

• **Building a cottage:** If you're looking for an architect who specializes in cottages, the ads in magazines dedicated to vacation properties are a good starting place. In the U.S., the American Institute of Architects is a useful general source on the profession, and it has an "architect finder" tool on its website, **www.aia.org**. In Canada, architects are self-regulating professionals governed by provincial legislation, and each province has its own association. (You can find Ontario architects, for instance, on the website of the Ontario Association of Architects: **www.oaa.on.ca**.)

• **Renting:** *The Cottage Rentals Directory* (formerly *Tyler's Cottage Directory*) is an extensive guide covering Canada's cottage rental market (though most of its listings are in Ontario). Listings are available on-line (**www.tylers.ca**), and the directory is also published in print form twice a year.

A good overview of U.S. tax law with respect to vacation property rental activity is available from San Francisco lawyer Andy Sirkin (**www.andysirkin.com**). (Also see the list of tax documents related to rental activity, above.)

• **Surveying:** To find a professional surveyor, and to learn more about surveying issues in Canada, go to the Canadian Council of Land Surveyors website (**www.ccls-ccag.ca**), which provides an index to provincial surveyors' associations and other useful links. In the U.S., consult the National Society of Professional Surveyors (**www.lsrp.com/proforg.html**), which provides a directory of state-level organizations. In addition, the Minnesota Society of Professional Surveyors (**www.mn surveyor.com/faq.cfm**) offers an exceptionally good overview of surveying issues affecting waterfront property owners.

• *Cottage Life* magazine's website, **www.cottagelife.com**, has a link to an area of the site called the "Cottage Wide Web," which lists helpful cottage-related web addresses.

Acknowledgments

A lot of brains were picked and busy people pestered for this project, sometimes (I am embarrassed to say) for entirely unnecessary reasons, as some information I gleaned, though I found it fascinating, turned out to be beyond the scope of this book. (Sorry, Steve.) I shall leave in the trenches but collectively thank the staffers in various municipalities and at state, provincial, and federal departments and agencies who answered my questions. And while I have to take ultimate responsibility for the opinions expressed in this book, a number of people do need to be singled out for the value they provided, even if you don't necessarily see their names in print somewhere within.

David Hellyer of Hellyer Engineering in Mississauga, Ontario, and James Livingstone of Central Home & Cottage Inspections of Bancroft, Ontario, helped inform my understanding of what accredited home inspectors do (and should do) in the cottage market. Shirley Davy, associate broker at ReMax Parry Sound Realty, took my questions about sprucing up a cottage for optimum resale seriously enough to pool the entire staff at the office and reply with detailed advice. Phil Chandler, an independent broker operating Phil Chandler Real Estate in Sudbury, Ontario, allowed me to pelt him with questions about the real estate biz in general and issues affecting both Canadian and American buyers. The Ontario Real Estate Association was likewise helpful with both information and forms. My thanks as well to the staff at Cottage Country Travel Services for providing an insider's view of the rental business. John Hiley, president of the Bracebridge, Ontario, land surveyors Coote, Hiley, Jemmett, and his staff were generous wth their time in searching for surveys to illustrate the points raised.

On the banking front, I was well informed by Gillian Riley, vice president, mortgages, at Scotiabank; and by two perpetually harried (by me) employees of my local CIBC: Shelley Blanchard, account manager, personal banking; and Veronica Smith, financial sales associate. They were invaluable in my quest to understand and explain risk management in bank lending practices with vacation properties and entertained my war-gaming scenarios of various financing situations.

Special thanks go to three lawyers: Fred Hacker of Hacker Gignac Rice in Midland, Ontario; Peter Lillico of Lillico Bazuk Kent Galloway in Peterborough, Ontario; and Stuart Hollander, whose eponymous firm is located in Suttons Bay, Michigan. All have practices strong in cottage properties and cottage succession and estate planning, and answered my queries with care and thoroughness.

And a tip o' the hat to partners and staff at Deloitte Touche, whom I've worked with in recent years, who inspired my thinking on vendor due diligence in vacation property sales.

Thanks as well go to *Cottage Life* magazine. Its 18 years' worth of back issues were an invaluable resource in helping to shape this book.

Last but not least, a thanks to editor Ann Vanderhoof, for keeping this project on the rails and rolling up her own sleeves where necessary.

Index

When looking for an item on a page, check the sidebars as well as the main text; the content of the sidebars has also been indexed.

A

aboriginal land claims, 112
access. *See*: road access; water access
agents. *See*: real estate agents
algae blooms, 45, 49
alternative power sources, 91–92, 220–21
alternative toilets, 94–95
American Society of Home Inspectors, 117
American tax law. *See*: taxation (U.S.)
Americans buying property in Canada, 37–39
anglers. *See*: fishing
asking price, 196–98

B

backlot property, 56–57
banker, choosing a, 21, 144
beaches
    natural vs. manmade, 50
    public access to, 57, 58, 110–11
    right of use and ownership, 57, 58
"beaver fever" (giardiasis), 49
bequest
    avoiding family friction, 233–34
    capital gains and, 224–28, 240–41, 243
    charitable bequest and public donations, 244
    chart summarizing options for, 240–41
    discussing plans with offspring, 224, 234
    family law and, 231–32
    "gifting," 225, 234–37, 240
    life insurance, use of in, 238
    mental incompetence and, 242
    non-profit organization, 239, 241
    power of attorney, 242
    practicalities of, 227–38
    pre-bequest ownership changes, 234–37, 240–41
    probate, 225, 239–43
    securing a "life interest," 236
    selling to offspring, 237, 240
    simple bequest (wills), 240
    trust, *inter vivos* (living), 236, 239–43
    trust, testamentary, 239
boathouses, 103, 112, 123
boating
    lake suitability for, 51–55, 81
    legal restrictions, 51, 53–54, 87, 89–90
    paddling, 52
    powerboating, 52–54
    sailing, 52–53
    traffic, 82, 89–90
    See also: boats
boats
    cottage rental and, 180
    surveying, 67
    "with contents" cottage sales and, 66–67, 202, 205
    See also: boating
broker, definition of, 68
budgeting, 20–23
    See also: financing
builder, choosing, 135
building-code violations, 121
building permits, 202
buyer agency agreement, 71–74, 76
buyer agents. *See*: real estate agents

C

Canada Mortgage and Housing Corporation, 50, 147
Canadian Association of Home and Property
    Inspectors, 116–17

Canadian Standards Association, 127
Canadian Yachting Association, 53
capital gains (Canada)
    calculation of, 140–42, 230–31, 232
    Canadian property purchased from U.S. citizen
        and, 39
    capital gains loophole (1994), 228
    donation of ecologically sensitive land and, 244
    "gifting" and, 225, 234–36
    "half hectare" rule, 227
    improvements offsetting gains, 225–26, 232
    Old Age Security clawback, 228, 235
    principal residence exemption, 140, 224, 226–27,
        228, 230–31, 232, 235
    tax obligations of U.S. owners of Canadian
        property, 226
    vacant land and, 140–42
    See also: bequest; renting out; selling a cottage;
        trusts
capital gains (U.S.)
    "gifting" and, 236–37
    improvements offsetting gains, 235
    main home exemption, 37, 138, 226
    payment of, on Canadian property, 226
    trusts and, 243
    See also: bequest; selling a cottage; taxation (U.S.)
carpenter ants, 122
children, 32–33
chimneys. See: woodstoves and fireplaces
closing issues. See: conditions of purchase; inspec-
    tion; surveys
collateralized mortgages, 147
communication systems, 95–96
composting toilet. See: alternative toilets
conditions of purchase, and survey results, 105
contents, purchasing a cottage with, 66–67
conventional mortgages, 146–147
co-ownership
    agreements, 168–69
    bequest and, 227–29, 233–34
    boats and, 166, 167
    changes in ownership, 166
    compatibility, 159–61, 168, 171
    discord, 166–70, 171
    dividing expenses, 165–67
    dividing usage, 163–65
    financing and, 162–63
    fractional ownership, 172
    legal structures, 161–62
    renting out and, 162, 165
    time-sharing, 170–172
cottage associations, as information source, 42–44,
    59
cottage logbook, 170
cottage operating manual, 119, 170, 180, 208–10
cottage wants checklist, 34–36

covenants, 109–11, 244
cross-border purchasing, 37–39

D
designated agent, 76–77
development issues, 58
disclosure documents. See: vendor disclosure
docks, 111–12, 123
down payment, 147
drinking water
    financing and, 150
    in winter, 220
    records, 202
    sources, 48–49, 92–93
    systems, 123–24, 220
    testing, 121
    treating, 48–49
    See also: water quality
drive-to vs. water-access properties, 26–27
"driveway test," 20
driving distance and time, 23–26
dual agency, dual agents, 76–77

E
easements
    charitable donation of, 244
    encroachments and, 106
    types, 109–11
electrical systems, 120–21, 123
encroachments, 103–06
Environmental Protection Agency, 127
estate planning: See: bequest
estate taxes: See: taxation (U.S.)

F
family law. See: bequest
Federal Emergency Management Agency, 50
Federation of Ontario Cottagers' Associations, 44
financing
    alternatives to conventional mortgage, 152–56
    Americans borrowing from Canadian banks, 39,
        147
    banker, choosing a, 21, 144
    calculating payments, 151
    conditions that concern banks, 148–51
    construction funding, 156
    co-ownership and, 162–63
    down payment, minimizing, 147
    home equity loans, 153
    how much to spend, 21, 151
    land purchase, funding of, 150, 156
    leased land and, 148
    line of credit, 154–55
    loan products for cottages, 146–48
    refinancing, 153–54
    risk assessment by lenders, 143–46, 149

second mortgage, 154–56
setting a budget, 20–23
tear-downs and, 150
using home as collateral, 152–156
vacant land and, 156
See also: mortgage
fireplaces. *See:* woodstoves and fireplaces
fish habitat, protection of, 112
fishing
    in front of cottages, 90–91
    lake types and, 45, 48, 54–55
    researching lakes for, 43, 48, 55
flooding, 50
"for sale by owner," 63, 68, 71, 74–75, 188–95
    See also: selling
fractional-ownership properties, 172
FSBO. *See:* "for sale by owner"

G
giardiasis, 49
"gifting." *See:* bequest; capital gains (Canada and U.S.)
grandfathering, 103, 132, 133
gray water, 93–95
guests
    accommodating, 29
    water access and, 27

H
"half hectare" rule, 227
handing down the cottage. *See:* bequest
health care, Americans in Canada, 39, 216
heating systems, 97, 126, 220–21
    See also: woodstoves and fireplaces
holdback, 120
holding tank, 94
home equity loans, 153

I
incinerating toilet. *See:* alternative toilets
insect infestation, 122
inspection (property)
    agreement of purchase and, 123
    building-code violations and, 121
    budgeting for, 22
    closing considerations, 120–21
    evaluating report, 121–26
    extent of, 118–19
    goals of, 115–16
    options for closing and, 128–29
    process of, 119–21
    reasons for, 113–15
    water quality and, 121
    when to inspect, 115
    See also: inspectors (home and property)

inspectors (home and property)
    accreditation of, 116–117
    agent recommendations of, 117
    finding an inspector, 117–18
    improper behavior of, 118
    See also: inspection (property)
insulation, 96–97, 221
insurance
    life, 238
    mortgage, 147
    property
        budgeting for, 23
        flood protection and, 50
        renting out and, 175, 182
        wood-burning appliances and, 127
    title, 104
interest deductibility. *See:* mortgage
Internet. *See:* communication systems
inter vivos trust, 236, 239–43
island properties
    pricing, 27
    renting and, 27, 176
    utilities and, 29
    See also: water access

J
joint tenancy, 161, 240–41

L
lake(s)
    finding information on, 43–44, 54–55
    restrictions on, 51, 53–54, 87, 89–90
    sleeper, 43
    suitability for types of boating, 51–55, 81
    traffic on, 82, 89–90
    types, 44–45, 54–55
land claims, 112
leased land, 108–09; financing, 148
license of occupation (encroachments), 106, 107
limnology, 44–45
location of cottage
    importance of, 80
    sun and, 80
    wind direction and, 81–82
lots. *See:* vacant land
"luxury quotient" test, 30

M
main home. *See:* capital gains (U.S.); mortgage interest deductibility (U.S.)
maintenance, budgeting for, 22–23
MapQuest, 25
maps, 44, 46–47
media,
    as information source, 59
    as source of real estate listings, 65–67

termites, 122
testamentary trust, 238, 239
"30-minute trap," 23
time-sharing properties, 170–72
title insurance, 104
transient boaters, 90
travel time, 23–26
trusts
    inter vivos (living), 236, 239–43
    testamentary 238, 239

U

Underwriters Laboratories, 127
U.S. Sailing Association, 53
utilities
    budgeting for, 23
    on vs. off grid, 29
    power sources, 82
    vacant lots and, 136–37

V

vacant land
    building to suit, 148
    capital gains on (in Canada), 136
    costs of developing, 136–38
    financing purchase, 150, 156
    lending risk, 149
    mortgage interest deductibility on (U.S.), 138–39
    pluses and minuses, 132–33
    zoning restrictions on, 134–36
vendor disclosure, 97, 110, 125–26, 200–01, 203
vendor due diligence, 123, 200–03

W

waste water
    financing and, 150
    treatment/storage types, 93–95
    See also: septic systems
water-access
    building and, 87, 136
    considerations, 86–87
    vs. drive-to, 26–27
    financing and, 148
    renting and, 27
waterfront
    measuring lot size and, 83–84
    ownership, 58, 111
    ownership of lake bottom, 111
    public access, 58, 110–11
    public right to adjoining waters, 91, 111
    public trust doctrine, 111
water-level changes, 49–50
water quality
    detritus, 81–82
    drinking, 48–49, 92–93, 121
    swimming, 49

    See also: drinking water
water system, 123–24, 208, 220
well record, 92, 202
wells, 92–93, 124
    inspection, 124
    records, 92
    types, 93
WETT, 127
wills. *See*: bequest
wind direction, prevailing, 81–83
winterizing, 96–97, 218–21
wish list, 25–36
"with contents" sales, 66–67, 205
Wood Energy Technology Training, 127
woodstoves and fireplaces, 97, 120, 126, 127

Y

year-round use, 26, 96–97
    See also: retirement to cottage country

Z

zoning
    covenants, 110
    limitations on
        additions and renos, 80
        boathouses, 112
        docks, 112
        new construction and tear-downs, 103, 132, 134–36
    maps, 47

About the author

Douglas Hunter has written widely on business, sports, and outdoor pursuits for publications ranging from *Cottage Life* magazine to *The Globe and Mail*. He is the author of 13 books, including *The Bubble & the Bear: How Nortel Burst the Canadian Dream*, which won the National Business Book Award in Canada. Hunter lives on Georgian Bay near Port McNicoll, in the heart of Ontario's cottage country.